Biographical Dictionary
of Sociologists

Biographical Dictionary of Sociologists

WILLIAM STEWART

McFarland & Company, Inc., Publishers
Jefferson, North Carolina, and London

LIBRARY OF CONGRESS CATALOGUING-IN-PUBLICATION DATA

Stewart, William, 1927–
Biographical dictionary of sociologists / William Stewart.
p.   cm.
Includes bibliographical references and index.

ISBN 978-0-7864-3328-5
illustrated case binding : 50# alkaline paper ∞

1. Sociologists — Biography — Dictionaries.   I. Title
HM478.S74   2008   301.092'2 — dc22   2008008025
[B]

British Library cataloguing data are available

On the cover: (clockwise from upper left) William Graham Sumner;
Max Weber; Franz Oppenheimer; Henry Pratt Fairchild; Thorstein Veblen;
Edward Cary Hayes; and William Hamilton Sewell; (lower center) Herbert
Spencer; (background photograph) Grand Central Station, New York, NY
©2008 Sandra Baker/Alamy

Front cover by TG Design

Manufactured in the United States of America

*McFarland & Company, Inc., Publishers
Box 611, Jefferson, North Carolina 28640
www.mcfarlandpub.com*

Contents

Preface

I was introduced to sociology when I was studying psychiatric social work, and later I took sociology as one my subjects for my open university degree. In my work as a counselor and teacher of counseling, I found that my knowledge of sociology gave me an all-around perspective of people. For me, then, sociology is essential in understanding people. Sociology is a social science that studies human societies, their interactions, and the processes that preserve and change them by examining the dynamics of constituent parts of societies such as institutions, communities, populations, and gender, racial, and age groups. Sociology also includes the study of social status or stratification, social movements, and social change, as well as societal disorder in the form of crime, deviance, and revolution. It is sociology's task to discover how organizations affect individual behavior how they are established, how they interact with one another, how they decay, and, ultimately, how they disappear. Among the most basic organizational structures are economic, religious, educational, and political institutions, as well as more specialized units such as the family, the community, the military, peer groups, clubs, and volunteer associations.

This is a biographical dictionary of sociologists and of people who have had a notable influence on sociology. Each entry is limited to 500 words, and presents (where possible, although after extensive research some dates of birth have been impossible to ascertain) personal details, career information, an overview of contributions to the field, and some of the person's main books. Limiting myself to 500 words was essential; otherwise the book would have run several volumes, for there is so much material available for most of the people profiled.

I consider it a privilege to have been able to compile this book, and researching the lives of the people in it has enriched my own professional body of knowledge. My hope is that readers will find the book both interesting and stimulating, as they read about the people men and women (some well-known, others not so well-known) who have all been sociologists or made contributions to sociology.

William Stewart
Bishopstoke
Eastleigh
Hampshire, England

The Sociologists

Addams, Jane (1860–1935)

SOCIAL REFORM

Jane Addams was born in Cedarville, Illinois, the daughter of a prosperous miller who served for sixteen years as a state senator and fought as an officer in the Civil War. After graduating from Rockford Female Seminary in 1881, Addams started medical studies but ill-health (owing to a congenital spinal defect) forced her to give up. While touring Europe with Ellen Starr (1859–1940) they were inspired by visiting Toynbee Hall, the settlement house in London's East End started in 1884 by friends of the social reformer Arnold Toynbee (1852–1883). Toynbee Hall served as a base for Charles James Booth (1840–1916) and his group of researchers working on the nine-volume *Life and Labor of the People in London* (1886–1903).

In 1889 Addams and Starr established Hull House, a center of excellence and education to improve conditions in the industrial districts of Chicago. By 1890 Hull House was catering to two thousand people a week, with kindergarten classes, club meetings for older children, and clubs and courses for adults in what became virtually a night school. There was an art gallery, a public kitchen, a coffee house, a gymnasium, a swimming pool, a cooperative boarding club for girls, a book bindery, an art studio, a music school, a drama group, a circulating library, an employment bureau, and a labor museum.

Addams led investigations on midwifery, narcotics consumption, milk supplies, and sanitary conditions; she accepted the official post of garbage inspector of the Nineteenth Ward, at an annual salary of a thousand dollars. An ardent feminist, Addams was passionate about women's suffrage. As a lecturer sponsored by the Carnegie Foundation, she spoke against America's entry into the First World War, was attacked in the press and expelled from the Daughters of the American Revolution.

She was appointed to Chicago's Board of Education and subsequently made chairman of the School Management Committee (1905); participated in the founding of the Chicago School of Civics and Philanthropy (1908); was first woman president of the National Conference of Charities and Corrections (1909); received the first honorary degree ever awarded to a woman by Yale University, New Haven, Connecticut (1910); was chair of the Woman's Peace party (1915); president of the International Congress of Women at The Hague, Netherlands (1915); and involved in the Women's International League for Peace and Freedom, which was established by The Hague congress (1915). She received a Nobel Peace Prize in Oslo (1931) (although she was too ill to attend), shared with the American educator Nicholas Murray Butler (1862–1947). Addams was admitted to a hospital the day of the Nobel award ceremony in Oslo, and died of cancer.

Major Literature

Addams, Jane. *Democracy and Social Ethics.* New York: Macmillan, 1902. The Echo Library, 2006.

___. *Newer Ideals of Peace.* New York: Macmillan, 1907. Champaign, Illinois: University of Illinois Press, 2006.

___. *Twenty Years at Hull House.* New York: Macmillan, 1910. Whitefish, Montana: R.A. Kessinger Publishing Co., 2004.

___. *The Second Twenty Years at Hull House,* New York: Macmillan, 1930.

Adorno, Theodor W. (1903–1969)

AUTHORITARIAN PERSONALITY

Theodor W. Adorno was born in Frankfurt, Germany, of Jewish and Italian Catholic descent and an accomplished musician. He studied philosophy with Hans Cornelius (1863–1947) and music composition with Alban Berg (1885–1935). After two years as a university instructor, Adorno was expelled by the Nazis, along with other professors of Jewish heritage. During the Nazi era he resided in Oxford, New York City, and southern California, where he wrote several books for which he later became famous, including *The Authoritarian Personality* (1950) (a collaborative project). Later he turned his father's Jewish surname (Wiesengrund) into a middle initial and adopted "Adorno," the maternal surname by which he is best known.

Returning to Frankfurt in 1949 to take up a position in the philosophy department, Adorno quickly established himself as a leading German intellectual and a central figure in the Institute of Social Research. He was one of the most important philosophers and social critics in Germany after World War II. He published numerous volumes of music criticism, several volumes of *Notes to Literature,* books on the philosopher Georg Wilhelm Friedrich Hegel (1770–1831) and on existential philosophy, and collected essays in sociology and in aesthetics.

Major Contributions

Adorno's major contribution is his work on the authoritarian personality, although it could be argued that his musical and philosophical works are of equal importance. Adorno's collaborative study began as an investigation of anti–Semitism in the U.S., but led to the discovery of numerous correlations between anti–Semitism and other attitudes associated with stereotyped behavior — although later work separated the attitudes toward authority from specific political views.

The hypothesis was that the origins of authoritarianism lay in childhood socialization when the parents — and especially the father — adopted a very harsh disciplinary approach toward their children. All transgressions, however minor, were severely punished. Aggressive feelings toward the parents would lead to displacing this aggression onto "safer targets." From their work developed the "F-scale," which became widely used as a measure of prejudice. People who are prejudiced against one group tend to be prejudiced against many groups with whom they do not agree; a hatred of Jews, for example, being associated with a hatred of Catholics.

The authoritarian personality may be usefully contrasted with the opposite — open-mindedness, which describes how flexible and responsive we are in examining new evidence about our belief systems. It partly describes our ability to receive, evaluate and act on information from the outside on its own merits. It also relates to how we are able to free ourselves from internal pressures that would obscure or interfere with incoming information.

Major Literature

Horkheimer, M., T.W. Adorno, G.S. Noerr, (Ed.), and E. Jephcott (trans.). *Dialectic of Enlightenment: Philosophical Fragments.* Stanford, California: Stanford University Press, 1947, 2002.

Adorno, T.W., et al. *The Authoritarian Personality.* New York: Harper and Brothers, 1950.

Adorno, T.W. *Notes to Literature* (1958, 1961, 1965, 1974). 2 vols., trans. S. Weber Nicholsen. New York: Columbia University Press, 1991, 1992.

Alberoni, Francesco (1929–)

SOCIOLOGY OF MOVEMENTS

Born in Piacenza, Italy, Francesco Alberoni graduated in medicine from Pavia in Northern Italy, where he was assistant to the Franciscan friar, physician and psychologist Agostino Gemelli (1858–1959). At the Catholic University of Milan he was adjunct professor of psychology and sociology (1960–1961) and professor of sociology (1964). He was at the Foundation Social Science Research Council (1964–1970); dean, University of Trento, Italy (1968–1970); professor, University of Lausanne, Switzerland, and the University of Catania, Sicily, then again at the University of Milan (1970–1978). A former teacher of Libera Università di Lingue e Comunicazione IULM, he was dean and chancellor until 2000 and founded the University Institute for Modern Languages. From 2002 to 2005, he was a board member of Cinecittà Cinema Holding of Rome, and since 2003, dean of the Experimental Center for Cinematography.

He has been a regular front page writer of *Corriere della Sera* (*Evening Mail*), Italy's most renowned newspaper since 1973, and since 1982 has written an editorial column titled "Public and Private" for the Monday edition. He is senior board member (chairman) of Rai, the national Italian television

(2002–2005); member of the Bi-national Committee Olivetti Foundation–Ford Foundation Social Science Research Council; past president of the Italian Association of Sociology; past president of CRS, an Italian research institute that forecasts future cultural and social trends; and president of ISTUR, an Italian center of studies on tourism and cultural differences.

Major Contributions

Alberoni has carried out numerous studies on sociology of movements and individuals, upon which his book *Movement and Institution,* published in 1977 and translated by Patricia C. Arden Delmoro for Columbia University Press in 1984, was based. It is among the first books on the sociological analysis of movements of people, their start, development and end, and is considered a milestone in the analysis of social movements. Alberoni explains how any historical process is the result of two forces at work, one utilitarian and economic in nature (the institution) and the other collective and liberating (the arising mass movement). If the former transforms and innovates society, it is the latter alone which can generate social solidarity. The concept he developed is the so-called *Statu Nascenti,* the "nascent state," the moment in which leadership, ideas, and communication come together and fuel the birth of movements.

In 1979 he published his worldwide bestseller, the scientific treatise *Falling in Love,* which was translated into more than twenty languages and published by Random House in 1983. After more than ten editions, it is still in print in Italy. In it he explores the subject in great detail, using as much as possible the language of love stories rather than the abstract language of psychoanalysis or sociology. More books followed, many developing the theme of falling in love and friendship, the majority in Italian.

Antonovsky, Aaron
(1923–1994)

STRESS AND HEALTH

Born in Brooklyn New York, and after serving in the U.S. army in World II, Aaron Antonovsky obtained his Ph.D. in sociology from Yale University, New Haven, Connecticut. He immigrated to Israel in 1960, settled in Jerusalem and worked at the Israel Institute for Applied Social Science and in the Department of Social Medicine of the Hebrew University of Jerusalem–Hadassah. He later became professor and head of the Department of Sociology of Health on the faculty of health sciences at Ben-Gurion University in Israel.

Major Contributions

Antonovsky's main contribution is in the field of health. His early work was directed toward the study of discrimination, inequality and minority groups, particularly the Jews. He was a medical sociologist whose basic premise was that we pay much more attention to illness and disease than to good health and well-being. His inquiring mind led him to pose the question: Why is that people who have come through trial and tribulation often have a greater sense of well-being and live longer than some others who have not suffered in the same way? He studied a group of women who were Holocaust survivors and found that those who did well physically and psychologically looked upon life as a gift, while others fared not so well and died younger. He called this defining difference the "sense of coherence" (SOC). Somehow these people made sense of what had happened. This ties in with logotherapy, the work of Viktor Frankl (1905–1997).

Antonovsky believed that a stronger SOC developed in individuals over time as confidence and had a direct influence on knowledge, self-esteem, and consistency that became integrated in the personality. Wellness does not mean attaining "perfect health" but a point on a continuum between perfect unhealth and perfect health. His concept of salutogenesis — how people stay healthy in spite of sometimes overwhelming odds — has three dimensions:

- *Meaningfulness*: How we make sense of life as a coping strategy.
- *Manageability*: The willingness to search out resources to help us cope.
- *Comprehensibility*: Perceiving the world as being understandable, meaningful, orderly and consistent rather than chaotic, random and unpredictable.

Antonovsky's salutogenic thinking is included in the education of many health professionals. He published over 100 papers and wrote or edited 12 books. In 1993 he was awarded an honorary doctorate from the Nordic School of Public Health, Sweden. Antonovsky retired from the medical school in 1992, but remained an active researcher end lecturer at meetings throughout the world.

Major Publications

Antonovsky, A. "The Sense of Coherence as a Determinant of Health." In J.D. Matarazzo (Ed.), *Behavioral Health: A Handbook of Health Enhancement and Disease Prevention*. New Jersey: John Wiley and Sons, Inc., 1984.
___. *Unraveling The Mystery of Health — How People Manage Stress and Stay Well*. London: Jossey-Bass Publishers, 1988.
___. "The Sctructural Sources of Salutogenic Strengths." In C.L. Cooper and R. Payne (Eds.), *Individual Differences: Personality and Stress*. New Jersey: John Wiley and Sons, Inc., 1991.

Aron, Raymond (1905–1983)

IDEOLOGY

Born in Paris, Raymond Aron was awarded a doctorate in philosophy from L'Ecole Normale Supérieure in Paris — the intellectual center of some of France's greatest thinkers — with a thesis on the philosophy of history. From 1930 to 1933 he lectured at the University of Cologne as well as studying at the French Institute, Berlin, and received a *state doctorat* in 1933. From 1934 to 1939 he was secretary to the Center of Social Information at the École Normale Supérieure. He was a professor of social philosophy at the University of Toulouse when World War II broke out in 1939, upon which he joined the French air force. He escaped to London in 1940 where, working under the pseudonym Rene Avord, he edited *La France Libre* (Free France), the monthly review of the Free French movements in London, founded at the invitation of General de Gaulle in 1940.

He became a professor at the École Nationale d'Administration (established by General De Gaulle in Paris in 1945, but now mainly situated in Strasbourg). From 1955 to 1968 he was professor of sociology at the Sorbonne, continuing as a journalist as well as holding the professorship of political science in Sorbonne between 1955 and 1968, and of sociology in the College de France from 1970 until his death. In his view on the war, he maintained that the Vichy government and Marshal Pétain had chosen the lesser of two evils in collaborating with the Nazis during World War II.

Major Contributions

Aron applied the methods of sociology to the study of economics, international relations, ideology, industrial society, and war. A political commentator, he is known for his skepticism of ideological orthodoxies. Crit-

ical of Marxism, he defended pluralism and the value of human freedom; he disapproved of the French left philosophy, and opposed those who promoted a centralized and idealized state. Aron delivered his Gifford Lectures at Aberdeen between 1965 and 1966 under the title *On Historical Consciousness in Thought and Action*. In 1947 Aron became an influential columnist for the conservative morning newspaper *Le Figaro*, a position he held for thirty years until he joined France's first news magazine *L'Express*, modeled on the American *Time*, for which he wrote a political column until his death.

Major Publications

Aron, Raymond, and Harvey C. Mansfield. *The Opium of the Intellectuals.* London, England: Random House Group, Ltd.: Secker and Warburg, 1957. New Jersey: Transaction Publishers, 2001.

Aron, Raymond. *Peace and War.* London, England: Weidenfeld and Nicolson, 1967. Malabar, Florida: Krieger Publishing Company, 1981.

___. *Eighteen Lectures on Industrial Society.* London, England: Weidenfeld and Nicolson, 1968.

___, and August Heckscher. *Diversity of Worlds: France and the United States Look at Their Common Problems.* Westport, Connecticut: Greenwood Press, 1973.

Aron, Raymond. *The Century of Total War.* Lanham, Maryland: Rowman and Littlefield Publishers, Inc., 1985.

___. *Great Debate: Theories of Nuclear Strategy.* Lanham, Maryland: University Press of America, 1985.

___. *Memoirs: Fifty Years of Political Reflection.* New Jersey: Holmes and Meier Publishing Inc., 1991.

Balch, Emily Greene (1867–1961)

GENDER INEQUALITY

Born into a prosperous Boston family, Emily Greene Balch graduated from Bryn

Mawr College, Pennsylvania, in 1889, a member of its first graduating class, then spent the next year in independent study of sociology. She was awarded a European fellowship by Bryn Mawr to study economics in Paris in 1890–1891. She also studied at Harvard University, Cambridge, Massachusetts, and the University of Chicago, Illinois, and worked in economics in Berlin (1895–1896). Between 1896 and 1913 she was on the faculty of Wellesley College, Wellesley, Massachusetts, rising to the rank of professor of economics and sociology.

Like Jane Addams (see entry), she worked tirelessly for peace and was a delegate to the International Congress of Women at The Hague in 1915, and helped found the Women's International Committee for Permanent Peace, later named the Women's International League for Peace and Freedom. As a result of her stance against America's entry into World War I, she lost her job at Wellesley College, and was on the editorial staff of the liberal weekly, the *Nation*. In the light of Nazi atrocities in Europe, during World War II she modified her pacifist stance but still campaigned for peace. She became a Quaker in 1921.

Major Contributions

Known mainly for her studies on immigration, women, and gender inequality, like many women academics of her day, her work was largely ignored by the male-dominated professions. Balch was one of the earliest sociologists to promote the use of the concept of role. She participated in movements for women's suffrage, for racial justice, for control of child labor, and for better wages and conditions of labor. She contributed to knowledge with her research, notably, *Our Slavic Fellow-Citizens* (1910), a study of the main concentrations of Slavs in America and of the areas in Austria and Hungary from which they emigrated. She helped in one way or another with many projects of the

League of Nations — among them, disarmament, the internationalization of aviation, drug control, and the participation of the United States in the affairs of the League.

She also worked for the United Nations and was awarded the Nobel Peace Prize in 1946. Although frail, she continued her work with the Women's International League for Peace and Freedom. In 1959 she served as a co-chairman of a committee to mark the centenary of the birth of Jane Addams, herself a winner of the Nobel Peace Prize in 1931.

Major Literature

Balch, Emily Greene. *Public Assistance of the Poor in France*. Baltimore, Maryland: American Economic Association, 1893.

___, Jane Addams, and Alice Hamilton. *Women at The Hague: The International Congress of Women and Its Results*. New York: Macmillan, 1915.

Balch, Emily Greene. *Approaches to the Great Settlement, With an Introduction by Norman Angell*. New York: Husbach, 1918.

Barchas, Patricia R. (1945–2003)
SOCIOPHYSIOLOGY

Patricia R. Barchas was a pioneer of sociophysiology — the study of the effects of social behavior on the brain. Born in Chickasha, Oklahoma, Barchas grew up in Los Angeles, gained a B.A. in English and history in 1956 from Pomona College, Claremont, California, an M.A. in education from the University of Chicago, Illinois, and a Ph.D. in sociology at Stanford University, California. Early in her career, Barchas taught emotionally disturbed children. She also spent many years studying neurophysiology and endocrinology, and was on the faculty of Stanford's Department of Sociology. She served as a senior research associate in the Department of Psychiatry and Behavioral Sciences, where she headed the program in sociophysiology of the Division of Child Psychiatry and Development, then later she was a member of the research staff at the University of California–Los Angeles School of Medicine. Barchas died of a long-standing brain tumor.

Major Contributions

Barchas demonstrated that electrical brain waves are activated by increasing social status and that the secretion of some hormones is changed by social behavior. She discovered that small amounts of alcohol could alter the way people relate to each other. She also showed that humans and non-human primates form new social hierarchies in comparable ways, and provided evidence that groups of human females and groups of human males use different social processes in solving problems, with the females being more likely to reach agreement. She was co-author of a report commissioned by Congress, dealing with aggression and violence, and was a co-author of an Institute of Medicine report dealing with mental disorders and substance abuse.

The Patricia R. Barchas Award, established in 1999 by the American Psychosomatic Society, is presented each year by the program committee, president, and editor of *Psychosomatic Medicine*. Recipients are chosen because they have helped expand knowledge of the interface of the social and physiological worlds.

Major Literature

Mendoza, Sally P., and Patricia R. Barchas (Eds.). *Social Cohesion: Essays Towards a Sociophysiological Perspective.* Westport, Connecticut: Greenwood Press, 1984.

Barchas, Patricia R. (Ed.). *Social Hierarchies: Essays Towards a Sociophysiological Perspective.* Westport, Connecticut: Greenwood Press, 1984.

___ (Ed.). *The Sociophysiology of Social Relationships.* New York: Oxford University Press, 1989.

Baudrillard, Jean (1929–)
STRUCTURAL SEMIOTICS

Born in Reims, France, Jean Baudrillard studied German at the Sorbonne University in Paris, taught German in a Lycée and completed his doctoral thesis in sociology (1966). He was assistant professor (1966–1972) at Nanterre University of Paris X; was habilitated (1972); professor of sociology (1972–1986); and scientific director at IRIS (Institut de Recherche et d'Information Socio-Économique), University of Paris IX (1986–1990). He is a professor of philosophy of culture and media criticism at the European Graduate School in Saas-Fee, Switzerland. He supports the work of the National Center for Scientific Research, Paris.

Major Contributions

Baudrillard is the best-known of the group of French thinkers and writers known as the postmodernists. Most of Baudrillard's writing centers on the twin concepts of "hyperreality" and "simulation," and with poststructuralism. According to Baudrillard, we live in a world dominated by simulated experience and feelings, and have lost the capacity to comprehend reality as it actually exists. We only experience prepared realities — edited war footage, meaningless acts of terrorism, and the destruction of cultural values. Baudrillard has also focused on the application of structural semiotics to understanding the consumer society and consumer satisfaction. He argues that individuals, in purchasing and consuming goods, necessarily place themselves within a system of signs and objects that always say something about those who use them.

Writing about the First Gulf War (1990–1991), Baudrillard achieved a certain notoriety by declaring that Saddam Hussein was not fighting the Allied Forces, but using the lives of his troops as a form of sacrifice to preserve his power, and that the Allied Forces fighting Saddam were merely dropping 10,000 tons of bombs a day as if to prove to themselves there was an enemy to fight. Little politically changed in Iraq; the enemy was not defeated, the victors were not victorious, there was no war: the Gulf War did not take place. In contrast to the "non-event" of the Gulf War, Baudrillard, in his essay *The Spirit of Terrorism*, characterized the attacks on the World Trade Center and Pentagon as the "absolute event." He sought to understand them in terms of an emotional response to the techno-political expansion of globalization, rather than in terms of a religious or civilization-based conflict.

Major Literature

Baudrillard, Jean. *Symbolic Exchange and Death*. London, England: Sage Publications, Ltd., 1993.
___. *The Gulf War Did Not Take Place*. Paul Patton (Translator). Indiana University, Bloomington: Indiana University Press, 1995. Australia, University of Sydney: Power Publications, 2004.
___. *Jean Baudrillard: Selected Writings*. Cambridge, England: Polity Press, 2001.
___. *The Spirit of Terrorism*. Chris Turner (Translator). London, England: Verso Books, 2003.
Baudrillard, Jean. *Passwords*. London, England: Verso Books, 2003.
___. *The System of Objects*. London, England: Verso Books, 2005.

Bauman, Zygmunt (1925–)

CONSUMERISM

Zygmunt Bauman was born to non-practicing Polish-Jewish parents in Poznan, Poland. The family escaped into the Soviet zone of occupation after Poland was invaded by Nazi troops in 1939. Bauman later served as a political education instructor in the Soviet-controlled Polish First Army, and later in the Corps for Domestic Security, in which he rose to the rank of major and was awarded the Polish Cross of Valor in 1950. Bauman studied sociology at the Warsaw Academy of Social Sciences, then philosophy at the University of Warsaw. He was suddenly dishonorably discharged in 1953, when his father made inquiries from the Israeli embassy in Warsaw about the possibility of immigrating to Israel. Bauman did not share his father's Zionist leanings, so there was a rift between father and son.

Bauman completed his M.A. degree, then became a lecturer at the University of Warsaw in 1954, where he remained until 1968. Influenced by the works of Antonio Gramsci and Georg Simmel (see entries), Bauman grew increasingly critical of the communist government and of Marxist theory. Faced with increasing political pressure and the anti–Semitic campaign, Bauman renounced his membership in the governing Polish United Workers' Party in January 1968 and immigrated to Israel to teach at Tel Aviv University. From 1971 to 1990 he was professor in sociology at the University of Leeds, England, where he is now emeritus professor.

Major Contributions

Bauman has become best known for his analysis of the links between modernity and the Holocaust and of postmodern consumerism. Central to Bauman's analysis is the notion that today's societies are held together by consumption rather than by production. Freedom, he says, is modeled on freedom to choose how one satisfies individual desires; one's identity is constructed via the medium of the consumer market. As a consequence, Bauman contends that freedom and individual fate have increasingly become "privatized." An increasingly privatized life feeds disinterest in politics, whether one can afford to partake in consumer freedom or not. And politics freed from constraints deepens the extent of privatization, thus breeding "moral indifference."

Bauman exerted a considerable influence on the anti- or alter-globalization movement. Since the turn of the millennium Bauman has disposed with any form of explicit reference to "postmodern" society (preferring the phrase "liquid modern" society). Bauman was awarded the European Amalfi Prize for Sociology and Social Sciences in 1992 and the Theodor W. Adorno Award of the city of Frankfurt in 1998.

Major Literature

Bauman, Zygmunt. *Modernity and the Holocaust.* Cambridge, England: Polity Press, new edition, 1991.
___. *Globalization: The Human Consequences.* New York: Columbia University Press, 1998.
___. *Liquid Modernity.* Cambridge, England: Polity Press, 2000.
___. *Liquid Love: On the Frailty of Human Bonds.* Cambridge, England: Polity Press, 2003.
___. *Wasted Lives: Modernity and its Outcasts.* Ames, Iowa: Blackwell Publishing, 2003.
___. *Identity.* Cambridge, England: Polity Press, 2004.
___. *Liquid Life.* Cambridge, England: Polity Press, 2005.

Becker, Gary Stanley (1930–)

ECONOMIC SOCIOLOGY

Born in Pottsville, Pennsylvania, Gary Stanley Becker gained an A.B. with honors at Princeton University, New Jersey (1951). At the University of Chicago, Illinois, he gained his A.M. (1953) and Ph.D. (1955) degrees and was assistant professor (1954–1957); visiting professor of economics (1969–1970); university professor, Department of Economics (1970–1983); university professor, Departments of Economics, Graduate School

of Business, and Sociology (1983 to present); and chairman, Department of Economics, 1984–1985. At Columbia University, New York, he was assistant and associate professor of economics (1957–1960); Arthur Lehman Professor of Economics (1968–1969); and professor of economics (1960–1968). Since 1990 he has been Rose-Marie and Jack R. Anderson Senior Fellow, Hoover Institution, Ford Foundation.

He was a member, senior research associate and research policy advisor to the Center for Economic Analysis of Human Behavior and Social Institutions, National Bureau of Economic Research (1957–1979); member, Academic Advisory Board, American Enterprise Institute for Public Policy Research (1987–1991); associate member, Institute of Fiscal and Monetary Policy, Ministry of Finance, Japan (since 1988); and member, Advisory Committee to the Secretary of Defense (since 2001). He received the Professional Achievement Award, University of Chicago Alumni Association (1968); Nobel Prize in Economics (1992); an honorary membership, Gente Nueva, Mexico City (1996); the Irene B. Taeuber Award for Excellence in Demographic Research, Population Association of America (1997); National Medal of Science (2000); American Academy of Achievement (2001); Medal of the Italian Presidency (2004); John von Neumann Lecture Award, Rajk College, Corvinus University, Budapest, Hungary (2004); and honorary degrees from nineteen universities around he world.

Major Contributions

Becker's central premise is that rational economic choices, based on self-interest, govern most aspects of human behavior — not just the purchasing and investment decisions traditionally thought to influence economic behavior. In his dissertation, published in 1957 as *The Economics of Discrimination* (University of Chicago Press; 2nd rev.

edition, 1971), Becker examined racial discrimination in labor markets, concluding that discrimination has costs for both the victim and the perpetrator. In *Human Capital* (University of Chicago Press, 1964, 1994) Becker argued that an individual's investment in education and training is analogous to a company's investment in new machinery or equipment.

In studies such as *A Treatise on the Family* (Harvard University Press, 1981, expanded edition, 1993), Becker analyzed the household as a sort of factory, producing goods and services such as meals, shelter, and child care. Applying theories of production to household behavior, he was able to make predictions about family size, divorce, and the role of women in the workplace. Subsequent work focused on such subjects as criminal behavior and addiction.

Major Literature

Becker, Gary Stanley. *Essays in the Economics of Crime and Punishment.* New York: Columbia University Press, 1974.
___. *The Essence of Becker.* Stanford, California: Stanford University, Hoover Institution Press, 1995.
___. *The Economic Way of Looking at Behavior: The Nobel Lecture.* Stanford, California: Stanford University, Hoover Institution Press, 1996.
___, and Kevin Murphy. *Social Economics: Market Behavior in a Social Environment.* Cambridge, Massachusetts: Harvard University Press, new edition, 2003.

Becker, Howard Saul (1928–)
SOCIOLOGY OF ART

Howard Saul Becker was born in Chicago, Illinois, and graduated from the University of Chicago, from where he also received his Ph.D. (1951). He went on to teach in the sociology departments at Northwestern University, Illinois, the University of Washington,

and the University of California at Santa Barbara. The majority of his research, writing, and teaching has been in the sociology of art, qualitative method, visual sociology and the practice of research and writing (composition theory) in social sciences. He has received several awards based on his lifetime contributions to sociology, including the Cooley-Mead Award from the Social Psychology section of the American Sociological Association in 1985, and the Charles H. Cooley and George Herbert Mead awards from the Society for the Study of Symbolic Interaction, which he served as president in 1977–1978, 1980 and 1987.

Major Contributions

While at the University of Chicago, Becker worked as a professional jazz pianist. Professor Everett C. Hughes encouraged Becker to undertake the study of jazz musicians as a professional group. He has researched individuals' development of identity through their occupations, conducted in-depth interviews with those who identify as marijuana users, and has written on the implications of society labeling substances as drugs and users as drug addicts. This research led Becker to write extensively about drug use, which he did in his book *Outsiders*, a critical work in the sociology of deviance and the foundation of labeling theory. This labeling theory (also known as social reaction theory) found in *Outsiders* is probably Becker's most important and influential contribution to sociology (the term "labeling" is also used in social psychology and in psychiatry).

Influenced by Charles H. Cooley and George Herbert Mead (see entries), Becker explains that deviance is based on the reactions and responses of others to an individual's acts. This theoretical approach to deviance has influenced criminology, gender, sexuality and identity research. One of Becker's achievements is to write in simple, yet precise and easily-understood language. He has written books for students on how to prepare theses, and for academics on how to write clear prose, clear prose and clear thinking being inseparable.

Major Literature

Becker, Howard Saul. *Outsiders: Studies in the Sociology of Deviance*. New York: The Free Press. 1963.

___. *Sociological Work: Method and Substance*. New Jersey: Transaction Publishers, 1984.

___. *Writing for Social Scientists: How to Start and Finish Your Thesis, Book or Article*. Chicago, Illinois: University of Chicago Press, 1986.

___. *Guides to Writing, Editing and Publishing*. Chicago, Illinois: University of Chicago Press, 1986.

Ragin, Charles C., Howard Saul Becker (Eds.). *What is a Case? Exploring the Foundations of Social Inquiry*. New York: Cambridge University Press, 1992.

Becker, Howard Saul. *Tricks of the Trade: How to Think About Your Research While You're Doing It*. Chicago, Illinois: University of Chicago Press, 1998.

Bell, Daniel (1919–)

CLASS CONFLICT

Born in Brooklyn, New York, to Jewish immigrant parents, Daniel Bell's early childhood was difficult. His father died when he was six months old and Bell's mother worked long hours in a factory to support herself and her son. In his childhood, Bell experienced poverty of a Jewish immigrant population drawn largely from Eastern Europe. He graduated from City College of New York in 1938, and after a year of graduate study at Columbia University he spent 20 years as a journalist and editor of *Common Sense, The New Leader,* and *Fortune.* In 1958 he became an associate professor at Columbia University, New York City, where, in 1960, he received a Ph.D. and was promoted to full professor in 1962. In 1969 he moved to Harvard University, Cambridge, Massachusetts, and he received a Henry Ford II endowed chair in 1980, from which he retired as emeritus professor in 1990.

Bell was among the original New York Intellectuals, a group of anti–Stalinist left-wing writers. He has written on contemporary capitalist society and the individual's place within it. His books, *The End of Ideology* and *The Cultural Contradictions of Capitalism,* appeared on the *Times Literary Supplement*'s list of the 100 most important books of the second half of the twentieth century.

Major Contributions

Bell is best known for his prediction in his book *The Coming of Post-Industrial Society* that the end of class conflict was in sight. He identified three stages:

- The Pre-industrial Society, a feudal society where people were mostly involved in agriculture.
- The Industrial Society, resulting from Industrial Revolution, still in evidence today, where the emphasis is on the production of massive amounts of material goods that society doesn't necessarily need, and their consumption.
- Information and Communication Technology (ICT).

Bell based ICT on the idea that what was emerging was a post-industrial society that would replace the industrial society as the dominant system. He identified three components of a post-industrial society: a shift from manufacturing to services; the centrality of the new science-based industries; the rise of new technical elites and the advent of a new principle of stratification.

While many of his predictions have come to pass, Bell modified his belief that conflict would cease; he could not have foreseen that mass consumption could cause conflict of values and would incur great social cost, such as loss of job security and high unemployment.

Major Literature

Bell, Daniel. *The End of Ideology: On the Exhaustion of Political Ideas in the Fifties*. Glencoe, Illinois: Free Press, 1965.
___. *The Coming of Post-Industrial Society: A Venture in Social Forecasting*. New York: Basic Books, 1976.
___. *The Cultural Contradictions of Capitalism*. New York: Basic Books. 1996.

Bellah, Robert Neelly (1927–)
SOCIOLOGY OF RELIGION

Born in Altus, Oklahoma, Robert Neelly Bellah gained a B.A. with honors (1950) at Harvard College, Cambridge, Massachusetts, and a Ph.D. in sociology and Far Eastern languages, Harvard University (1955). He was research associate, Institute for Islamic Studies, McGill University, Montreal, Quebec, Canada (1955–1957). At Harvard University he was research associate, Center for Middle Eastern Studies (1957–1958); lecturer, Department of Social Relations (1958–1961); Fulbright research grantee, Tokyo, Japan (1960–1961); associate professor of sociology and regional studies (1961–1966); and professor of sociology (1966–1967).

From 1964 to 1965 he was a fellow at the Center for Advanced Studies in the Behavioral Sciences, Stanford University, California. At the University of California, Berkeley, he was Ford professor of sociology (1967–1997); chairman, Center for Japanese and Korean Studies (1968–1974); director, National Endowment for the Humanities summer seminars for college teachers (1975, 1976, 1978) and residential seminar (1976–77); and chairman, Department of Sociology (1979–1985). His awards and honors include the Harbison Award for Gifted Teaching (1971); Sorokin Award of the American

Sociological Association for *The Broken Covenant* (1976); *Los Angeles Times* book prize, winner of Current Interest Division, for *Habits of the Heart* (co-authored with Richard Madsen, William M. Sullivan, Ann Swidler and Steven M. Tipton) (1985); Skirball Values Award, Skirball Institute for American Values (1999); National Humanities Medal (2000); and honorary degrees from seven universities in America and Japan.

Major Contributions

Bellah, the Elliott Professor of Sociology, emeritus, at the University of California, Berkeley, won fame as a public intellectual with his 1967 essay "Civil Religion in America," an examination of the use of religious symbolism by U.S. political figures from the founders through John F. Kennedy and a plea for "an awareness that our nation stands under higher judgment." The essay grew out of his opposition to the Vietnam war, a moral and political crisis he argued had sparked America's "third time of trial," a period of testing and soul-searching akin to those of the Revolution and the Civil War. Bellah has raised awareness of the values that are at the core of the American democratic institutions and of the dangers of individualism unchecked by social responsibility. He spent 50 years studying religion, and although retired, he continues to battle gloom, preaching hope, though in his writings he admits to a deepening gloom over the perilous state of the nation and the world.

Major Literature

Bellah, Robert N. *Beyond Belief: Essays on Religion in a Post-Traditional World*. Berkeley, California: University of California Press, 1970.
___. *The Broken Covenant: American Civil Religion in Time of Trial*. New York: Harper Collins Publishers, Inc., 1975.
___, and Richard Madsen (Eds.). *Individualism and Commitment in American Life: Readings*

on the *Themes of Habits of the Heart*. New York: Harper Collins Publishers, Inc., 1987.

Bellah, Robert N., et al. *The Good Society*. New York: Alfred A. Knopf, 1991.

Bellah, Robert N. *Imagining Japan: The Japanese Tradition and its Modern Interpretation*. Berkeley, California: University of California Press, 2003.

___, and Steven M. Tipton (Eds.). *The Robert Bellah Reader*. Durham, North Carolina: Duke University Press, 2006.

Bendix, Reinhard (1916–1991)

HISTORICAL SOCIOLOGY

Born in Berlin, Germany, Reinhard Bendix immigrated to the U.S. in 1938 and received his B.S., M.A., and Ph.D. degrees from the University of Chicago, Illinois, where he taught from 1943 to 1946. He then taught for a year in the Sociology Department of the University of Colorado, Boulder. He went on to teach at the Department of Sociology at the University of California, Berkeley, from 1947 until he retired. He was elected president of the American Sociological Association in 1969 and from 1968 to 1970 he served as director of the University of California Education Abroad Program in Göttingen, Germany. In 1972 he joined the Department of Political Science at Berkeley, and was guest professor at several universities in America, England, Germany, and Israel.

Bendix received many prestigious awards in America and in Germany and had honorary doctorates from three universities. He was elected to serve as the 61st president of the American Sociological Association. His presidential address, titled "Sociology and the Distrust of Reason," was delivered at the association's annual meeting on August 31, 1970, in Washington, D.C. In his honor as professor of sociology and political science at the University of California, Berkeley, the Institute of International Studies there established the Reinhard Bendix Memorial Research Fellowship for Berkley graduate students who are working for their Ph.D. in the field of political and social theory or historic studies of society and politics.

Major Contributions

Bendix wrote in the areas of political and social theory as well as historical studies of society and politics. He had a keen interest in working with other disciplines; throughout his career, Bendix saw himself as someone who lived between cultures, building connections between academic disciplines in the United States and Germany. Bendix is known for his full-scale study of the work of Max Weber (see entry) in *Max Weber: An Intellectual Portrait* (Doubleday, 1960), in which he explored some of Weber's major themes of enquiry. Bendix was at work on a manuscript to be entitled *Unsettled Affinities* at the time of his death. In his role as a teacher, he worked to promote scholarship and intellectual exploration.

Major Literature

Bendix, Reinhard, and Seymour Martin Lipset (Eds.). *Class, Status and Power*. New York: Free Press, 1966.

Bendix, Reinhard. *Embattled Reason: Essays on Social Knowledge*. New York: Oxford University Press, 1974.

___. *From Berlin to Berkeley: German-Jewish Identities*. New Jersey: Transaction Publishers, 1990.

___. *Social Mobility in Industrial Society*. New Jersey: Transaction Publishers, 1992.

___. *Force, Fate and Freedom: On Historical Sociology*. Berkeley, California: University of California Press, 1992.

___. *Unsettled Affinities*. New Jersey: Transaction Publishers, 1993.

___. *Nation-building and Citizenship: Studies of Our Changing Social Order*. New Jersey: Transaction Publishers, 1996.

Berger, Peter Ludwig (1929–)

SOCIOLOGY OF CONSCIOUSNESS

Born in Trieste, Italy, and raised in Vienna, Peter Ludwig Berger immigrated to America shortly after World War II. He earned a B.A. at Wagner College, New York City (1949), and an M.A. (1950) and Ph.D. (1952) from New School for Social Research, New York City. He was assistant professor or associated professor at various universities, including five years at Hartford Theological Seminary, Connecticut (1955–1973). Since 1973 Berger has been professor at Rutgers University, New Jersey, and Boston College, Massachusetts; professor of sociology and theology at Boston University; and director of the Institute for the Study of Economic Culture, which Berger reformed in 1985 as the Institute on Culture, Religion and World Affairs at Boston University. Berger holds honorary degrees from Loyola University, Chicago; Wagner College, New York City; University of Notre Dame, Indiana; University of Geneva (Switzerland); and University of Munich (Germany). From 1966 to 1967 he was president of the Society for the Scientific Study of Religion.

Major Contributions

Central to Berger's work is the relationship between society and the individual. Berger's "subjective reality" describes how our understanding of reality is produced by how we interact with social structures. Much of Berger's work is related to understanding what it means to live in a multi-faith society. A lay Lutheran theologian, he is also a leading scholar in the sociology of religion and the sociology of knowledge, noted for the breadth and depth of his work and for his lucid style. Berger first gained a national profile in the United States with the publication of two books in 1961: *In The Noise of*

Solemn Assemblies and *The Precarious Vision* (published by Doubleday), in which he accused Protestant clergy of the day of smug conservatism and spiritual emptiness of the Protestant establishment. Berger went beyond a mere interpretation of religion to explore its social and psychological implications, seeking to integrate religion into the general structure of society.

For Berger, religion is a kind of "canopy" that shields individuals and, by implication, society from the ultimately destructive consequences of a seemingly chaotic, purposeless existence. But he was cautious; he insisted that religious truth claims must always be "bracketed" in the sense that they cannot be verified using the tools of the social scientist. For Berger, an important goal for both sociologists and theologians is to understand modern pluralism's characteristics, limitations, and likely impact on religious institutions and faith.

Major Literature

Berger, Peter Ludwig. *The Sacred Canopy: Elements of a Sociological Theory of Religion*. New York: Bantam Doubleday Dell Publishing Group, 1967.

___. *Homeless Mind: Modernization and Consciousness*, New York: Random House, Inc., 1974.

___. *The Precarious Vision: Sociologist Looks at Social Fictions and Christian Faith*. Westport, Connecticut: Greenwood Press, 1976.

Gay, Craig M., and Peter L. Berger. *With Liberty and Justice for Whom? The Recent Evangelical Debate Over Capitalism*. Vancouver, British Columbia: Regent College Publishing, 2000.

Berger, Peter L., and Samuel P. Huntington. *Many Globalizations: Cultural Diversity in the Contemporary World*. New York: Oxford University Press, Inc., 2003.

Bernard, Jessie Shirley (1903–1996)

MARRIAGE AND FAMILY

Jessie Shirley Ravitch was born in Minneapolis, Minnesota, gained a B.A. (1923)

and M.A. (1924), and married the sociologist Luther Lee Bernard (see entry) in 1925. After obtaining her Ph.D. at Washington University, St. Louis, Missouri, in 1935, she worked as a social science analyst for the U.S. Bureau of Labor Statistics in the late 1930s. She taught at Lindenwood College for Women, St. Charles, Missouri, from 1940 to 1947, and was professor of sociology at Pennsylvania State University (1947–1964). After resigning from Pennsylvania State University she was an independent scholar and writer who wrote influential feminist literature. Syracuse University awarded her an honorary doctor of laws degree in 1980. The American Sociological Association Jessie Bernard Award is given in recognition of scholarly work that has enlarged the horizons of sociology to encompass fully the role of women in society.

Major Contributions

Bernard is best known for her work on marriage, the family, the status of women, communities, social problems and public policy. It was she who explored the phenomenon of "his" and "hers" marriages, arguing that women fared much worse in marriage than men and advantages for men are not always shared by women. Bernard suggested that in marriages "his" is much better than "hers" on almost every indicator — demographically, socially, and psychologically. The debate still rumbles on. Researchers argue that married people are happier, healthier and better off financially than unmarried people. (This does not take account of the more recent trend of cohabiting rather than getting married.) A related health point is that married people are less likely to suffer from mental ill-health.

Bernard amassed a huge amount of data related to the lives of women in different contexts. What Bernard champions is a marriage of equality, but admits that this goal is not always easily reached. She is also known

for her work on the history of sociology and as a co-founder (1951) of the Society for the Study of Social Problems, which produces a *Social Problems Journal.*

Major Literature

Bernard, Jessie. *American Family Behavior.* Harper and Brothers, 1942; reprinted 1973.
___. *Academic Women.* University Park: Pennsylvania State University Press, 1964.
___. *Marriage and Family Among Negroes* (Spectrum Books). Prentice Hall, 1966.
Broderick, Cailfred B., and Jessie Bernard. *Individual, Sex and Society.* Johns Hopkins University Press, 1969.
___. *The Future of Marriage.* World Publishing, 1972, Yale University Press, 1982.
Lipman-Blumen, Jean, and Jessie Bernard. *Social Policy and Sex Roles.* Sage Publications, Ltd., 1979.
Bernard, Jessie. *Sex Game Communication Between the Sexes.* Macmillan Publishing Co., 1972.
Bernard, Jessie. *Sociology of Community.* Longman Higher Education, 1973.
___. *The Female World from a Global Perspectiv.* Indiana University Press, 1987.

Bernard, Luther Lee (1881–1951)
SOCIAL ATTITUDES

Born in Kentucky, Luther Lee Bernard gained a B.S. at Missouri's Pierce City Baptist College (1900); an A.B. at the University of Missouri, St. Louis (1907); and a Ph.D. in sociology at the University of Chicago, Illinois (1910). Bernard was professor of languages, Lamar College, Missouri (1903–1905); instructor in sociology, Western Reserve University, Cleveland, Ohio (1910–1911); professor of history and social science, University of Florida, Gainesville, (1911–1914); professor of sociology, University of Missouri (1914–1917); associate professor and professor, University of Minnesota, Minneapolis (1918–1925); professor at Cornell

University, Ithaca, New York (1925–1926); professor of sociology at Tulane University, New Orleans (1927–1928); professor of sociology, University of North Carolina, Chapel Hill (1928–1929); professor of sociology, Washington University, St. Louis, Missouri (1929–1946); and lecturer and visiting professor, Pennsylvania State College, Lewistown, Pennsylvania (1947–1950).

Bernard was visiting professor in the summers at Chicago, North Carolina, and the University of Washington, and was research counsel fellow in Argentina. He held many positions on committees and in associations in sociology and social welfare work, the most important of which was the presidency of the American Sociological Society in 1932. The Masaryk Sociological Society of Czechoslovakia conferred a medal upon him for his work in sociology.

Major Contributions

Bernard was known as America's favorite peripatetic professor of sociology, as evidenced by this career pattern. Bernard, the twenty-second president, was instrumental in founding the American Sociological Society's official journal, the *American Sociological Review*, in 1936. It was Bernard who invented the term "sociological science," a systematic classification of the environments:

- *Inorganic*, including the cosmic, climatic, geographic, and inorganic resource factors which condition man's behavior directly and indirectly (mainly the latter).
- *Organic natural environments*, including fauna and flora that made such a strong direct impact upon the collective behavior of primitive man and that have received so much emphasis from anthropologists.
- *Cultural environments*, including the material cultural environment; the bicultural environment, consisting of

learned overt behavior patterns, mainly neuro-muscular skills; the psychocultural or symbolic cultural environment, consisting of language forms and their accumulated cultural forms; the derivative control (chiefly institutional) cultural environments, so called because it is derived from the other three.

Major Literature

Bernard, L.L. "The Teaching of Sociology in the United States." *American Journal of Sociology* 15 (1909).
___. "Instincts and the Psychoanalysts." *Journal of Abnormal and Social Psychology* 17 (1923): 345–55.
___. *Instinct: A Study in Social Psychology*. New York: Henry Holt, 1924, republished by New York: Arno Press, 1979.
___. *An Introduction to Social Psychology*. New York: Henry Holt, 1926.
___ "Social Attitudes." In Alvin S. Johnson and Edwin R.A. Seligman (Eds.), *Encyclopedia of the Social Sciences*. New York: Macmillan, 1930.
___. *An Introduction to Sociology*. New York: Thomas Y. Crowell, 1942.

Bernstein, Basil (1924–2000)
SOCIOLINGUISTICS

The son of a Jewish immigrant family, Basil Bernstein was brought up in the East End of London, England. Although under age, he served with the Royal Air Force during World War II. After the war, he worked in Stepney, East London, with boys' clubs for underprivileged Jewish children age 9 and 18. In 1947 he attended the London School of Economics and supported himself by doing any job he could get while he studied sociology. He then trained as a teacher at Kingsway Day College, London, and between 1954 and 1960 he taught at the City Day College, in Shoreditch, London; his students were almost all working class young men.

In 1960 Bernstein became a research assistant in phonetics at University College, London, and gained his Ph.D. in linguistics. He spent the rest of his career at the Institute of Education, London, and in 1967 he was appointed to a professorship and head of the sociological research unit. Bernstein was awarded a number of honorary doctorates, including ones from universities in Athens, Greece and Lund, Sweden. His work has had a huge effect on reforming educational practice abroad, particularly in Chile and Mexico. Just before he died he joined in a video link to Lisbon where a conference was being held in his honor.

Major Contributions

Bernstein is renowned for his work in sociolinguistics, the study of the relationships between language and social and cultural factors. The fact that humans speak is taken for granted; what Bernstein did was to highlight the link between language and culture and the different ways people use words. He developed the idea of "elaborated" and "restricted speech" codes linked to social class. The *elaborated code*, which uses standard English with correct grammar, is a more formal and public language that can be used to communicate in ways that most people would understand. The *restricted code* is used in informal ways and tends to be understood only by people who share an understanding of the context, and where the grammar is less formal. For example, a speaker using restricted code might say "I ain't done it" as against "I haven't done it." Or "It weren't me that done it" as against "I didn't do it." Bernstein argued that children from middle-class families have more opportunity to become familiar with both codes, and children from lower class backgrounds do not have the same opportunities to learn the elaborated code and that this will affect tasks such as those involving abstract thinking. Some theorists do not fully support Bernstein's theories but at the time they were revolutionary.

Major Literature

Bernstein, Basil, and Julia Brannen (Eds.). *Children, Research and Policy*. London, England: Taylor and Francis, 1996.

Bernstein, Basil. *Pedagogy, Symbolic Control and Identity*. Lanham, Maryland: Rowman and Littlefield Publishers, 2000.

Bernstein, Basil. *Class, Codes and Control*. 4 vols. London: Routledge, 2003.

Bielby, William T.

PSYCHOLOGY OF ROCK AND ROLL

William T. Bielby gained a B.S. in electrical engineering with high honors (1970) and an M.A. in social sciences (economics) (1972) from the University of Illinois, Urbana. He was research associate, Institute for Research on Poverty (1975–1977), and gained a Ph.D. in sociology (1976) from the University of Wisconsin, Madison. At the University of California, Santa Barbara, he was assistant professor, Department of Sociology (1977–1981); associate professor (1981–1983); chair, department of sociology (1992–1998); professor (1983–2005); professor (affiliated), Department of Statistics and Applied Probability (1993–2005); affiliated faculty, Center for Film, Television, and New Media (2002–2005); undergraduate chair (since 2005); professor emeritus, Department of Sociology (since 2005).

He was visiting professor, Graduate School of Management, University of California, Los Angeles (1985); 98th president, American Sociological Association (2002–2003); visiting scholar, American Bar Foundation, Chicago, Illinois (2003–2004); fellow, University of California Washington Center, Washington, D.C. (2004); and visiting distinguished John D. MacArthur Professor of Sociology, Northwestern University, Evanston, Illinois (2004). He received the Kathleen Gregory Klein Award for Excellence in Feminist Studies, Popular and American

Culture Associations (1986), and the Reuben Hill Research and Theory Award, National Council on Family Relations (1992).

Major Contributions

Professor Bielby (called the Rock and Roll Sociologist) entitled his presidential address (2002) "Rock in a Hard Place: Grass-Roots Cultural Production in the Post-Elvis Era" (*American Sociological Review*, 69 [February 2004]: 1–13). The emergence of rock and roll in the mid–1950s inspired many teenagers to consider making music themselves. They invented a new cultural form, predominantly male, the teen rock and roll band.

Drawing on research on cultural capital, status attainment, and deviant subcultural involvements, Bielby shows how participation in grassroots cultural production affects life-course paths. Much of his work has since focused on how men and women are differently employed, and differences that exist even when employed on the same job. Many employers appear to reserve some jobs for men and others for women. In a series of reports, Bielby and his wife, Denise, detailed the barriers facing female, minority, and older writers, which led to another line of research on how the social organization of the industry shapes the careers of creative workers. Bielby has been involved in several high profile cases of discrimination against female employees where his expert testimony has swung the case in favor of the plaintiff. His most recent interest is a comparison of white bands in the area where he grew up with nearby black bands.

Major Literature

Bielby, William T., and James N. Baron. "A Woman's Place is With Other Women: Sex Segregation Within Organizations." In *Sex Segregation in the Workplace*, edited by Barbara Reskin. Washington, D.C.: National Academy, 1984, pp. 27–55.
___. "Men and Women at Work: Sex Segregation and Statistical Discrimination." *The American Journal of Sociology* 91, No. 4 (1986): 759–799.
Bielby, William T. "Cumulative Disadvantage in an Unstructured Labor Market: Gender Differences in the Careers of Television Writers." *Work and Occupations* (1992).
___. "Organizational Mediation of Project-Based Careers: Talent Agencies and the Careers of Screenwriters." *American Sociological Review*, 64 (1999).

Blackmar, Frank Wilson (1854–1931)
Sociology Pioneer

Born at Springfield, Erie County, Pennsylvania, Frank Wilson Blackmar graduated with an A.B. degree (1881) from the University of the Pacific at San Jose, California, where he was professor of mathematics until 1886. He then joined Johns Hopkins University, Baltimore, Maryland, as a graduate student and was an instructor in history (1887–1888) and a fellow in history and politics (1888–1889). In 1889 he received his Ph.D. and moved to the University of Kansas, Lawrence, first as professor of history and sociology (1889–1899), then professor of sociology and economics, establishing it as one of the oldest departments in the country. When the Lawrence graduate school was organized in 1896, Blackmar was elected dean and served until 1922. He served as the 9th president of the American Sociological Society (Association, 1959). His presidential address, "A Working Democracy," was delivered at the organization's annual meeting in Chicago in 1919.

Major Contributions

In 1890, at Lawrence, Blackmar started a course called "Elements of Sociology," which is still offered in the prospectus, and was the first of its kind offered in the United States. Blackmar believed wholeheartedly in serving the community by putting to use his sociological knowledge. To this end he gave countless lectures to adult groups all over the state. With others, Blackmar wrote much of the Kansas Juvenile Code, and he also served in official advisory roles for state government.

Students virtually forced Blackmar out of office on account of his autocratic style. His last full academic year was 1928–1929, and the university took the unusual step of paying him a pension, 13 years before a pension plan would begin for all faculty. On April 5–6, 1991, the Department of Sociology at the University of Kansas recognized Blackmar and the dozens of sociologists who followed him by holding a Centennial celebration, "Sociology as a Vocation."

Major Literature

Blackmar, Frank Wilson. *Spanish Colonization of the Southwest*. 1890. New York: AMS Press, Inc., 1940.
___. *Spanish Institutions in the Southwest*. Baltimore: Johns Hopkins University Press, 1891.
___. *The Story of Human Progress*. Leavenworth, Kansas: Press of Ketcheson and Reeves, 1896.
___. *History of Higher Education in Kansas*. Washington, D.C.: Government Printing Office, 1900.
___. *Life of Charles Robinson*. Manchester, New Hampshire: Ayer Co. Publishers, 1900.
___. *Elements of Sociology*. New York: MacMillan, 1905.
___. *The Purposes and Benefits of Social Surveys*. Lawrence, Kansas: League of Kansas Municipalities, 1915.
___. *Justifiable Individualism*. New York: Thomas Y. Crowell, 1922.

Blau, Peter Michael (1918–2002)

FORMAL ORGANIZATIONS

Born in Vienna, Austria, the son of secular Jews, Peter Michael Blau was convicted in 1935 of high treason and given a 10-year sentence in federal prison for writing in the underground newspaper of the Socialist Worker's Party. When the National Socialists came to power he was released. His family remained in Austria after Hitler annexed Austria in 1938, although his sister was evacuated to Britain. Blau escaped and immigrated to the United States in 1939, where he attended Elmhurst College in Illinois on a refugee scholarship, majoring in sociology. He graduated with a B.A. in 1942 — the year his family was killed in Auschwitz — then spent three years in the U.S. Army, where he served as an interrogation officer in Europe. He gained his Ph.D. from Columbia University, New York, in 1952 and was professor at the University of Chicago, Illinois, from 1953 to 1970, and was then professor at Columbia until he retired in 1988, although he carried on teaching until 2001.

He was 65th president of the American Sociological Association in 1974. Blau is considered one of the founders of contemporary American sociology and one of the most prominent scholars of his time. Among his many honors, he was an honorary professor at the Tianjin Academy of Social Sciences in China.

Major Contributions

Blau's Ph.D. dissertation was on bureaucracy, which led to his book *The Dynamics of Bureaucracy: A Study of Interpersonal Relations in Two Government Agencies* (Chicago: University of Chicago Press, 1955). For the next 50 years, Blau studied the visible characteristics of society; his theories seek to explain how social phenomena such as upward mobility, occupational opportunity, heterogeneity, and population structures influence human behavior.

Another area of his work is social exchange theory, which is based on a central premise that the exchange of social and material resources is a fundamental form of human interaction. All relationships have give and take, although the balance of this exchange is not always equal. Social exchange theory explains how we feel about a relationship with another person as depending on our perceptions of:

- The balance between what we put into the relationship and what we get out of it.
- The kind of relationship we deserve.
- The chances of having a better relationship with someone else.

Exchange varies from setting to setting and would be different at work and at home, between siblings, and between children and parents.

Major Literature

Blau, Peter M. *Inequality and Heterogeneity*. New York: The Free Press, 1978.
___, Otis Dudley Duncan, and Andrea Tyree. *The American Occupational Structure*. New York: The Free Press, 1978.
Blau, Peter M. *Exchange and Power in Social Life*. Transaction Publishers, 1986.
Blau, Peter M., and Marshall W. Meyer. *Bureaucracy in Modern Society*. McGraw-Hill Education, 1987.
Blau, Peter M., and Joseph E. Schwartz. *Crosscutting Social Circles: Testing a Macrostructural Theory of Intergroup Relations*. New Jersey: Transaction Publishers, 1997.

Bloemraad, Irene

SOCIOLOGY OF IMMIGRATION

Irene Bloemraad gained a B.A. in political science with first class honors (1995) and an M.A. in sociology (1996) from McGill University, Montreal, Quebec, Canada, and Ph.D. in sociology at Harvard University, Cambridge, Massachusetts (2003). She was assistant professor, Department of Sociology, University of California, Berkeley (2003), and since 2006 she has been research fellow at the Institute for the Study of Labor, an independent research agency based in Bonn, Germany, that focuses on the economic analysis of national and international labor markets.

Her awards and honors include the Oswald Hall Prize for the best first-year graduate student, Department of Sociology, McGill University (1996); Sawyer Fellowship in the Performance of Democracies, Weatherhead Center for International Affairs, Cambridge, Massachusetts (2000); Social Science Research Council International Migration Dissertation Fellowship, New York (2000–2001). Bloemraad is a reviewer for *American Journal of Sociology*, *Contexts*, *Du Bois Review*, *International Migration Review*, *Perspectives on Politics*, *Sociological Forum*, Harvard University Press, Canadian Social Science and Humanities Research Council, and U.S. National Science Foundation.

Major Contributions

Bloemraad's main research interests are citizenship (including naturalization and dual nationality), immigrants' civic and political incorporation, multiculturalism and comparative political sociology. Bloemraad's work has appeared in journals such as *Social Forces*, *Social Science Quarterly*, *International Migration Review* and *Journal of Ethnic and Migration Studies*. Her 2006 book, *Becoming a Citizen*, compares immigrants' acquisition of citizenship and political participation in the United States and Canada. She argues that government settlement and multiculturalism policies have led to better outcomes in political incorporation in Canada over the last thirty years compared to the United States. In the context of current debates around immigration in the United States, her work suggests that any effective immigration policy must examine not just border control, but also integration and settlement policies. Current research focuses on immigrants' civic and political engagement in the United States and the political socialization of Mexican-origin residents of the San

Francisco Bay area, both projects funded by the Russell Sage Foundation.

One question of particular interest is whether non-profit community organizations provide alternative, accessible avenues to leadership and advocacy for women. Bloemraad has developed immigration seminars at the graduate and undergraduate levels and runs an informal immigration workshop for those researching immigrant-related topics.

Major Literature

Bloemraad, Irene. "Portuguese Immigrants and Citizenship in North America." *Lusotopie* 5 (1999): 103–120. Published in Paris by Kartha.
___. "Outsiders and Insiders: Collective Identity and Collective Action in the Quebec Independence Movement, 1995." *Research in Political Sociology (The Politics of Social Inequality)* 9 (2001): 271–305. Published in Amsterdam by Elsevier.
___. "Who Claims Dual Citizenship? The Limits of Postnationalism, the Possibilities of Transnationalism, and the Persistence of Traditionalism." *International Migration Review* 38 (2) (2004): 389–426.
___. *Becoming a Citizen: Incorporating Immigrants and Refugees in the United States and Canada.* Berkeley, California: University of California Press, 2006.
___. "Citizenship Lessons from the Past: The Contours of Immigrant Naturalization in the Early Twentieth Century." *Social Science Quarterly* 87, Issue s1 (2006): 927.

Bogardus, Emory Stephen (1882–1973)

SOCIAL DISTANCE SCALE

Born near Belvidere, Illinois, Emory Stephen Bogardus graduated with B.A. (1908) and M.A. (1909) degrees from Northwestern University, Illinois, where he majored in psychology. He received his Ph.D. from Chicago, Illinois, in 1911. He became assistant professor at Southern California University in 1911 and was soon appointed professor and head of the department of sociology. He edited the sociological monographs *Journal of Applied Sociology, Journal of Sociology and Social Research*, and *Research News*.

He was the twenty-first president of the American Sociological Society, 1931; his presidential address was "Social Process on the Pacific Coast." He believed that the meeting of the East and the West would, through overlapping and interpenetration, bring into existence a new culture. The breadth of his work was heightened by face-to-face contact with groups in England, Europe, China, Japan, the Philippines and South America.

Major Contributions

Bogardus' contributions are in the fields of race relations, occupational attitudes, public opinion, the consumer cooperative movement, and leadership, plus thirty-six years as head of the department of sociology, dean of a school of social work, and dean of a graduate school. Bogardus founded the University of Southern California Department of Sociology in 1915. He was a prolific writer over more than fifty years, in general sociology, leadership, social distance, race and ethnic groups, social psychology, and social research. His study of immigration and social inequality led to his publication of several books on the subject.

In 1929, he helped found the Pacific Sociological Association and served as its first president. He also founded Alpha Kappa Delta (AKD), the sociology honor society, in 1920. The Bogardus Award was established by AKD to honor outstanding faculty in the Department of Sociology at Iowa State and is presented annually to the faculty member who students feel is most deserving based on the criteria of creativity in teaching and high standards of scholarship.

He produced the "Bogardus Social Distance Scale," used in social research to measure people's willingness to have contact of varying degrees of closeness with members of diverse social groups, such as other racial, religious and ethnic groups, sex offenders, and homosexuals. This research was developed during the 1920s, when Bogardus was the director of the Pacific Coast Race Relations Survey.

Major Literature

Bogardus, Emory Stephen. *Introduction to Sociology.* Los Angles, California: University of Southern California Press, 1917.

___. "A Social Distance Scale." *Sociology and Social Research* 3 (1933): 265–271.

___. *Dictionary of Cooperation* (Including Supplementary Materials). Cooperative League of the United States of America, 1943.

___. *The Development of Social Thought.* New York: Longmans Green, 1952. Westport, Connecticut: Greenwood Press, 1979.

___. *The Mexican in the United States.* Manchester, New Hampshire: Ayer Co. Publishers, 1970.

Bourdieu, Pierre (1930–2002)

EDUCATION AND CULTURE

Born in Denguin, southwest France, Pierre Bourdieu studied philosophy in Paris at the École Normale Supérieure, and after qualifying in philosophy he worked as a teacher for a year, then served in the French army during the Algerian War of Independence (1958–1962). In 1959–1960 he lectured at the University of Algiers and studied traditional farming and ethnic Berber culture. In 1960 he returned to France and studied anthropology and sociology, then taught at the University of Paris (1960–1962) and at the University of Lille (1962–1964), after which he joined the faculty of the École pratique des Hautes Études, Paris.

In 1968 he became director of the Centre de Sociologie Européenne, Paris. In 1975 Bourdieu launched the journal *Actes de la Recherche en Sciences Sociales.* In 1981 he was appointed to the prestigious chair of sociology at the Collège de France, Paris. By the late 1980s Bourdieu had become one of the French's most respected social scientists. In 1980 he launched a new European review, *Liber,* to coincide with the fall of the Berlin Wall and the beginning of a new era. In 2001 a documentary film about Pierre Bourdieu — *Sociology Is a Combat Sport*— was a hit in Paris.

Major Contributions

Bourdieu studied the economic and sociological life of the peasantry in the Béarn, where he had been brought up, with particular reference to the number of peasants who did not marry. He and his colleagues studied how the transmission of a dominant culture maintains a system of power, and argued that the French educational system reproduces the cultural division of society because it affirms the differences between social classes. He supported striking rail workers, spoke for the homeless, was a guest on television programs, and in 1996 he founded the publishing company Liber/Raisons d'agir.

One of Bourdieu's arguments was that the struggle for social distinction is fundamental to all social life. Another is that all human actions take place within social fields, which are arenas for the struggle for the resources. Individuals, institutions, and other agents try to distinguish themselves from others, and acquire capital that is useful or valuable in the arena. Bourdieu considered television a serious danger for all the various areas of cultural production; in his view television degrades journalism because it must attempt to be inoffensive. He also regarded television journalism as coming under political control.

Major Literature

Bourdieu, Pierre, and Richard Nice (Trans.). *Distinction: A Social Critique of the Judgment of Taste.* London, England: Taylor and Francis Books, Ltd., 1986.

___. *The Logic of Practice*. Cambridge, England: Polity Press, 1992.

Bourdieu, Pierre, Gino Raymond, and Matthew Adamson (Translators). *Language and Symbolic Power*. Cambridge, England: Polity Press, 1992.

Bourdieu, Pierre. *The Field of Cultural Production: Essays on Art and Literature*. Cambridge, England: Polity Press, 1993.

___. *The Social Structures of the Economy*. Cambridge, England: Polity Press, 2005.

Brym, Robert J. (1951–)

POLITICAL SOCIOLOGY

Born in Saint John, New Brunswick, Canada, Robert J. Brym earned a B.A. with honors at Dalhousie University, Halifax, Nova Scotia and Hebrew University of Jerusalem (1972); an M.A. at Dalhousie (1973), and a Ph.D., at the University of Toronto (1976). He was assistant professor in the Department of Sociology at the Memorial University of Newfoundland (1976–78). At the University of Toronto's Department of Sociology, he was assistant professor (1978–80); associate professor (1980–84); and professor (since 1984). He was an associate at the Center for European, Russian and Eurasian Studies, University of Toronto (1980), and Desmond Pacey Memorial Lecturer, University of New Brunswick (1990).

His awards and honors include the Dean's Excellence Award, University of Toronto (1991, 1994, 1996, 1997, 2004, 2006); Oswald Hall Prize for Undergraduate Teaching Excellence, Department of Sociology, University of Toronto (1992–93); Outstanding Contribution Award, Canadian Sociology and Anthropology Association, for the first edition of *New Society: Sociology for the 21st Century* (1995); Hawthorn Lecture, Canadian Sociology and Anthropology Association (1996); Distinguished Service Award, Canadian Sociology and Anthropology Association (2001).

Major Contributions

Brym studies the social bases of politics and ethnic relations, in Canada, Russia, and Israel. A recent research project made policy recommendations to the office of the president of Russia to improve the efficiency of the Russian civil service. Brym is currently leading a research project on collective violence in Israel, the West Bank and Gaza, between 2000 and 2005. He has published about 100 articles in edited collections and scholarly journals, including *Slavic Review, Europe-Asia Studies, Canadian Journal of Sociology, Canadian Review of Sociology and Anthropology, British Journal of Sociology, East European Jewish Affairs, International Sociology, Social Forces*, and *Political Science Quarterly*.

Brym has presented his work extensively across Canada, the United States, Brazil, Israel, and other countries. He served as sociology editor of the *Canadian Review of Sociology and Anthropology* from 1986 until 1989, general editor of Sage Studies in International Sociology from 1990 until 1993, editor of *Current Sociology* from 1993 until 1997, and co-editor of *East European Jewish Affairs* from 2001 until 2005. He is also interested in promoting sociological knowledge through media other than books. He has published interactive web sites to accompany sociological texts.

Major Literature

Brym, Robert, and Bonnie J Fox. *From Culture to Power: The Sociology of English Canada*. Toronto: Oxford University Press, 1989. World Wide Web edition (2005), http://www.chass.utoronto.ca/brym/cpALL.html.

Brym, Robert, with the assistance of Rozalina Ryvkina. *The Jews of Moscow, Kiev and Minsk: Identity, Antisemitism, Emigration*. London: Macmillan. New York: New York University Press, 1994.

Brym, Robert. *Intellectuals and Politics*. London and Boston: George Allen and Unwin, 1980. World Wide Web edition (2005), http://www.chass.utoronto.ca/brym/ipALL.html.

___, and John Lie. *Sociology: Your Compass for a New World.* 3rd ed. Belmont, California: Wadsworth, 2007; also in Canadian and Brazilian editions.

Brym, Robert. *Sociology as a Life or Death Issue.* New York and Toronto: Penguin, 2007.

Burgess, Ernest Watson (1886–1966)

URBAN SOCIOLOGY

Born in Tilbury, Ontario, Canada, the son of a minister in the Congregational Church, Ernest Watson Burgess gained a B.A., at Kingfisher College, Kingfisher County, Oklahoma (1908), and a Ph.D. at the University of Chicago's Department of Sociology, Illinois (1913). His dissertation was "The Function of Socialization in Social Evolution." He was assistant professor of sociology at the University of Kansas, Lawrence (1913–1915) and at Ohio State University, Athens (1915–1916). At University of Chicago, he was assistant professor (1916–1921); associate professor (1921–1927); professor (1927); chairman of the department (1946–1951); and professor emeritus (1951).

He was 24th president of the American Sociological Association (1934); his presidential address was "Social Planning and the Mores." He was editor of the *American Journal of Sociology* (1936–1940).

Major Contributions

Throughout his career, Burgess worked hard to encourage specialists from all the different social science areas to work together on joint research projects. Burgess's scientific inquiry into the nature of the family led him to investigate marriage stability and the possibility of predicting success or failure in marriage. He theorized that the quality of adjustment depended on the gradual fusing of attitudes and social characteristics of the husband and wife. He edited *Aging in Western Societies*, a work that considered the effects of retirement and the efficacy of government programs for the aged.

Burgess' groundbreaking social ecology research, in conjunction with his colleague, Robert E. Park (see entry), provided the impetus for the development of the Chicago School founded in 1892 by Albion Small (see entry). *Introduction to the Science of Sociology* (Chicago: University of Chicago Press, 1967) was a highly influential sociology text and became the "Bible of Sociology" for many sociology students. Much of Burgess's collaborative research with Park focused on urban land use and the social aspects of the urban community.

In 1942, Burgess was elected president of the National Conference on Family Relations, an organization he had helped found in 1938 after his involvement with the White House Conference on Child Health and Protection. His final project, the study of old age, combined the efforts of medical doctors, psychiatrists, psychologists, anthropologists, and sociologists in a single all-inclusive effort.

Major Literature

Park, Robert E., and Ernest Watson Burgess. *Introduction to the Science of Sociology.* Chicago, Illinois: University of Chicago Press, 1921, 1970.

Burgess, Ernest Watson (Ed.). *Aging in Western Societies.* Chicago, Illinois: University of Chicago Press, 1960.

___, and Donald J. Bogue (Eds.). *Contributions to Urban Sociology.* Chicago, Illinois: University of Chicago Press, 1964.

Burgess, Ernest Watson. *Urban Sociology.* Chicago, Illinois: University of Chicago Press, 1967.

___. *The Family.* New York: Van Nostrand Reinhold, 1971.

___. *Community, Family and Delinquency.* Chicago, Illinois: University of Chicago Press, 1974, 1977.

Park, Robert E., and Ernest Watson Burgess. *The City.* Chicago, Illinois: University of Chicago Press, 1984.

Cadge, Wendy (1975–)

SOCIOLOGY OF RELIGION

Born in Somerville, Maryland, Wendy Cadge gained a B.A. in sociology, anthropology and religion at Swarthmore College, Swarthmore, Pennsylvania (1997). At Princeton University, New Jersey, in the Department of Sociology she gained an M.A. in religion, gender and sexuality, and economic development in South Asia (2000), and a Ph.D. in sociology (2002). Her Dissertation was "Seeking the Heart: The First Generation Practices Theravada Buddhism in America." She was acting associate director, Center for the Study of Religion (2002–2003). Cadge was also assistant professor of sociology, Bowdoin College, Brunswick, Maine (2003–2006); Robert Wood Johnson Foundation Scholar in Health Policy Research, Harvard University, Cambridge, Massachusetts (2004–2006); and assistant professor of sociology, Brandeis University, Waltham, Massachusetts (since 2006).

Major Contributions

Cadge's focus of research is sociology of religion, culture, health and medicine, immigration, gender, sexuality, organizations and research methods. Her research focuses broadly on questions about meaning and identity in the contemporary United States. Her book *Heartwood* is an ethnographic study of how immigrant Buddhists from Thailand and mostly white convert Buddhists in the U.S. understand and practice Buddhism in their everyday lives.

Her current project, *Paging God: Religion in the Halls of Medicine* (book in progress) examines the historical and current institutional presence of religion and spirituality in hospitals. It draws from historical materials and the evolving policies of the Joint Commission for the Accreditation of Healthcare Organizations as well as from more than one hundred interviews with hospital chaplains, nurses, and physicians in large academic medical centers in the greater Boston area and across the country.

With the support of the Metanexus Institute on Religion and Science (an educational center based in Philadelphia, Pennsylvania, that promotes the engagement between science and religion from a religious perspective) Cadge is also working with several colleagues on a research project about spiritual capital in three small cities (Portland, Maine; Olympia, Washington; and Danbury, Connecticut) where large numbers of immigrants have settled since 1990.

Major Literature

Cadge, Wendy, Paul DiMaggio, Lynn Robinson, and Brian Steensland. "The Role of Religion in Public Conflicts Over the Arts in the Philadelphia Area, 1965–1997." In Crossroads: Art and Religion in American Life. Alberta Arthurs and Glenn Wallach, Eds. New York: The New Press, 2001.

Cadge, Wendy. "Vital Conflicts: The Mainline Protestant Denominations Debate Homosexuality." In The Hand of God: Faith Based Activism and the Public Role of Mainline Protestantism. Robert Wuthnow and John Evans, Eds. Berkeley, California: University of California Press, 2002.

Cadge, Wendy, Sara Curran, Chang Chung, and Anchalee Varangrat. "Boys and Girls' Educational Opportunities in Thailand: The Effects of Siblings, Migration, and Accessibility of Schools." Research in Sociology of Education 14 (2004): 59–102.

Cadge, Wendy. "Reconciling Congregations Bridging Gay and Straight Communities." In Gay Religion. Edward R. Gray and Scott Thumma. Lanham, Maryland: Alta Mira Press, 2004.

____. Heartwood: The First Generation of Theravada Buddhism in America. Chicago, Illinois: The University of Chicago Press, 2005.

____, and Sidhorn Sangdhanoo. "Thai Buddhism in America: A Historical and Contemporary Overview." *Contemporary Buddhism* 6 (1) (2005).

Carr-Saunders, Sir Alexander Morris (1886–1966)

DEMOGRAPHY

Born in Reigate, Surrey, England, Alexander Morris Carr-Saunders gained a zoology degree at Magdalen College, Oxford (1908), and in 1909 he was Naples Table scholar in biology and demonstrator at Oxford. He studied biometrics (1910) under the statistician Karl Pearson (1857–1936); read for the bar (1910–1914); was secretary of the Eugenics Education Society; social worker and sub-warden at Toynbee Hall, in the East End of London and member of Stepney Borough Council; served in the Royal Army Service Corps in Egypt (1914–1918); worked in the zoology department Oxford University with a particular interest in population (1919); was Charles Booth Chair of Social Science, University of Liverpool, England (1923–1937); chairman of the Population Investigation Committee (1936); director, London School of Economics, succeeding Sir William Beveridge (1879–1963), architect of the British Welfare State (1937–1955); and was on the Commission on Higher Education in the Colonies (1943) under Sir Cyril Asquith (later Lord Asquith of Bishopstone) (1890–1954).

He served on the Royal Commission on Population (1944–1949); was chairman in of the commission which promoted the University of Malaya (1947); and was chairman of the commission that led to the foundation of the multi-racial University College of Rhodesia and Nyasaland (1952–1953). His awards and honors include Fellow of the British Academy (1946); Eugenics Society, first Galton medal (1946); and created Knight of the British Empire (1957). He received honorary doctorates from ten universities in the U.K., South Africa, America, France and Malaya, and was made honorary fellow of Peterhouse, Cambridge; the University College of East Africa, and the London School of Economics.

Major Contributions

The Population Problem published in 1922 was one of the earliest significant historical studies in demography. At Liverpool, Carr-Saunders established a reputation for the teaching of social sciences and furthered the role of social science as a university discipline. As vice chancellor of the University of London, he was largely responsible for establishing several overseas university colleges, some of which became independent universities. Among them were the universities of Khartoum, the Sudan; Malaya at Kuala Lumpur; Ibadan, Nigeria; the West Indies at Kingston, Jamaica; and East Africa in Kenya, Tanzania, and Uganda. He was also chairman of the Inter-University Council through which the help of all the British universities was given to the colleges and universities of the dependent territories.

Major Literature

Carr-Saunders, A.M. *The Population Problem: A Study in Human Evolution.* Oxford, England: Clarendon Press, 1922. Manchester, New Hampshire: Ayer Co. Publishers, 1974.

___. *World Population.* Oxford, England: Clarendon Press, 1936.

___. *Young Offenders.* New York: Cambridge University Press, 1942.

___. *A Survey of Social Conditions in England and Wales as Illustrated by Statistics.* Oxford, England: Clarendon Press, 1958.

___. *New Universities Overseas.* London, England: Allen and Unwin, 1961. Westport, Connecticut: Greenwood Press Reprint, 1977.

___. *A Survey of Social Conditions in England and Wales.* Oxford, England: Clarendon Press, 1965.

Castells, Manuel (1942–)

URBAN SOCIOLOGY

Born in Hellín, Albacete, Spain, Manuel Castells graduated from the faculty of law and economics, Sorbonne, Paris (1964), and gained a Ph.D. in sociology at the University of Paris (1967), where he taught methodology of social research. He gained a *doctorat d'etat ès lettres et sciences humaines* (human sciences) at the University of Paris (Sorbonne) and doctorate in sociology from the University of Madrid.

He was assistant professor of sociology, University of Paris, Nanterre Campus (1967–1970); associate professor of sociology, École des Hautes Études en Sciences Sociales, University of Paris (1970–1979); professor and director, Institute for Sociology of New Technologies Universidad Autonoma de Madrid (1988–1993); research professor, Consejo Superior de Investigaciones Cientificas, Barcelona (on permanent leave since 1996).

At University of California, Berkeley, he was professor of sociology and professor of city and regional planning (since 1979) and chair of the Center for Western European Studies (1994–1998). He was research professor at the Universitat Oberta de Catalunya, Barcelona (2000); professor of communication and the first Wallis Annenberg endowed chair of communication and technology, University of Southern California Annenberg School for Communication, Los Angeles (since 2003). His awards have been numerous, from France, Finland, Chile, Portugal, Catalonia, America and Spain. In 1994, he was appointed member of the European Academy.

Major Contributions

Castells was one of the intellectual founders of what came to be known as the "New Urban Sociology." In 2000, he addressed the United Nations' Economic and Social Council on information technology and global development. *The Informational City* is an analysis of the urban and regional changes brought about by information technology and economic restructuring in the United States. In the early 1980s, Castells began to focus on the role of new technologies in economic restructuring. In 1989, he introduced the concept of the "space of flows"—the various components of the global information networks.

In the 1990s, he combined both strands of his research into a massive study, *Information Age*, published by Blackwell as a trilogy between 1996 and 1998; a second edition was published in 2000. In his trilogy he puts forward the view that societies are now structured around the net and self—the multiple practices through which people try to reaffirm identity. Castells also coined the term Fourth World.

Major Literature

Castells, Manuel. *The Informational City*. Cambridge, Massachusetts: Blackwell, 1989.
___. *The City and the Grassroots*. Berkeley, California: University of California Press, 1992.
___. *The Internet Galaxy: Reflections on the Internet, Business and Society*. Oxford, England: Oxford University Press, 2002.
___, and Himanen Pekka. *The Information Society and the Welfare State: The Finnish Model*. Aberdeen, Scotland: Aberdeen University Press, new edition, 2004.
Castells, Manuel, Jack Linchuan Qiu, Mireia Fernandez-Ardevol and Araba Sey. *Mobile Communication and Society: A Global Perspective*. Cambridge, Massachusetts: MIT Press, 2006.

Chapin, Francis Stuart (1888–1974)

SOCIAL CHANGE

Born in Brooklyn, New York, Francis Stuart Chapin gained a B.A. (1909) and M.A. in sociology (1910) and a Ph.D. (1911) from Columbia University, New York. He taught economics at Wellesley College, Wellesley, Massachusetts, for one year and then moved to Smith College, Northampton, Massachusetts, where he taught sociology and was department chair (1912–1921). He was also director of the Smith College School for Social Work (1918–1921), then professor of sociology and chair of the department University of Minnesota, Minneapolis (1922–1953), where he directed the social work program at the university and the Training Course for Social Work (1922–1950) and served as the first director of the newly developed School of Social Work in 1941.

Chapin retired in 1953 as professor emeritus, though he continued to write and edit works on sociology and social work during his retirement until his death. He served as the 25th president of the American Sociological Society (1935). His presidential address was "Social Theory and Social Action."

Major Contributions

Chapin played a key role in the creation of a quantitative, statistical sociology in the United States in the years 1920 to 1940. He devised "living room scales" to measure social class by items in the home, undertook studies of civic participation as a key to social adjustment, and proposed methods for the comparative study of social situations using experiment and control groups. Chapin proposed a cyclical view of social change, and anticipated later work on latent and manifest functions and on bureaucratic personality. Chapin also helped professionalize American sociology, being a prime mover in the creation of the Social Science Research Council and an active participant in the American Sociological Society (Association, 1959).

In 1929, Chapin took leave from Minneapolis to serve as editor of *Social Science Abstracts*, with which he had been involved

since its inception. A decline in subscriptions during the early years of the Depression was a major influence in the Social Science Research Council's decision on September 13, 1932, to discontinue its support of the journal, which ceased publication at the end of 1932. Chapin was a member of many social science and social work associations, including American Sociological Association, which he served as president in 1936, and the Minnesota Council on Social Agencies.

Major Literature

Chapin, Francis Stuart. *An Introduction to the Study of Social Evolution: The Prehistoric Period.* New York: The Century Co., 1905.
___. *Contemporary American Institutions.* New York, Harper and Brothers, 1935.
___. *Research Memorandum on Social Work in the Depression.* New York: Social Science Research Council, 1937.
___. *Experimental Designs in Sociological Research.* New York, Harper and Brothers, 1947.
___, and S.F. Weiss (Eds.). *Urban Growth Dynamics.* New Jersey: John Wiley and Sons, Inc., 1962.
Chapin, Francis Stuart. *Human Activity Patterns in the City.* New Jersey: John Wiley and Sons, Inc., 1974.
___, and Edward J. Kaiser. *Urban Land Use Planning.* University of Illinois Press, 1979.

Chodorow, Nancy Julia (1944–)

PSYCHOANALYSIS OF FEMINISM

Born in New York, the daughter of Marvin Chodorow, a professor of applied physics, Nancy Julia Chodorow graduated from Radcliffe College, Cambridge, Massachusetts (1966), before it became an integral part of Harvard University. She earned her Ph.D. in sociology from Brandeis University, Waltham, Massachusetts (1975) (a privately controlled non-sectarian university sponsored by the Jewish community), and received her psychoanalytic training at the San Francisco Psychoanalytic Institute.

Throughout her career Chodorow has been a sociologist, psychoanalyst, and an educator, and is a leading theorist in feminist thought, especially in the field of psychoanalysis and feminist psychology. In 1973 she taught Women's Studies at Wellesley College, Massachusetts, then from 1974 to 1986 she was assistant professor of sociology at California University, Santa Cruz. She is a member of the American Sociological Association and the National Women's Study Association.

Chodorow has received fellowships from the Stanford Center for Advanced Study, Stanford, California, the Guggenheim Foundation, the American Council of Learned Societies, and the National Endowment for the Humanities. In of 2000, she was the recipient of the Distinguished Contribution to Women and Psychoanalysis Award from the American Psychological Association. For her book *The Power of Feelings* she was awarded the L. Bryce Boyer Prize of the Society for Psychological Anthropology. She retired from the University of California at Berkeley in 2005.

Major Contributions

Chodorow is best known for her work on the central role that mothers play in child rearing and how the family is the prime focus for gender socialization. In her book *Psychoanalysis and the Sociology of Gender*, she challenges the traditional view that females are biologically predisposed toward nurturing infants. She also argues that it is the woman's need for reciprocal intimacy that is the drive to want to have a baby. Chodorow further argues that although the relationship a mother has with her infant son is close, mothers do not experience the same "oneness" as they do with female infants. The reason that women take on the mothering role is that men who have not been accustomed to close intimacy avoid such a role.

Chodorow proposes some radical views on the Oedipus complex and how it is worked through. She argues that a girl's pre-oedipal bond with her mother can continue after she develops a fascination with her father. She believes that Freud was much too general in his statements about women and men. She also maintains that psychoanalysis must take more account of the social and historical influences on the person.

Major Literature

Chodorow, N.J. *The Reproduction of Mothering: Psychoanalysis and the Sociology of Gender.* Berkeley, California: University of California Press, 1978, 1999.
____. *Feminism and Psychoanalytic Theory.* New Haven, Connecticut: Yale University Press, 1989.
____. *Femininities, Masculinities, Sexualities: Freud and Beyond.* London, England: Free Association Books, 1994.
____. *The Power of Feelings: Personal Meaning in Psychoanalysis, Gender, and Culture.* New Haven, Connecticut: Yale University Press, 1999.

Christakis, Nicholas Alexander (1962–)

MEDICAL SOCIOLOGY

Nicholas Alexander Christakis gained a B.S. in biology with honors Yale University, New Haven, Connecticut (1984). From 1987 to 1988, he was teaching fellow in the Department of the History of Science at Harvard University, Cambridge, Massachusetts. He gained a master of public health degree, Harvard School of Public Health, Boston, Massachusetts (1988) and an M.D., with honors, at Harvard Medical School, Boston, Massachusetts (1989).

At the University of Pennsylvania, Philadelphia, he was assistant instructor, Department of Medicine (1990–1991); resident in medicine, Medical Center (1989–1991); Robert Wood Johnson Foundation Clinical Scholar (1991–1993); National Research Service Award Fellow, Department of Sociology and Division of General Internal Medicine (1993–1995); fellow, Department of Medicine (1991–1994); instructor, Department of Medicine (1994–95); Ph.D., sociology (1995). He gained his final licensure and certification in 2002. At the University of Chicago, Illinois, he was assistant professor of medicine (1995–1998); associate professor of sociology (1999–2001); associate professor of medicine (1999–2001); professor of sociology (2000–2001); and professor of medicine (2000–2001). Since 2001 he has been professor of medical sociology, Department of Health Care Policy, Harvard Medical School, Boston, Massachusetts, and since 2005, professor of sociology, Harvard University, Cambridge, Massachusetts, where he co-directs the Robert Wood Johnson Scholars in Health Policy program.

He received the Distinguished Researcher Award, National Hospice and Palliative Care Organization (2006). He was a member of the editorial boards of *Law, Medicine and Ethics* (1988–1995), *IRB: A Review of Human Subjects Research* (1993–2000), *Journal of Palliative Medicine* (1998–2006), and *British Medical Journal* (1999–2006). He has been associate editor, *American Journal of Sociology* (2000–2001) and *Palliative Medicine* (since 2002).

Major Contributions

Christakis' research makes use of his medical, sociological, statistical, and public health training to study social factors that influence the delivery, uptake, and outcomes of medical care. His research has both practical and theoretical implications for patient care and public health, as well as for the fields of demography, sociology, and health care policy. In his recent work, he has been concerned with various aspects of the care of patients who are seriously, chronically or terminally ill, including prognosis and consequences of hospice use.

A related study focuses on the health of a couple when one is terminally ill. Having a spouse fall ill or die has powerful implications for the individuals involved, for society, and for health policy. It seems likely that improving the health of one partner in a marriage can have meaningful effects on the health of the other, and that both parties would value this — in a way that influences health policy.

Major Literature

Christakis, N.A. "Prognostication and Death in Medical Thought and Practic" (Ph.D. dissertation). Ann Arbor, Michigan: University Microfilms, 1995.
___. *Implicit Purposes of Proposals to Reform American Medical Education*. Philadelphia, Pennsylvania: Medical College of Pennsylvania Press, 1995.
___. *Death Foretold: Prophecy and Prognosis in Medical Care*. Chicago, Illinois: University of Chicago Press, 1999, 2001.

Clark, Samuel Delbert (1910–2003)

POLITICAL SOCIOLOGY

Born at Lloydminster, Alberta, Canada, Samuel Delbert Clark gained a B.A. in political science and history (1930) and an M.A. (1931) from the University of Saskatchewan, Saskatoon, Saskatchewan, Canada. From 1932 to 1933 he studied on an Imperial Order Daughters of the Empire Scholarship at the London School of Economics and Political Science. He gained an M.A. at McGill University, Montreal, Quebec, Canada (1935), and was lecturer in political science and sociology, University of Manitoba, Canada (1937–1938). At the University of Toronto, Canada, he gained a Ph.D. (1938), then worked in the Department of Political Economy (1938–1976) and was professor emeritus from 1976.

Clark was president of the Canadian Political Science Association (1958) and helped found the Sociology Department (1963), in which he was first chair until 1969. He was president of the Royal Society of Canada in 1975–1976. His awards and honors include the J.B. Tyrrell Historical Medal (1960); honorary president, Canadian Sociology and Anthropology Society (1967); honorary member, American Academy of Arts and Sciences (1976); officer of the Order of Canada (1978); and honorary doctorate, University of Toronto (1988).

Major Contributions

Clark was known for studies that interpreted Canadian social development through various states of disorganization and reorganization on a several fronts. His professionalism won him acceptance when Canadian academics were still skeptical of sociology as an emerging discipline, and with John Porter (see entry) he was joint founder of Canadian sociology. In the 1960s his interest shifted to contemporary consequences of economic change, especially suburban living and urban poverty. Clark established a distinct, interdisciplinary Canadian sociology, with roots in history and political economy as well as in American and European sociology.

He recruited many young and mid-career talents with a variety of theoretical perspectives and created the dynamic Department of Sociology at the University of Toronto; it won worldwide respect for the research carried on there. The University of Toronto became the leading producer of new Canadian Ph.D.s in sociology. After retiring from University of Toronto, Clark taught briefly at the universities of Edinburgh, Scotland; Lakehead, Thunder Bay, Ontario, Canada;

and Dalhousie, Halifax, Nova Scotia. His approach is essentially Canadian, in which he sees Canada as a vast set of hinterland communities; hinterlands, by their nature, love and hate the heartland. In Clark's hinterlands, people struggle to overcome the disabilities of distance, poverty, and outside control. Clark's work provides an understanding of this clash of civilizations — of hinterland against heartland — and the continuing struggle for political and economic power.

Major Literature

Clark, S.D. *The Canadian Manufacturers' Association: A Study in Collective Bargaining and Political Pressure.* Toronto, Canada: University Press of Toronto, 1939.
___. *The Social Development of Canada.* Toronto, Canada: University Press of Toronto, 1942. New York: AMS Press, Inc., 1975.
___. *Church and Sect in Canada.* Toronto, Canada: University Press of Toronto, 1948.
___. *Movements of Political Protest in Canada.* Toronto, Canada: University Press of Toronto, 1959.
___. *The Developing Canadian Community.* Toronto, Canada: University Press of Toronto, 1962, 2nd ed. 1968.
___. *The Suburban Society.* Toronto, Canada: University Press of Toronto, 1966.
___. *Canadian Society in Historical Perspective.* Whitby, Ontario, Canada: McGraw-Hill Ryerson, 1976.
___. *The New Urban Poor.* Columbus, Ohio: McGraw-Hill Education, 1978.

Coleman, James S. (1926–1995)

Sociology of Education

Born in Bedford, Indiana, James S. Coleman received his bachelor's degree in chemical engineering from Purdue University, West Lafayette, Indiana (1949), and his Ph.D. from Columbia University, New York (1955). He taught at Stanford University, California; the University of Chicago; Johns

Hopkins University, Baltimore, Maryland; and at Chicago, where he directed the National Opinion Research Center. In 1991 he was elected president of the American Sociological Association.

Coleman founded the interdisciplinary journal *Rationality and Society* to serve as a forum for discussion and debate of these issues. He was a member of the National Academy of Sciences, the American Philosophical Society, the American Academy of Arts and Sciences, the National Academy of Education and the Royal Swedish Academy of Sciences. From 1970 to 1973, he was a member of the President's Science Advisory Committee. Coleman was the author of nearly 30 books and over 300 articles and book chapters. Among his numerous awards were the Paul Lazarsfeld Award for Research (1983), the Educational Freedom Award (1989) and the American Sociological Association Distinguished Publication Award (1992) for Foundations of Social Theory.

Major Contributions

Coleman and several other scholars produced a report of over 700 pages — "Equality of Educational Opportunity" (often simply called the "Coleman Report, 1966"). It is one of the largest studies in history, with more than 150,000 students in the sample. One of the study's most prominent conclusions was that lower-class black children benefited academically from being in integrated schools. Coleman published the results of further research into the effects of school busing systems intended to bring lower-class black students into higher-class mixed race schools. His conclusion was that white parents moved their children out of such schools in large numbers; this is known as "white flight." Some prominent members of the American Sociological Association moved to have Coleman expelled for daring to reach this conclusion.

His other contributions lay in sociology theory — including the analysis of social change, collective action and rational choice — along with the sociology of education and of public policy. In 1980 Coleman headed a research team that launched the largest American survey ever conducted on the effects of schooling. The study, "High School and Beyond," continues to be conducted by the National Opinion Research Center at the university. The survey follows 75,000 people who were sophomores and seniors in high school in 1980 and examines how their education affected their lives and careers.

Major Literature

Coleman, James S. *The Adolescent Society*. Westport, Connecticut: Greenwood Press, 1961.
___. *An Introduction to Mathematical Sociology.* New York, Simon and Schuster, Inc., 1964. New York: MacMillan Publishing Company, 1978.
___. *Mathematics of Collective Action*. Chicago: Aldine Publishing Co., 1973, 2005.
___. *Youth: Transition to Adulthood*. Boulder, Colorado: Westview Press, Inc., 1973. Chicago, Illinois: University of Chicago Press, 1999.
___. *The Asymmetric Society*. New York: Syracuse University Press, 1982.

Collins, Patricia Hill (1948–)
SOCIOLOGY OF BLACK WOMEN

Patricia Hill was born in Philadelphia, Pennsylvania, and gained her B.A. degree from Brandeis University, Waltham, Massachusetts (1969), her M.A. in teaching from Harvard University, Cambridge, Massachusetts (1970), and her Ph.D. from Brandeis (1984). She was a teacher and curriculum specialist and director of the African American Center at Tufts University, Medford, Massachusetts, between 1976 and 1980. Collins became an assistant professor at the University of Cincinnati, Ohio, in 1982. She is married to Roger L. Collins, a professor of education at the University of Cincinnati.

Collins has published several books and over 40 articles and essays in a wide range of fields, including philosophy, history, psychology and sociology. She was appointed professor of African-American studies at the University of Cincinnati in 1993. The University of Cincinnati named Collins the Charles Phelps Taft Professor of Sociology in 1996, the first African-American and second woman to hold this position.

She was appointed professor emeritus of sociology at the University of Maryland, College Park, in 2005, and she was named a Distinguished University Professor there in 2006. Collins has taught at several institutions, held editorial positions with professional journals, lectured widely in the United States and abroad, served in many capacities in professional organizations, and has acted as consultant for a number of businesses and community organizations.

Major Contributions

Collins is widely regarded as one of America's leading black feminists. Her research and scholarship have focused on gender, race and social class, specifically related to African-American women. Some of her other sociological specialist topics are the sociology of knowledge, organizational theory, social stratification and work and occupations. She came to national attention for her book *Black Feminist Thought,* in which she makes the following assertions:

- Oppressions of race, class, gender, sexuality and nation are interconnected.
- Black women have often been restricted because of external definitions of black womanhood expressed through controlling images.
- Black women have created world views out of a need for self-definition and to work on behalf of social justice.

Collins's current research interests lie in investigating the current status of racial theory; analyzing how race, class, gender, sexuality, ethnicity and nation intersect as concepts and as social phenomena; and examining how issues of globalization and transnationalism affect black male and female youth.

Major Literature

Collins, Patricia Hill. *Fighting Words: Black Women and the Search for Justice.* Minneapolis: Minnesota University Press, 1998.
___. *Black Feminist Thought: Knowledge, Consciousness and the Politics of Empowerment.* London, England: Taylor and Francis Books, Ltd., Routledge, 2000.
Andersen, Margaret, and Patricia Hill Collins. *Race, Class and Gender: An Anthology.* Belmont, California: Wadsworth, 2003.
Collins, Patricia Hill. *Black Sexual Politics: African Americans, Gender, and the New Racism.* London, England: Taylor and Francis Books, Ltd., Routledge, 2005.
___. *From Black Power to Hip Hop: Racism, Nationalism, and Feminism.* Philadelphia, Pennsylvania: Temple University Press, 2006.

Comte, Auguste (1798–1857)
PIONEER OF SOCIOLOGY

Known as the "Father of Sociology," Auguste Comte was born in Montpellier, in southwestern France. He studied at the École Polytechnique until 1816, and when the school closed for re-organization he continued his studies at the medical school in Montpellier. He appears not to have settled consistently to anything and he earned money by doing small jobs and depended on sponsors and financial help from friends.

One period of stability was from 1817 to 1824, when he became a student and secretary for Claude Henri de Rouvroy, Comte de Saint-Simon (1760–1825)—the founder of French socialism—who brought Comte into intellectual society. His personal life was beset with many difficulties in personal relationships with some hint of mental instability, which involved a term in an asylum, yet he was unquestionably a man of genius and a great thinker. He died in Paris and is buried at the famous Cimetière du Père Lachaise, the largest cemetery in Paris.

Major Contributions

Comte saw one universal law at work in all sciences, which he called the "law of three phases"—theological, metaphysical, and scientific; to the last phase he also gave the name "positive." It was one of the first theories of the social evolutionism:

1. *Theological phase.* This preceded the Enlightenment of the 17th century, in which man's place in society and society's restrictions upon man were decided by the will God.
2. *Metaphysical phase.* This followed the Revolution and involved the justification of *universal rights.*
3. *Scientific phase.* This followed the failure of the Revolution and the defeat of Napoleon, and involved people finding solutions to social problems, despite proclamation of universal rights and the will of God.

His "law of three phases" developed into a systematic and hierarchical classification of all sciences, which he called *sociologie.* The idea was not unique but the way Comte organized it was. For Comte, this new science — sociology — based on positivism was the last and greatest of all sciences, one that would include all other sciences, and which would integrate and relate their findings into a cohesive whole. His emphasis on the interconnectedness of different social elements was a forerunner of modern functionalism.

Time has proved that sociology is but one science of many and not the central one as Comte envisioned. However, his emphasis on a quantitative, mathematical basis for decision-making is a foundation of the modern notion of positivism, modern quantitative statistical analysis, and business decision-making. Comte began to regard positivism as a religion, and he referred to himself as the Pope of Positivism.

Major Literature

Comte, Auguste. *Introduction to Positive Philosophy.* Translated by Frederick Ferre. Indianapolis, Indiana: Hackett Publishing Co., Inc., 1988.
___. *The Catechism of Positive Religion.* Boston, Massachusetts: Adamant Media Corporation, 2000.
___. The Positive Philosophy of Auguste Comte. Translated by Harriet Martineau. London, England: Continuum International Publishing Group Ltd., Thoemmes, 1853 edition, 2002.

Cooley, Charles Horton (1864–1929)

Socio-Psychology

Born in Ann Arbor, Michigan, the son of a highly successful Supreme Court justice and professor of law, Charles Horton Cooley received a B.A. (1887) and Ph.D. (1894) from the University of Michigan, Ann Arbor, for his dissertation on human ecology. He turned to sociology and started teaching at the University of Michigan in 1892, becoming a full professor of sociology in 1907, and remained there until the end of his life, devoting his work to the study of the self. He was one of the founder members of the American Sociological Society in 1905 (Association, 1959), and became president of the Society in 1918.

Major Contributions

Cooley merged history, social psychology and philosophy, and was associated with the

Chicago school of sociology formed in 1892, the first in the United States. He is best known for his work on the development of personality through the relationship between self and others. More precisely, through the concept of the "looking-glass self." He also developed the key concepts of primary and secondary relationships, which are crucial concepts in the study of groups, organizations and the family.

According to Cooley, primary relationships are long-lasting, founded upon strong emotional ties and a sense of commitment to each other. Primary relationships are such that one member cannot simply replace the other with a new person. A primary relationship exists between parent and offspring. Secondary relationships are relatively short-lived relationships between people, characterized by limited interaction, clear rules for relating and well-defined social roles. They rarely have much in the way of emotional involvement, and the members in the relationship can be replaced rather easily.

In the notion of the looking-glass self, Cooley emphasized that the self and society are bound together with bonds that are indissoluble. Thus Cooley forged a link between psychology and sociology. He argued that a person's self-identity grows out of relationship with other people. In order to develop the concept of "I" there has to be an accompanying concept of "you" or "they." Cooley's looking-glass self is based on how we think other people see us, although how we think they see us may not be an accurate reflection of how they actually see us. He identified six phases of the looking-glass self:

- My real person known only to God.
- My idea of myself.
- My idea of what you think of me.
- My idea of what you think of yourself.
- Your idea of me.
- What you actually think of me.

Major Literature

Cooley, Charles H. *Human Nature and the Social Order*. New York: Charles Scribner's Sons, 1902. New Jersey: Transaction Publishers, 1992.

___. *Social Organization: A Study of the Larger Mind*. New York: Charles Scribner's Sons, 1909. New York: Transaction Publishers, 1992.

___. "Roots of Social Knowledge." *American Journal of Sociology* 32: (1926–27) 59–79. New York: Irvington Publishers, 1993.

___. *On Self and Social Organization*. Chicago, Illinois: University of Chicago Press, 1998.

Coser, Lewis Alfred (1913-2003)

SOCIAL CONFLICT

Born Ludwig Cohen in Berlin (his father later changed the family name), Lewis Alfred Coser fled in 1933 from the Nazis to Paris, where he studied comparative literature and sociology at the Sorbonne. Active in Marxist politics, he was arrested by the French government in 1940 and placed in an internment camp in the South of France. In 1941, with the assistance of the International Relief Association, he traveled through Marseilles and Portugal and boarded a boat to New York, and on the advice of an immigration officer, changed his name to Lewis.

For the next ten years he supported himself largely as a left-wing journalist. He met and married Rose Laub (she died in 1994), the social worker for the International Relief Association who had arranged his visa. In the fifties, he enrolled as a graduate student in sociology at Columbia University and gained a Ph.D. in 1954. He taught from 1951 to 1968 at Brandeis University, Waltham, Massachusetts, where he founded the sociology department, and at State University of New York, Stony Brook, from 1969 until he retired in 1987.

He was elected 66th president of the American Sociological Association in 1974.

His presidential address was "Two Methods in Search of a Substance." Coser collected many honors and distinctions but always considered himself an intellectual first and a sociologist second. He retired to Cambridge, Massachusetts, where he was professor emeritus, first at Boston College and then at Boston University.

Major Contributions

Coser was the first sociologist to try to bring together structural-functionalism and conflict theory; his work was focused on finding the functions of social conflict. He argued that conflict might serve a useful purpose to fuse fragmenting groups together. In a society that seems to be disintegrating, conflict with another society may restore the group's identity and cohesion — uniting against a common enemy. This can be seen in the longstanding Israeli-Palestinian conflict, where both sides are united in their fight. Further back, there was the unity experienced by the British allies against Nazi Germany during World War II. The Vietnam protests united thousands of young people to take political action against the war. Conflict, tension and ambivalence had been so much a part of Coser's life that thriving on them became central to his identity.

Major Literature

Coser, Lewis A. *Continuities in the Study of Social Conflict.* New York: Simon and Schuster, Inc. The Free Press, 1967.

___. *Sociology Through Literature.* New Jersey: Prentice Hall, 1972.

___. *Masters of Sociological Thought: Ideas in Historical and Social Context* (2nd Ed.). Fort Worth: Harcourt Brace Jovanovich, Inc., 1977.

___. *Coser Introduction to Sociology.* London, England: Thomson Learning, 1983.

___. *A Handful of Thistles: Collected Papers in Moral Conviction.* New Jersey: Transaction Publishers, 1988.

___. *Men of Ideas: A Sociologist's View.* New York, Simon and Schuster, Inc., The Free Press, 1997.

Cottrell, Leonard Slater, Jr. (1899–1985)

EMPATHY IN SOCIOLOGY

Born in Richmond, Virginia, Leonard Slater Cottrell, Jr., graduated (1922) from Virginia Polytechnic Institute, Blacksburg, Virginia, and earned a master's degree in sociology (1926) from Vanderbilt University, Nashville, Tennessee. He moved to Chicago, where he earned his living as a probation officer, then gained his Ph.D. from the University of Chicago (1933). From 1935 to 1951, Cottrell was in the Department of Rural Sociology at Cornell University, Ithaca, New York, as a professor of sociology.

Soon after the attack on Pearl Harbor (December 1941), the War Department set up a Research Branch where Cottrell helped organize surveys of the morale problems of people in uniform. After the war, Cottrell expanded the department at Cornell by recruiting several colleagues from the research branch and was named dean of arts and sciences. He was secretary and research director of the Russell Sage Foundation in New York City from 1951 to 1968. His task was to help re-orient the foundation from social work education to applying the social science to other professions and to public policy studies. In his seventeen years there, he was sponsor and adviser for dozens of ventures in applied sociology. Much of the triumph of medical sociology traces back to the foundation (and also of the National Institute of Mental Health, which Cottrell long served also as consultant).

He was a visiting professor of sociology at the University of North Carolina, Chapel Hill, from 1968 to 1972, when he retired. He served as the 40th president of the American Sociological Association (1950). His presidential address, "Some Neglected Problems in Social Psychology" (*American Sociological Review*, 15, No. 6 [December 1950]:

705–712), focused on empathy. He argued that if empathy is a crucial element in human interaction, then why has it not been studied by social psychologists and sociologists? He posed seven crucial questions:

1. Is empathy a general capacity or is it specific to situations?
2. What type of early formative social relations are associated with varying levels of empathic responsiveness? in general? in specified types of situations?
3. What types of social situations heighten and depress empathic responsiveness?
4. What kinds of social relations and adjustments are made by persons of varying empathic capacity?
5. Is it possible to modify empathic responses by deliberate training?
6. If so, are solutions to certain problems in human relations facilitated by increasing decreasing the level of responsiveness?
7. Are there optimal levels of empathic responsiveness for the various social roles called for in our society?

Major Literature

Cottrell, Leonard S. *Developments in Social Psychology, 1930–1940*. New York: Beacon House, 1941.

___, and Sylvia Eberhart. *American Opinion on World Affairs in the Atomic Age*. New Jersey: Princeton University Press, 1948. Westport, Connecticut: Greenwood Press Reprint, 1969.

Foote, Nelson Northrup, and 'Leonard S. Cottrell. *Identity and Interpersonal Competence*. Chicago, Illinois: University of Chicago Press, 1955.

Dahrendorf, Ralf, Baron (1929–)

CLASS CONFLICT

Ralf Dahrendorf was born in Hamburg, Germany. Between 1947 and 1952, he studied philosophy, classical linguistics and sociology at Hamburg University and became a doctor of philosophy and classics in 1952. He continued his academic research at London School of Economics, England, as a Leverhulme Research Scholar, and gained a Ph.D. in 1956. He taught at the University of Saarbrücken in the then Federal Republic of Germany before becoming a fellow at the Center for Advanced Study in the Behavioral Sciences, Palo Alto, California (1957–1958). He was a professor of sociology at the universities of Hamburg (1957–1960), Tübingen (1960–1964), and Konstanz (1966–1969).

From 1969 to 1970 he was a member of the German Parliament for the Free Democratic Party (the German liberals), and a parliamentary secretary of state in the Ministry of Foreign Affairs. In 1970 he became a commissioner in the European Commission in Brussels. From 1974 to 1984 he was director of the London School of Economics, then returned to Germany to become professor of social science, Konstanz University (1984–1986). In 1987 he was appointed warden of St. Antony's College, Oxford; he was knighted in 1982, became a British citizen in 1988, and was made a life peer in 1993. He has received 26 honorary degrees from various universities.

Major Contributions

Dahrendorf's main argument is that Karl Marx defined class too narrowly and that his definition was limited by history. Whereas Marx described the fundamental differences of class in terms of property — those who own the means of production, and those who work for wages — Dahrendorf claimed that power and authority are at the root of differences in class. However, power is not absolute: a person may have power in one sphere but not in another. Thus, society could be split up into those who give orders and those who take orders. Dahrendorf's theory is that although there are inequalities of authority, excesses can, to some extent, be moderated by the political rights of the people.

In cooperation with Vienna's Institute for Human Sciences, "Project Syndicate" features Ralf Dahrendorf as one of its thought leaders to address such questions as: Why, after decades of peace and prosperity, are so many people in rich societies so profoundly unhappy? Why is there hardship in the midst of plenty? Are democracy and liberalism on a collision course?

Major Literature

Dahrendorf, Ralf. *Class And Class Conflict in an Industrial Society.* London, England: Taylor and Francis, Routledge, 1959, 1972.
___. *Society and Democracy in Germany.* Westport, Connecticut: Greenwood Press, 1980.
___(Ed.). *Europe's Economy in Crisis.* New Jersey: Holmes and Meier Publishing, Inc., 1982.
Dahrendorf, Ralf, and Theodore C. Sorensen. *A Widening Atlantic: Domestic Change and Foreign Policy.* New York: Council on Foreign Relations, 1986.
Dahrendorf, Ralf, et al. *Trust and Civil Society.* New York: Palgrave, 2003.

Davis, Kingsley (1908–1997)

DEMOGRAPHY

Born in Tuxedo, Texas, Kingsley Davis gained a B.A. in English (1930) and an M.A. in philosophy (1932) at the University of Texas, Austin; he earned an M.A. (1933) and Ph.D. in sociology (1936) at Harvard University, Cambridge, Massachusetts. Davis was assistant professor, Clark University, Worcester, Massachusetts (1936–1937); head of the Division of Sociology, Pennsylvania State University, Philadelphia (Penn State) (1937–1940); Social Science Research Council postdoctoral fellow in demography (1940–1942); conducted a fertility survey in Puerto Rico; worked at the Bureau of the Census; was visiting research associate, Office of Population Research (OPR), Princeton University, New Jersey; associate professor of Public Affairs, Penn State and research associate, OPR (1942–1944); associate professor of a new Department of Sociology and Anthropology, Princeton University (1945–1948).

He was on the graduate faculty of political science, Columbia University, New York City, rising from associate professor to professor of sociology; associate director, then director of the Bureau of Applied Social Research (1948–1955); professor of sociology, University of California, Berkeley; chairman of the Department of Sociology; founder of a program in international population and urban research, and helped establish the Berkeley Department of Demography (1955–1977); distinguished professor of sociology, University of Southern California, Los Angeles (1977–1981); and senior research fellow (part-time), the Hoover Institution, Stanford University, California (1981).

He was the first sociologist in the nation to be elected to the National Academy of Sciences (1966). He received the Irene B. Taeuber Award for outstanding research in demography (1978); Commonwealth Award for distinguished work in sociology (1979); and Career of Distinguished Scholarship Award from the American Sociological Association (1982).

Major Contributions

Davis was internationally recognized for his expertise in world population growth, the theory of international migration, world urbanization, demographic transition and population policy. He contributed to studies of American and worldwide societies, and coined the terms "population explosion" and "zero population growth." He was president of the Population Association of America and the 49th president of the American Sociological Association. He represented the United States on the United Nations

Population Commission and was a member of the Advisory Council of the National Aeronautics and Space Administration and the Advisory Committee on Population for the U.S. Bureau of the Census.

He was a principal exponent of the use of incentives in fertility control policies and a member of the American Eugenics Society. Davis led a social-science team sponsored by the Carnegie Corporation to 10 countries in Africa and directed studies of societies in India, Europe, and Latin America.

Major Literature

Davis, Kingsley. *Human Society*. New York: Macmillan, 1970.

___. *World Urbanization, 1950–70*. Westport, Connecticut: Greenwood Press, 1977.

___, Mikhail S. Bernstam, and Rita Ricardo-Campbell, (Eds.). *Below-Replacement Fertility in Industrial Societies: Causes, Consequences, Policies*. Cambridge, England: Cambridge University Press, 1987.

Davis, Kingsley, and Amyra Grossbard-Shechtman (Eds.). *Contemporary Marriage*. New York: Russell Sage Foundation, 1987.

Davis, Kingsley, and Mikhail S. Bernstam (Eds.). *Resources, Environment and Population: Present Knowledge, Future Options*. New York: Oxford University Press Inc., 1991.

Dilthey, Wilhelm (1833–1911)

HISTORICAL CONSCIOUSNESS

Born in Biebrich, Nassau-Wiesbaden, Germany, the son of a Reformed Church theologian, Wilhelm Dilthey studied theology, first at Heidelberg, then at Berlin, where he transferred to philosophy. In 1864 he gained his doctorate at the University of Berlin and was appointed to a chair at the University of Basel, Switzerland, in 1866; appointments to Kiel, in 1868, and Breslau, in 1871, followed. In 1882 he was appointed to the University of Berlin, where he spent the remainder of his career.

Major Contributions

Dilthey searched for the philosophical foundation of what he first and rather vaguely summarized as the "sciences of man, of society, and the state," which he later called *Geisteswissenschaften* ("human sciences"), a term that eventually gained general recognition to collectively mean the fields of history, philosophy, religion, psychology, art, literature, law, politics, and economics. He was the first to maintain that human sciences could not be subject to the same methodological investigations as the natural sciences and must be independent of the natural sciences; in so doing he broke new ground. His study involved the relations between several elements:

- personal experience in creative expression and the understanding of that experience;
- the interdependence of self–knowledge and knowledge of other persons; and
- the logical development from these to the understanding of social groups and historical processes.

Dilthey emphasized that the essence of human beings cannot be grasped by introspection but only from a knowledge of all of history. This knowledge can never be final, for history is constantly evolving. In all of this, Dilthey emphasized that there are some questions that can never be answered, and if this "not knowing" proves uncomfortable, it is often the spur for greater research.

His work reminded sociologists (although he did not call himself one) that the focus of their work is the human being, not something to be analyzed by some psychological theory but by languages and literatures, actions, and institutions. Above all, the social world can be understood only through the people who participate in it. For example, a study of groups must also try to understand the people who comprise the group. In this, sociologists have to be aware that they themselves are a part of the group and what they do must form a part of their observations.

Major Literature

Dilthey, Wilhelm. *Introduction to the Human Sciences: An Attempt to Lay a Foundation for the Study of Society and History* (1923). Detroit, Michigan: Wayne State University Press, 1988.

Dilthey, Wilhem. *Essence of Philosophy* (North Carolina University Studies in the Germanic Languages and Literature, No. 13). New York: AMS Press, Inc., 1954.

___, et al. *Wilhelm Dilthey, Selected Works: Poetry and Experience* Vol. 5 (Selected Works). New Jersey: Princeton University Press, 1997.

Du Bois, William Edwards Burghardt (1868–1963)

RACIAL OPPRESSION

Born in Great Barrington, Massachusetts, W.E.B. Du Bois earned a bachelor's degree (1888) at Fisk University, Nashville, Tennessee, and a bachelor's degree (1890), master's degree (1891) and Ph.D. (1895) at Harvard University, Cambridge, Massachusetts. He was the first African-American to earn a Ph.D. from Harvard. His dissertation was published as *The Suppression of the African Slave Trade to the United States of America, 1638–1870* (Mineola, New York: Dover Publications, Inc., 1970). After studying in Berlin he taught at Wilberforce College, Ohio, and then at Atlanta University, where he was professor of economics and history (1897–1910). While there he conducted extensive studies of the social conditions of black people in America.

In 1905 Du Bois helped found the Niagara Movement, which called for full civil liberties, an end to racial discrimination, full economic opportunities, and full education. The movement recognized that rights also demanded duties and responsibilities, which

were outlined as the duty to vote, respect the rights of others, work, obey the laws, be clean and orderly, send their children to school, and respect themselves, even as they respect others. The Niagara Movement became the National Association for the Advancement of Colored People (NAACP) in 1909, and in 1910 the historic magazine *The Crisis* was launched.

The teachings of Du Bois were an important influence on the Civil Rights Movement of the '50s and '60s. He embraced leftist ideology, was awarded the Lenin Peace Prize in 1958 and formally joined the Communist Party in 1961. For sixty-six years he functioned not only as a mentor, model, and spokesman for generations of black Americans but also as the conscience of black and white Americans alike who wanted racial equality and social justice. He conducted pioneering surveys that helped to dispel the white mythology about black people, on which racial prejudice is based.

He organized the first Pan-African Congress in 1919. In the last year of his life he moved to Ghana and took citizenship in that nation. Du Bois died on the eve of the historic civil rights march on Washington, August 28, 1963, addressed by Martin Luther King, who gave his famous "I have a dream..." speech. Actor and playwright Ossie Davis read an announcement of the death of Du Bois to the 250,000 people gathered the next day at the Washington Monument. On Jan. 31, 1992, a 29-cent stamp was released honoring W.E.B. Du Bois.

Major Literature

Du Bois, W.E.B. *The Philadelphia Negro: A Social Study.* New York: Lippincott, 1899. Philadelphia, Pennsylvania: University of Pennsylvania Press, 1996.

Du Bois, W.E.B., et al. *The Souls of Black Folk.* Chicago, Illinois: A.C. McClurg and Co., 1903. New York: W.W. Norton and Co., Ltd., 1999.

Du Bois, W.E.B. *Black Reconstruction in America 1860–1880*. New York, Athenaeum, 1935. New York: Simon and Schuster, Inc., The Free Press, 1999.

___. *Darkwater: Voices from Within the Veil*. New York: AMS Press, Inc., 1920. Mineola, New York: Dover Publications, Inc., 1999.

Duncan, Otis Dudley (1921–2004)

SOCIAL STRATIFICATION

Born in Nocona, Texas, Otis Dudley Duncan received his B.A. (1941) at Louisiana State University, Baton Rouge, and an M.A. (1942) at the University of Minnesota, Minneapolis. After three years in the U.S. Army during World War II, he was awarded his Ph.D. in sociology (1949) at the University of Chicago. He was on the sociology faculties at Pennsylvania State University, Philadelphia, Pennsylvania; the University of Wisconsin, Madison; University of Chicago; University of Michigan, Ann Arbor; University of Arizona, Tucson; and the University of California–Santa Barbara.

He was elected to membership of the National Academy of Sciences; the American Academy of Arts and Sciences; the American Philosophical Society; was awarded honorary degrees by three American universities, and was president of the Population Association of America (1968–1969). After retirement in 1987, Duncan wrote articles on the prevalence of creationism, the rising public toleration of atheists, the increasing number of people who specify "none" as their religion, the increasing public approval of euthanasia and suicide for terminally ill persons, and on some controversial statistics regarding gun use.

Major Contributions

Duncan was an early leader in the field of quantitative sociology, as distinct from qualitative sociology. Duncan and Peter M. Blau (see entry) carried out quantitative analyses of the first large national survey of social mobility in the United States. They showed how parents transmit their social standing to their children, which affects the children's education. This study led to later work to include the role of cognitive ability, race, and other factors in the transmission of social standing from one generation to the next. One conclusion was that education is more influential than social status in determining future success.

Duncan's work helped inspire a new generation of sociologists to follow and pursue quantitative sociology. In the 1980s Duncan adapted and introduced Georg Rasch's measurement theory and models for the evaluation of social surveys. Rasch (1901–1980) was a Danish mathematician, statistician, and psychometrician. Duncan introduced an index of residential segregation between whites and blacks and conducted a thorough study of racial segregation in Chicago. He laid the foundation for the United States General Social Survey, developed the Duncan Socioeconomic Index for measuring the social standing of individuals, and introduced structural equation models into sociology. These instruments and methods became established as standard tools for empirical sociologists worldwide.

Major Literature

Hauser, Philip M., and Otis Dudley Duncan. *The Study of Population*. Chicago, Illinois: University of Chicago Press, 1959.

Blau, Peter M., and Otis Dudley Duncan. *American Occupational Structure*. New Jersey: John Wiley and Sons, Ltd., 1967.

Goldberger, Arthur S., and Otis Dudley Duncan (Eds.). *Structural Equation Models in the Social Sciences*. London: Reed Elsevier Group, Academic Press Inc., 1973.

Duncan, Otis Dudley. *Notes on Social Measurement: Historical and Critical*. New York: Russell Sage Foundation, 1984.

___. *The Measurement of Population Distribution*

(Reprint in Social Sciences). New York: Irvington Publishers, 1993.

Durkheim, Émile (1858–1917)

SUICIDE

Émile Durkheim was a French social theorist, along with Karl Marx and Max Weber (see entries), who is widely regarded as one of the founders of sociology as a discipline, and founder of the French School in particular. Born in Épinal, France, from a long line of Jewish scholars, he graduated from the École Normale Supérieure, Paris (1882), and taught law and philosophy at a number of state secondary schools (1882–1887). While in Germany (1885–1886) Durkheim was impressed by the pioneering experimental psychology work of Wilhelm Wundt (1832–1920). From 1887 to 1902 he taught sociology at the university of Bordeaux and was professor of social philosophy until 1902. He moved to the University of Paris, where he wrote some of his most important works and influenced a generation of scholars.

Major Contributions

One of Durkheim's guiding philosophies was that spiritual progress is enhanced more by effort and sorrow than by pleasure or joy. Durkheim underwent a dramatic change in his religious beliefs and, like many of his day, turned to science and in particular to social science to provide the answers. Durkheim is the pioneer of the structural-functionalism perspective of sociology, which focuses on social systems as a whole, how they operate, how they change, and the social consequences they produce. Atomism is a different perspective — a social system is no more than a collection of individuals. A third

perspective is positivism — society can be changed by observing it and using the knowledge gained to improve the social condition.

For Durkheim, the common values shared by a society — the "collective conscience" — are the cohesive bonds that hold the social order intact. A breakdown of these values leads to a loss of social stability, or anomie (lawlessness) and to individual feelings of anxiety and dissatisfaction.

Durkheim on suicide

Suicide is an important subject in psychology and sociology. In Durkheim's systematic study on suicide, published in 1897, he argued that weak social ties resulted in higher rates of suicide. He predicted that Protestants would have higher rates of suicide than Catholics, since Protestantism emphasized personal autonomy and achievement more than did Roman Catholicism. Durkheim's classification of suicide is egoistic, altruistic, and anomic suicide.

Through Durkheim, sociology became an influential discipline in France that broadened and transformed the study of law, economics, linguistics, ethnology, art history, and history.

Major literature

Durkheim, Émile. *The Division of Labor in Society.* 1893, translated 1933. New York: Simon and Schuster, Inc., The Free Press, 1984.
___. *The Rules of Sociological Method.* 1895, translated 1938. New York: Simon and Schuster, Inc., The Free Press, 1965.
___. *Suicide: A Study in Sociology.* 1897, translated 1951. New York: Simon and Schuster, Inc., The Free Press, 1966.
___. *The Elementary Forms of Religious Life.* 1912, translated 1915. Montana: R.A. Kessinger Publishing Co., 2005.

Duster, Troy (1936–)
SOCIOLOGY OF RACE

Born in Chicago, Illinois, the grandson of Ida B. Wells-Barnett (see entry), Troy Duster gained a B.S. in journalism at Northwestern University, Evanston, Illinois (1957); an M.A. in sociology, University of California, Los Angeles (1959); and a Ph.D. in sociology, Northwestern University (1962). Duster was assistant professor, Department of Sociology, University of California, Riverside (1963–1965); research sociologist, Stockholm University, Stockholm, Sweden (1966–1967); assistant research sociologist, Center for Research and Development in Higher Education, University of California, Berkeley (1967–1970); and visiting associate professor, Department of Sociology, University of British Columbia, Vancouver, B.C., Canada (1969).

At University of California, Berkeley, he was associate professor, Department of Sociology (1970–1978); director, Institute for the Study of Social Change (1979–1997); professor, Department of Sociology (1979–1999); and chair, Department of Sociology (1985–1988). Since 1999 he has been professor, Department of Sociology, and director of the Institute for the History of the Production of Knowledge, New York University. He was president, American Sociological Association (2004). His awards: doctor of letters, Williams College, Williamston, Massachusetts (1991); chancellor's professor, University of California, Berkeley (1998); DuBois-Johnson-Frazier Award, American Sociological Association (2001); and Hatfield Scholars Award (2002).

Major Contributions

Duster's research and writing have ranged across a variety of subject areas: the sociology of law, science, deviance, inequality, race and education. In 1970, his first book, *The Legislation of Morality: Drugs, Crime, and Law*, became a classic in the drug field. In 1997, Duster threw into confusion the meeting at the National Human Genome Research Institute, where scientists were proclaiming that because the DNA of people with different skin colors and hair textures is 99.9 percent alike, the notion of race had no meaning in science. Duster then presented a forensics paper which claimed that criminologists could find out whether a suspect was Caucasian, Afro-Caribbean or Asian Indian merely by analyzing three sections of DNA. Race is a biological reality, with important biological outcomes, such as sharply higher rates of hypertension and prostate cancer in different racial populations

In addition to his books and book chapters, he contributed to national and international journals. Duster has been an editor for *Theory and Society*, *Sociological Inquiry*, *Contemporary Sociology*, *The American Sociologist*, and the American Sociological Association's Rose Monograph Series. He was chair of the Ethical, Legal and Social Issues Committee of the Human Genome Project. With his siblings, Duster has established the Ida B. Wells Foundation, which gives awards to journalists and researchers working in Wells' tradition of writing and speaking out for civil rights, civil liberties and social justice.

Major Literature

Duster, Troy. *The Legislation of Morality: Drugs, Crime, and Law*. New York: The Free Press, 1972.
___, and Garrett, Karen. *Cultural Perspectives on Biological Knowledge*. Norwood, New Jersey: Ablex Publishing Corporation, 1984.
Duster, Troy. *Backdoor to Eugenics*. New York: Taylor and Francis Group, Routledge, 2003.
Brown, Michael K., Troy Duster et al. *Whitewashing Race: The Myth of a Color-Blind Society*. Berkeley, California: University of California Press, 2003.

Elias, Norbert (1897–1990)

PROCESS SOCIOLOGY

Born in Breslau, Germany (now Wroclaw, Poland), of Jewish parents, Norbert Elias later became a British citizen. From 1915 to 1917, he served as a telegrapher in the German army, invalided out, and posted to Breslau as a medical orderly. He studied philosophy, psychology and medicine at the University of Breslau (1917–1919), spending three terms at the university of Heidelberg, and completed the pre-clinical part of medical training. He was deeply involved in the German Zionist movement and the German-Jewish youth movement "Blau-Weiss" (Blue-White). He gained a doctorate in philosophy, Breslau University (1924); studied sociology at the University of Heidelberg (1925); was accepted as a candidate for habilitation by Alfred Weber; and was academic assistant to his friend Professor Karl Mannheim (see entry), Sociological Institute, Frankfurt (1929).

In 1933, the Nazis closed Mannheim's clinic and Elias fled to Paris, then to London in 1935, where he was senior research assistant under Karl Mannheim at the London School of Economics (1939). He was detained at internment camps in Liverpool and on the Isle of Man as an alien (1940–1941). His father died in Breslau in 1940; his mother died in Auschwitz in 1941. Elias moved to Cambridge in 1941, taught evening classes for the Workers' Educational Association, trained as a group therapist under the psychoanalyst Siegfried Heinrich Foulkes, with whom he co-founded the Group Analytic Society in 1952, and then worked as a group therapist.

From 1954 to his retirement in 1962 he was lecturer at the Department of Sociology the University of Leicester, England, and was professor emeritus of sociology, University of Ghana in Legon near Accra, West Africa (1962–1964). Elias moved to Amsterdam (1965) and traveled much as a visiting professor, mainly at German universities. From 1978 to 1984, he worked at the Center for Interdisciplinary Research at the University of Bielefeld, Germany. He received the Theodor W. Adorno Award (1977) and the European Amalfi Prize for Sociology and Social Sciences (1987).

Major Contributions

Elias's work focused on the relationship between power, behavior, emotion, and knowledge over time. He developed what is called figurational sociology. In his study of the development of European societies from the middle ages, he called the changes in behavior and manners "the civilizing process." Elias maintained that social life is not based on individuals by themselves nor on social systems, but is made up of patterns (figures) all interacting in a sort of network.

Major Literature

Elias, Norbert. Reflections on a Life. Edmund Jephcott (Translator). Cambridge, England: Polity Press, 1994.
___, et al. The Germans: Power Struggles and the Development of Habitus in the Nineteenth and Twentieth Centuries. Cambridge, England: Polity Press, 1997.
___. On Civilization, Power and Knowledge. Chicago, Illinois: University of Chicago Press, 1998.
Elias, Norbert. The Civilizing Process. Edmund Jephcott (Translator). Oxford: Blackwell Publishers, 2000.
___. The Society of Individuals. London: Continuum International Publishing Group, 2001.

Ellwood, Charles Abram (1873–1946)

PSYCHOLOGICAL SOCIOLOGY

Born in New York, Charles Abram Ellwood graduated from Cornell University,

Ithaca, New York (1896), studied in Czechoslovakia, France, Italy, Austria, Germany, England, and in other places beyond the United States, and received his Ph.D. degree under Albion Small (see entry) at Chicago (1899). After a short period as secretary of a charity at Lincoln, Nebraska — where he also lectured in sociology at the University of Nebraska — he became professor of sociology at the University of Missouri, St. Louis, where he stayed until 1929, and where he became one of the leading American sociologists.

From 1929 to 1944 he was at Duke University, Durham, North Carolina, where he built up another successful sociology department. Along the way he was visiting professor, largely in summers, at several other universities, including Harvard University, Cambridge, Massachusetts. He was president of the State Conference of Charities and Corrections; president, International Congress of Sociology, Brussels, (1935); president, International Institute of Sociology (1935–1936); and member of National Education Association and director of the Department of Social Studies, (1922–1924). Ellwood was advisory editor of *The American Journal of Sociology* and an associate editor of the journal of *Criminal Law and Criminology*. In 1922, Bethany College in Bethany, West Virginia, awarded him an honorary LL.D. degree.

Major Contributions

Ellwood's sociological outlook is probably best described as psychological sociology, in which psychic forces are more of a cultural, than a biological, product. In 1925, Ellwood became the 14th president of the American Sociological Society (Association, 1959); the theme of his presidential address was intolerance. He was the first of the presidents who came all the way up through university training in sociology. Ellwood was concerned that intolerance seemed to be growing in every form of American life and he concluded that intolerance was a handicap to social progress. "But the worst examples of intolerance are to be found, not in our business and industrial world, but in the religious world," he said. Intolerance breeds separation, misunderstanding, and hostility between groups, which may lead to civic disorder and revolution. His remedy was to convert the people to a scientific attitude of mind. The aggregate sale of his books, Ellwood estimated, ran into more than a million copies, including foreign translations of several of them.

Major Literature

Ellwood, Charles A. *Public Relief and Private Charity in England*. St. Louis, Missouri: University of Missouri, 1903.
___. *Sociology and Modern Social Problems*. Woodstock, Georgia: American Book Company, 1905. Whitefish, Montana: R.A. Kessinger Publishing Co., 2004.
___. *The Reconstruction of Religion*. New York: Macmillan, 1922.
___. *Christianity and Social Science*. New York: Macmillan. 1923.
___. *The Psychology of Human Society*. New York: Appleton, 1925.
___. *Cultural Evolution*. New York: The Century Co., 1927.
___. *Man's Social Destiny*. Nashville, Tennessee: Abingdon-Cokesbury Press, 1929.
___. *Social Problems*. Woodstock, Georgia: American Book Company, 1932.
___. *The World's Need of Christ*. Nashville, Tennessee: Abingdon-Cokesbury Press, 1940.

Engels, Friedrich (1820–1895)

Dialectic Materialism

As with Karl Marx (see entry), Friedrich Engels, although not a sociologist, has exercised a profound influence on sociological thought. He was born in Barmen, Rhine Province, Prussia, the son of a Protestant textile manufacturer in Barman, with a cotton plant in Manchester, England. From 1838 to 1841, Engels worked as a clerk in the manufacturing town of Bremen. While in Bremen, Engels converted from an agnostic into a militant atheist and converted to communism in 1842. Not having had a university education, Engels had a flair for publishing radical articles under the pseudonym of Friedrich Oswald. Engel's friendship with Marx began in Berlin just before he left Germany in 1842 to help manage his father's cotton factory in Manchester (1842–1844).

In 1845, Engels published his classic *Die Lage der arbeitenden Klasse in England* (*The Condition of the Working Class in England in 1844*). In the summer of 1845 he escorted Marx on a tour of England, where his major purpose was that of attempting to convert various émigré German worker groups — among them a socialist secret society, the League of the Just — as well as leading French socialists to his and Marx's views. In 1847, when the league held its first congress in London in June 1847, Engels helped transform it into the Communist League; the *Communist Manifesto* followed in 1848, and Marx was exiled to England in 1849.

Engels sold his flourishing partnership in the Manchester business in 1869. He received enough for it to live comfortably until his death and to provide Marx with an annual grant of £350, with the promise of more to cover all contingencies. After Marx's death (1883), Engels became the authority on Marx and Marxism, and from Marx's uncompleted manuscripts and rough notes he completed volumes 2 and 3 of *Das Kapital* (1885 and 1894).

Although the names of Engels and Marx are always linked, Engels's ideas were significantly different. For example, he believed that although equality of wealth and incomes were possible under communism, efficient functioning of division of labor, in all its complexity, would always depend on inequality of power and authority. In addition to developing dialectic materialism, Engels explored the relationship between economic systems and male dominance and female subordination of women within families. Engels died before he could complete the final volume of *Das Kapital*.

Major Literature (See also, Karl Marx)

Engels, Friedrich. *The Origin of the Family*. London, England: Lawrence and Wishart, Ltd., 1940.

___. *Engels On Capital*. London, England: Lawrence and Wishart, 1941.

___. *The Condition of the Working Class in England*. London, England: Penguin Books, Ltd., 1987.

Marx, Karl, Friedrich Engels, and Martin Milligan (Translator). *The Economic and Philosophic Manuscripts of 1844*. Loughton, Essex, England: Prometheus Books, 1988.

Feuerbach, Ludwig, Karl Marx and Friedrich Engels. Wolfgang Schirmacher (Editor, Translator). *German Socialist Philosophy*. London, England: Continuum International Publishing Group, Ltd., 1997.

Engels, Friedrich. *Peasant War in Germany*. New York: International Publishers, 2000.

Erikson, Kai T. (1931–)

HUMAN DISASTERS

Kai T. Erikson was born in Vienna, Austria, the son of the psychoanalyst Erik Erikson (1902–1994) who immigrated with his family to the United States in 1933. Kai gained a B.A. from Reed College, Portland, Oregon (1953) and a Ph.D. at the University of Chicago, Illinois (1963). He joined the faculty at Yale (1966), where he edited the *Yale Review* (1979–89). Erikson is past president of the American Sociological Association, the Society for the Study of Social Problems, and of the Eastern Sociological Society. He has been a Fellow of the Center for Advanced Study in the Behavioral Sciences, Stanford, California and a Visiting

Scholar of the Russell Sage Foundation. His research and teaching interests include American communities, human disasters, and ethnonational conflict. He has been Master of Trumbull College, Yale University, New Haven, Connecticut; Chair of the American Studies program at Yale, editor of *The Yale Review*, and Chair of the Department of Sociology. Erickson served as the 76th President of the American Sociological Association (ASA). His Presidential Address, entitled "On Work and Alienation," was delivered at the Association's 1985 Annual Meeting in Washington, D.C. and was later published in the *American Sociological Review* (ASR February 1986, Vol. 51 No 1, pp 1–8). He is visiting professor of sociology, teaches in the department of sociology and American studies at Yale and has also taught at the University of Pittsburgh, Pittsburgh, Pennsylvania and Emory University, Atlanta, Georgia. His *Wayward Puritans* won the MacIver Award of the ASA; and *Everything in Its Path* won the Sorokin Award of the ASA; he twice won the top award of the ASA for the best book of the year.

Major Literature

Erikson, Kai T. *Wayward Puritans: A Study in the Sociology of Deviance*. Boston: Allyn and Bacon, 1966; rev. ed., 2004.

___. *Everything in Its Path: Destruction of Community in the Buffalo Creek Flood*. New York: Simon and Schuster, 1976.

___. *A New Species of Trouble: The Human Experience of Modern Disasters*. New York: W.W. Norton, 1994.

___ (ed.). *Sociological Visions*. Lanham, Md.: Rowman & Littlefield, 1997.

Etzioni, Amitai (1929–)

SOCIOECONOMICS

Born in Cologne, Germany, Amitai Etzioni fled Germany to Palestine in the 1930s. He gained a B.A. (1954) and M.A. (1956) at the Hebrew University, Jerusalem (where he studied with Martin Buber [1878–1965]), and a Ph.D. in sociology (1958) at the University of California, Berkeley. He was on the staff of Columbia University, New York (1958–1980) and was professor of sociology from 1967. He has been a professor since 1980 at George Washington University, Washington, D.C., where he also serves as the director of the Institute for Communitarian Policy Studies. He joined the Brookings Institution (think tank) in Washington, D.C., in 1978 and in 1979–1980 served as senior advisor to the White House on domestic affairs.

He held the Thomas Henry Carroll Ford Foundation Professorship (as visiting professor) in the Graduate School of Business Administration at Harvard University, Cambridge, Massachusetts (1987–1989), and was visiting scholar in sociology at Harvard (1996). Etzioni received the seventh James Wilbur Award for Extraordinary Contributions to the Appreciation and Advancement of Human Values, Conference on Value Inquiry (1998), and in the same year the Sociological Practice Association Outstanding Contribution Award. In 2001, Etzioni was named among the top 100 American intellectuals as measured by academic citations in Richard Posner's book, *Public Intellectuals: A Study of Decline*, Harvard University Press. In 2001, Etzioni was awarded the John P. McGovern Award in Behavioral Sciences as well as the Officers' Cross of the Order of Merit of the Federal Republic of Germany.

Major Contributions

Etzioni is famous for his work on socioeconomics (the study of the relationship between economic activity and social life). He was a founder of the communitarian movement in the early 1990s and established the Communitarian Network to disseminate the movement's ideas. Communitarianism is a group of related but distinct philosophies that oppose classical liberalism , capitalism and socialism while advocating phenomena such as civil society. Communitarianism focus on communities and societies rather than on individuals as the basis for determining and affirming people's basic values. Etzioni argues that people who claim rights must be willing to balance them with responsibilities to help others; people must all sacrifice, take care of their responsibilities, and do their share. According to Etzioni, what we need is a revival of the idea that small sacrifices by individuals can create large benefits for everyone. His writings emphasize the importance for all societies of a carefully crafted balance between rights and responsibilities and autonomy and order.

Major Literature

Etzioni, Amitai. *The Monochrome Society.* Princeton, New Jersey: Princeton University Press, 2001.

___. *My Brother's Keeper: A Memoir and a Message.* Lanham, Maryland: Rowman and Littlefield, 2003.

___(Ed.). *Rights vs. Public Safety After 9/11: America in the Age of Terrorism.* Lanham, Maryland: Rowman and Littlefield, 2003.

___(Ed.). *Voluntary Simplicity: Responding to Consumer Culture.* Lanham, Maryland: Rowman and Littlefield, 2003.

___. *From Empire to Community: A New Approach to International Relations.* New York: Palgrave MacMillan, 2004.

Fairchild, Henry Pratt (1880–1956)

EUGENICS

Born in Dundee, Illinois, Henry Pratt Fairchild received his A.B. degree from Doane College, Nebraska, then taught at the International College, Smyrna, Turkey (moved to Beirut in 1936) in 1900, then served on the faculty at Bowdoin College, Brunswick, Maine. He gained his Ph.D. from Yale University, New Haven, Connecticut (1912), and was a professor of sociology at Yale (1912–1918). From 1918 to 1919 Fairchild was the associate director of the personnel department at War Camp Community Service, a U.S. government service for care and training of servicemen.

From 1919 to 1924, Fairchild was director of the Bureau of Community Service and Research, City University New York, where he was professor of sociology (1924–1951) and served as the chairman of the sociology graduate school department (1938–1945). Fairchild served on the National Research Council and as a special investigator on immigration for the Department of Labor. He was the first president of the Population Association of America, from 1921–1925. From 1934 to 1940, he served as the Town Hall Club president and was the 26th president of the American Sociological Society in 1936.

Major Contributions

During the years 1929–1931, Fairchild was president of the American Eugenics Society, and from 1934 to 1938, president of the Population Association of America. One of Fairchild's most famous contributions was the development of the Planned Parenthood of America Federation — called the Birth Control Federation of America until 1942. There he served on the board of directors in 1932 and later was vice president (1939–1948). Fairchild was also an active member of the National Council of American-Soviet Friendship Club. He gave a well-known speech, "Race Building in a Democracy," to the Birth Control Federation of America and the National Committee on Planned Parenthood during their annual meeting in 1940.

Of his sixty major articles, 20 were on immigration, 15 on population, and 25 related to the family, social work, and world organization. He believed that one of the functions of a sociologist is to make the findings of sociology intelligible to the general public. Always an independent thinker, he did not hesitate to speak forthrightly on leading social and economic problems.

Major Literature

Fairchild, Henry Pratt. *Outline of Applied Sociology.* New York: Macmillan, 1905.
___. *General Sociology.* New York: John Wiley and Sons, Inc., 1905, 1934.
___. *Survey of Contemporary Sociology.* London, England: Thomas Nelson and Sons, 1905.
___. *The Melting Pot Mistake.* Boston, Massachusetts: Little, Brown, 1926. Manchester, New Hampshire: Ayer Co. Publishers, 1977.
___. *Economics for the Millions.* New York: Modern Age Books, 1940.
___. *Race and Nationality as Factors in American Life.* New York: Ronald Press Company, 1947.
___. *Dictionary of Sociology and Related Sciences.* Lanham, Maryland: Rowman and Littlefield Publishers, Inc., 1965, 1980.

Fanon, Frantz Omar (1925–1961)

DISCRIMINATION

Born in Fort-de-France on the Caribbean island of Martinique, Frantz Omar Fanon was the son of a native Martiniquan father and a French (Alsace) mother. Between 1939 and 1943 he studied at the Lycée Schoelcher, Fort-de-France, then traveled to the island of Dominica to rally the free French forces in the Caribbean. In 1944 he fought on the European front, was wounded near the Swiss border and received a citation for his courage. After the war he completed his studies in medicine and psychiatry at the University of Lyon.

From 1953 to 1956 he served as head of the psychiatry department of Blida-Joinville Hospital in Algeria. There Fanon applied the ideas of the French psychiatrist François Tosquelles, an innovative practitioner of group therapy, instituted reform in patient care and desegregated the wards. Sympathetic to the Algerian revolution from the start in 1954, Fanon joined the National Liberation Front, whose goal was independence from France. In 1956 he resigned his medical post and became an editor of the movement's newspaper, *El Moudjahid*, published in Tunis.

Fanon traveled to guerrilla camps from Mali to Sahara, hid terrorists at his home and trained nurses to dress wounds. In 1959, on the border of Algeria and Morocco, he was severely wounded. In 1960 he was appointed ambassador to Ghana by the rebel provisional government, and founded Algeria's first psychiatric clinic. Fanon died of leukemia in Washington, D.C., not living to see Algerian independence gained on 5 July 1962. His body was flown back to Algeria to be buried on Algerian soil.

Major Contributions

Fanon argued that racism harms and alienates the black man psychologically and blinds him to how he is dominated by the norms of white people. A racist culture stultifies psychological health in the black man. Language plays a subtle but important part in this domination, particularly where black is associated with evil and sin. Fanon believed that people's status depends on their economic and social position, and that violent revolution is the only means of ending colonial repression and cultural trauma in the Third World. Further, he argued that violence, like fire, is a force that cleanses people from their inferiority complex, from despair and inaction, and restores their self-respect. The film *Black Skin, White Masks,* based on his book, was released in 1996 by California Newsreel.

Major Literature

Fanon, Frantz. *Black Skin, White Masks.* London, England: Pluto Press, 1952, translated

1967, 1988. A psychoanalytic study of black life and the internalization of racism in a white-dominated world.

___. *The Wretched of the Earth*. London, England: Weidenfeld and Nicolson, Grove Press, 1961, translated, 1963, 2005. According to Fanon, a new type of humanity, modern yet proud of its nonwhite heritage, would emerge from this violent struggle.

Ferguson, Adam (1723–1816)

EARLY SOCIOLOGY

Born in Logierait, Perthshire, Scotland, Adam Ferguson was a "Scottish Enlightenment" historian and philosopher of the "common sense" school of philosophy. (The Scottish Enlightenment was a period of intellectual upheaval in Scotland, from approximately 1740 to 1800.) He is also remembered as a forerunner of modern sociology. Educated at the University of St. Andrews (M.A., 1742), Ferguson was deputy chaplain to Scotland's Black Watch Regiment (1745). In 1757 he succeeded David Hume (1711–1776) as keeper of the Advocates' Library in Edinburgh. Ferguson held successive chairs at the University of Edinburgh, first in natural philosophy (1759), then in moral philosophy and pneumatics (1764).

In 1778 Ferguson traveled to Philadelphia with a British commission sent to negotiate with American revolutionaries. He spent his later years in retirement at St. Andrews. Sir Walter Scott composed Ferguson's epitaph. Ferguson is also remembered for his *Essay on the History of Civil Society*, an intellectual history that traces humanity's progression from barbarism to social and political refinement. Ferguson wrote the article on history for the second edition of the *Encyclopedia Britannica* (1780), which included the first timeline presented in the encyclopedia. In 1783, he helped found the Royal Society of Edinburgh.

Major Contributions

Ferguson rejected social contract theory, arguing instead that the forces of society arise from the instincts, not the speculations, of philosophy. He also rejected the hedonism of David Hume, arguing that human behavior is driven not only by the peaceful pursuit of pleasure, but also — possibly primarily — by a will to power, aggressiveness, animosity and a instinctive desire for conflict and a susceptibility to corruption. Ferguson's focus was the individual; he had no time for analyzing institutions and constitutions in terms of natural rights and laws. As regards capitalism, he argued that the more a manufacturer can subdivide the tasks of his workmen, and the more hands he can employ on separate articles, the more are his expenses diminished, and his profits increased. Division of labor, he argued, was necessarily accompanied by inequality, where some are exalted and others depressed. Division of labor is also the cause of ignorance, alienation, misery and vices like envy and servility, he wrote in *An Essay on the History of Civil Society*: "The beggar, who depends upon charity; the laborer, who toils that he may eat; the mechanic, whose art requires no exertion of genius, are degraded by the object they pursue, and by the means they employ to attain it." Ferguson's pessimism influenced Adam Smith (1723–1790) and Karl Marx (see entry).

Major Literature

Ferguson, Adam. *Institutes of Moral Philosophy* (1769). New York: Garland Publishing, 1978.

___. *An Essay on the History of Civil Society* (1767). Indypublish.com, 2003.

___. *The History of the Progress and Termination of the Roman Republic* (1778). Ann Arbor: Scholarly Publishing Office, University of Michigan Library, 2005.

___. *Principles of Moral and Political Science* (1792). London, England: Continuum International Publishing Group Ltd., Thoemmes, 1999.

Related Literature

Lehmann, William C. *Adam Ferguson and the Beginnings of Modern Sociology*. New York: Columbia University Press, 1930.

Form, William Humbert (1917–)

INDUSTRIAL SOCIOLOGY

William Humbert Formicola (around 1935 he changed his name to William Form) was born in Rochester, New York, the son of Italian immigrants. He gained an A.B. (1938) and M.A. in sociology (1939) from University of Rochester, New York. He studied sociology at Hood College, Frederick, Maryland, and the American University in Washington (1939–1944), and gained a Ph.D. at the University of Maryland, College Park (1944). He was assistant professor of sociology, Stephens College, Columbia, Missouri (1944–1945), and associate professor, Kent State University, Ohio (1945–1947), where he began working on analyses of organizational politics in industry.

At Michigan State University, East Lansing, Michigan, Form was assistant professor (1947–1953); continued researching industrial sociology; associate professor (1953); and chaired the sociology department (1965–1968). In 1971 he married Joan Huber (see entry) and was appointed to Institute of Labor and Industrial Relations, University of Illinois at Champaign–Urbana (1945–1947). He was secretary of the American Sociological Association 1973–1979. In 1984, Form and Huber left Illinois to take positions at the Ohio State University, Form as dean in sociology. He retired in 1996 as professor emeritus.

Major Contributions

Form's doctoral dissertation, under the direction of Charles Wright Mills (see entry), was "The Sociology of a White-Collar Suburb: Greenbelt, Maryland." In 1954 he published an influential concise study of the politics of land-use, analyzing zoning decisions over time. Another sociological study was of the consequences of a disaster, when the Rio Grande flooded in the fall of 1954. He studied autoworkers in Turin, Italy; Lansing, Michigan; Cordoba, Argentina, and at Mombai (then Bombay), India.

Form clashed with Marxist sociologists, arguing that working-class solidarity did not increase with industrialization, but rather that the working classes became increasingly heterogeneous and stratified, and he found extensive evidence of job satisfaction, rather than alienation. From 1986 to 1990, he was editor of the *American Sociological Review*. This service culminated in further academic sparring with Marxist sociologists over the journals direction and content.

Major Literature

Miller, Delbert C., and William H. Form. *Industrial Sociology: An Introduction to the Sociology of Work Relations*. New York: Harper and Brothers, 1951.

Form, William H. "The Place of Social Structure in the Determination of Land Use." *Social Forces* 32 (1954): 317–323.

___, and Sigmund Nosow. "Community in Disaster." *Social Forces* 37, No. 4 (1959): 366–367.

Form, William H. "Industry, Labor and Community." *Industrial and Labor Relations Review*, 14, No. 4 (1961): 643–645.

D'Antonio, William V., and William H. Form. "Influentials in Two Border Cities: A Study in Community Decision-Making." *Social Forces* 44, No. 4 (1966): 606–607.

Form, William H., and Joan Huber. *Income and Ideology*. New York: The Free Press, 1973.

Form, William H. "Blue Collar Stratification: Autoworkers in Four Countries." *Contemporary Sociology* 6, No. 2 (1977): 159–160.

___. "Divided We Stand: Working-Class Stratification in America." *Industrial and Labor Relations Review* 41, No. 4 (1988): 645–646.

___. *Segmented Labor, Fractured Politics: Labor Politics in American Life*. New York: Springer-Verlag, 1995.

___. *Work and Academic Politics: A Journeyman's Story*. New Jersey: Transaction Publishers, 2001.

Frazier, Edward Franklin (1894–1962)

SOCIOLOGY OF RACE

Born in Baltimore, Maryland, Edward Franklin Frazier graduated with honors from Howard University, Washington, D.C. (1916). He taught in Alabama, Virginia and Maryland (1916–1919). He gained a master's degree at Clark University, Worcester, Massachusetts (1920); was a Russell Sage Foundation fellow, New York School of Social Work (later Columbia University School of Social Work) (1920–1921); fellow of the American Scandinavian Foundation, University of Copenhagen (1921–1922); director, School of Social Work; and instructor of sociology, Morehouse College, Atlanta, Georgia (1923–1927).

Frazier worked at the Department of Sociology, University of Chicago, Illinois (1927–1931), and earned a Ph.D. (1931). He worked at Fisk University, Nashville, Tennessee (1931–1934), and at Howard University, where he was director, Department of Sociology and the African Studies Program, and professor emeritus (1934–1959). From 1951 to 1953 Frazier was part of the United Nations Educational, Scientific and Cultural Organization (UNESCO) efforts in Paris, Africa and the Middle East. In 1948 he was the first black president, American Sociological Society (Association, 1959).

His awards and honors include Guggenheim Fellowship study of family life in Brazil (1941–1942); founding member, District of Columbia Sociological Society, and president (1943–1944); president, Eastern Sociological Society (1944–1945); and member of Alpha Phi Alpha. He received the American Sociological Association MacIver Award for his contributions in the field of sociology.

Major Contributions

In 1927, his article "The Pathology of Race Prejudice" (*Forum*, June 1927, 856–862), which argued that racial prejudice was analogous to insanity, stirred such strong reactions among residents in Atlanta that Frazier was removed from his position. His Ph.D. dissertation, published as the book *The Negro Family in Chicago,* analyzed the cultural and historical forces that influenced the development of the African-American family from the time of slavery. The book was awarded the 1939 Anisfield Award for the most significant work in the field of race relations.

At Howard University Frazier's work focused on the environment of black colleges, especially that of Howard University. He has been ranked among the top African-Americans for his influence on institutions and practices to accept the demands by African-Americans for economic, political and social equality in American life. In 2000 Howard University School of Social Work created in his honor the E. Franklin Frazier Research Center. Reproductions of many of Frazier's essays and journal articles are available in the Moorland-Spingarn Research Center, Howard University.

Major Literature

Frazier, E. Franklin. *The Negro Family in Chicago*. Chicago, Illinois: University of Chicago Press, 1932.

___. *The Negro Family in the United States*. Chicago, Illinois: University of Chicago Press, 1939.

___. "Sociological Theory and Race Relations." *American Sociological Review*, 12, No. 3 (1947): 265–271.

___. *Black Bourgeoisie: The Rise of a New Middle Class in the United States*. New Jersey: Prentice Hall, 1962.

___. *Race and Culture Contacts in the Modern World*. Boston Massachusetts: Beacon Press, 1965.
___. *Free Negro Family: A Study of Family Origins Before the Civil War*. Manchester, New Hampshire: Ayer Co. Publishers, 1979.

Gans, Herbert J. (1927–)

URBAN SOCIOLOGY

Born in Cologne, Germany, Herbert J. Gans immigrated to the United States in 1938 and became a U.S. citizen in 1945. He gained a Ph.B. (1947), an M.A. in social sciences (1950) from the University of Chicago, Illinois, and earned Phi Beta Kappa honors (1950). From 1950 to 1956 he was involved in planning in Chicago and Washington. At the Department of City Planning, University of Pennsylvania, Philadelphia, he was lecturer, (1956–1957) and gained a Ph.D. (1957). He was assistant sociologist, Department of Psychiatry, Massachusetts General Hospital and Harvard Medical School, Boston (1957–1958); assistant professor of city planning, Institute for Urban Studies and Department of City Planning (1958–1961); and lecturer, Department of Sociology (1961–1964) at University of Pennsylvania, Philadelphia.

At Teachers College, Columbia University, New York, he was associate professor of sociology and education (1964–1966); research associate, Institute of Urban Studies, (1964–1965); Center for Urban Education (1965–1966); senior staff sociologist, Center for Urban Education; and adjunct professor of sociology and education (1966–1969). He was professor of sociology and planning, Department of Urban Studies and Planning, Massachusetts Institute of Technology (M.I.T); faculty associate, Harvard Joint Center for Urban Studies, Cambridge, Massachusetts (1969–1971); professor of sociology, Columbia University (Ford Foundation Urban Chair) (1971–1985); Robert S.

Lynd Professor of Sociology, Columbia University (since 1985); president, Eastern Sociological Society (1973); 78th president, American Sociological Association (1988); and advisory editor of *Social Policy* (1971–2002), *Ethnic and Racial Studies* (1977–1989, 1995–2003), and the Rose Monograph Series, American Sociological Association (since 1996).

His awards and honors: fellow, American Academy of Arts and Sciences (1982); Robert and Helen Lynd Award for Lifetime Contributions to Research, Community and Urban Sociology Section, American Sociological Association (1992); honorary doctor of science, University of Pennsylvania (2003); Distinguished Career Award, International Migration Section, American Sociological Association (2004); and Career of Distinguished Scholarship Award of the American Sociological Association (2006).

Major Contributions

Gans' presidential address, "Sociology in America: The Discipline and the Public," was published in the *American Sociological Review* (54, No. 1 [1989]: 1–16). Gans' early experience was hands-on, working for an architectural firm where he did social research to help plan two new towns. He worked at the Housing and Home Finance Agency, now the U.S. Department of Housing and Urban Development. His research and teaching activities have concentrated on urban and community studies, urban poverty and antipoverty planning, social planning and social policy, equality and stratification, ethnicity, the news media and popular culture.

Major Literature

Gans, Herbert J. *The Urban Villagers*. New York: Free Press, 1962.
___. *The Levittowners: Ways of Life and Politics in a New Suburban Community*. New York: Pantheon Books, 1967. New York: Columbia University Press, 1982.

___. *Making Sense of America: Sociological Analyses and Essays*. Lanham, Maryland: Rowman and Littlefield Publishers, Inc., 1998.

___. *Popular Culture and High Culture*. Jackson, Tennessee: Basic Books, 2nd revised edition, 1999.

___. *Democracy and the News*. New York: Oxford University Press Inc., 2003.

___. *Deciding What's News: A Study of CBS Evening News, NBC Nightly News, Newsweek, and Time*. Evanston, Illinois: Northwestern University Press, 1979, 25th anniversary edition, 2004.

Garfinkel, Harold (1917–)

ETHNOMETHODOLOGY

Born into a large Jewish community in New Jersey, Harold Garfinkel studied accounting at the University of Newark, New Jersey. Having become interested in sociology, after completing his accounting degree, Garfinkel was offered a graduate fellowship at the department of sociology, University of North Carolina, Chapel Hill, and received his M.A. in 1942. From 1946 to 1952, after military service during World War II, Garfinkel trained in the Department of Social Relations at Harvard University, Cambridge, Massachusetts, under the supervision of Talcott Parsons (see entry) and gained his Ph.D. in 1952. He was affiliated with the U.S. Public Health Service from 1957 to 1966. After teaching at several universities, he spent most of his career at the University of California in Los Angeles, until his retirement as professor emeritus in sociology in 1987.

Major Contributions

In his doctoral dissertation, Garfinkel examined the different approaches to social action. He was searching for a theoretical framework that would directly relate to the procedures people use to analyze their circumstances and carry out courses of action.

In a study of juries, he found that jurors often brought their own methods to the proceedings, improvising upon the judge's instructions by means of practices that they would use at home with their peers. While this might create doubts whether the verdicts are well founded, Garfinkel used this observation to investigate other forms of social interaction and found similar procedures were used elsewhere.

Garfinkel is one of the key developers of the phenomenological tradition in American sociology; his own development of this tradition he terms *ethnomethodology*. Ethnomethodologists primarily examine particular encounters and attempt to uncover the common practices that people may assume or not consciously consider. While ethnomethodologists provide great insight into what these are and how they work, it may be difficult to connect this approach to more comprehensive theoretical approaches to sociology.

More than the other interactionist perspectives, ethnomethodologists focus on methods of social action and may not attempt to understand social people in the way that Max Weber, Talcott Parsons, or George Herbert Mead did (see entries). But the ethnomethodological perspective provides useful insight. Ethnomethodological studies come in a wide variety of forms, including: the sequential analysis of conversation (conversation analysis); the study of social categorization practices (membership category analysis); studies of workplace settings and activities (studies of work). One of the principal contributions of Garfinkel's work is the impression it has on the way we conduct, and think about, social research.

Major Literature

Garfinkel, Harold. *Studies in Ethnomethodology*. Upper Saddle River, New Jersey: Pearson Education, Longman Group, 1967. Cambridge, England: Polity Press, 1984.

___. *Ethnomethodological Studies of Work*. New

York: Taylor and Francis Group, Routledge, 1986.

___. *Ethnomethodology's Program: Working Out Durkheim's Aphorism*. Lanham, Maryland: Rowman and Littlefield Publishers, Inc., 2002.

___, and Rawls, Anne (Eds.). *Seeing Sociologically: The Routine Grounds of Social Action*. Boulder, Colorado: Paradigm Press, 2005.

___. *Sociology of Information*. Boulder, Colorado: Paradigm Press, 2006.

Gartner, Rosemary (1952–)

SOCIOLOGY OF CRIME

Born in Pomona, California, Rosemary Gartner gained a B.A. in sociology (with highest honors) at the University of California, Santa Cruz (1974). At the University of Wisconsin, Madison, she gained an M.S. in sociology (1977); a Ph.D. in sociology (1985); and was research specialist (1978–1982) and project specialist, Institute for Research on Poverty (1982–1985). She was visiting lecturer, Department of Sociology, Brunel University, England (1983–1984), and assistant professor, Department of Sociology, University of Iowa, Iowa City (1985–1988).

At the University of Toronto, Canada, she was assistant professor (1988–1989) and associate professor (1989–1992). She was associate professor in the Department of Sociology, University of Minnesota (1992–1993). At the University of Toronto, she was professor, Department of Sociology and Centre of Criminology (1993–1998 and 2003–present), and director, Centre of Criminology, and professor, Department of Sociology (1998–2003). In 1999 Gartner was appointed a member of the (U.S.) National Consortium on Violence Research.

Gartner's awards and honors include the Gordon Allport Intergroup Relations Prize, Society for the Psychological Study of Social Issues (shared with Dane Archer) (1975); Behavioral Science Research Prize, American Association for the Advancement of Science (shared with Dane Archer) (1985); and Dean's Excellence Award, Faculty of Arts and Science, University of Toronto (1991, 1992, 1993, 1994, 1997, 1998, 1999, 2000, 2001, 2002).

Major Contributions

Gartner has spent most of her career focusing on women and crime, specifically women who are homicide victims and women who commit homicide. She is also investigating how women respond to incarceration, and how patterns of violence in women's lives can result in their imprisonment. She is also heavily involved in an examination of women in two very different prisons in California. Women in the oldest women's prison in California were interviewed during the 1960s to see how women adjust to prison life differently from men. Gartner and a co-investigator returned to that prison 35 years later to see how women's adjustments to prison might have changed since the '60s. *Violence and Crime in Cross-National Perspective* (1984) won a Distinguished Scholarship Award from the American Sociological Association and an Outstanding Scholarship Award from the Society for the Study of Social Problems.

In addition to her many books and two chapters in the *Blackwell Encyclopedia of Sociology*, Garner has published numerous articles, has served on the editorial boards of several prestigious journals, including the *American Journal of Sociology*, and has addressed the Senate of Canada on the implications of cross-national research on homicide.

Major Literature

Gartner, R., and C. Kruttschnitt. "A Brief History of Doing Time: The California Institution for Women in the 1960s and 1990s." *Law and Society Review* 38 (2004): 267–304.

Kruttschnitt, C., and R. Gartner. *Marking Time*

in the Golden State: Women's Imprisonment in California. New York: Cambridge University Press, 2004.

Phillips, J., and R. Gartner. *Murdering Holiness: The Trials of Franz Creffield and George Mitchell*. Vancouver: University of British Columbia Press and Seattle: University of Washington Press, 2003.

Archer, D., and R. Gartner. *Violence and Crime in Cross-National Perspective*. New Haven: Yale University Press, 1984.

Geiger, Theodor (1891–1952)

SOCIAL MOBILITY

Born in Munich, Germany, Theodor Geiger served in World War I, then returned to Munich and gained his doctorate in law (1918). In 1920 Geiger became a member of the Social Democratic Party of Germany, and between 1924 and 1933 he worked in its statistics office in Munich. He edited the information magazine of the newly founded Berlin *Volkshochschule* (adult education center), where he had begun to work as a teacher, and in 1924 he took over as manager. Geiger joined the Brunswick University of Technology in 1924, progressing from visiting lecturer to associate professor, and finally to becoming a full professor of sociology from 1928 to 1933 — the first professorship of the department for cultural studies.

An early critic of the Nazis, Geiger fled to Copenhagen, where he was awarded a Rockefeller Foundation fellowship. He was appointed to the Institute of History and Economics, and in 1938 became Denmark's first professor of sociology at the University of Århus, Denmark. He took on Danish nationality and married a Dane. He studied social stratification and mobility, examining Danish intellectuals and the people of Århus. His posthumous *Democracy Without Dogma* (1964) expressed his vision of a society depersonalized by ideology but redeemed by human relationships.

In 1940, during the German occupation of Denmark in World War II, Geiger fled to Odense, Denmark, then in 1943, to Sweden, where he taught at the universities of Stockholm and Uppsala. Geiger returned to Århus in 1945, where he was a co–founder of the International Sociological Association (1949). He founded and directed the first Scandinavian institute of sociological research and developed the academic journal *Acta Sociologica* (now in its 49th volume). He died on a passage from Canada to Denmark.

Major Contributions

Geiger is considered the founder of social stratification, a term for the hierarchical arrangement of social classes, castes, and strata within a society. According to stratification, society is divided into an indefinite number of social levels or groups, defined according to attributes such as profession, education, upbringing, living standard, power, dress, religion, race, political opinion and organization. Stratification is closely connected to the concept of social mobility and the criteria for an industrial society. Social mobility is the degree to which, in a given society, an individual's social status can change throughout the course of his or her life, or the degree to which that individual's offspring and subsequent generations move up and down the class system. Stratification is closely linked to another sociological concept — inequality — a core concept in sociology. Inequality may refer to race, ethnicity, and gender; differences in pay between males and females; and inequality changes from generation to generation.

Major Literature

Geiger, Theodor. *Welfare and Efficiency: Their Interactions in Western Europe and Implications for International Economic Relations*. Washington, D.C.: National Planning Association, 1978.

_____. *The Future of the International System: The United States and the World Political Economy.* Boston, Massachusetts: Unwin Hyman, 1988.

Gellner, Ernest André (1925–1995)

ETHNOGRAPHY

Born in Paris, Ernest André Gellner was brought up in Prague, Czechoslovakia, where he attended the English grammar school. In 1939 his Jewish family moved to St. Albans, just north of London, England, where Gellner attended St. Albans county grammar school. In 1942 he won a scholarship to Balliol College, Oxford, and in 1944 he served for one year with the Czech army. He returned briefly to Prague but was disillusioned by the Communist takeover of Czechoslovakia and returned to Oxford, where he gained a first class honors degree in philosophy, politics and economics (1947). He was appointed assistant to Professor John MacMurray in the Department of Moral Philosophy, the University of Edinburgh.

He joined the sociology department of the London School of Economics in 1949, at which he was the professor of philosophy, logic and scientific method (1962–1984). From 1988 to 1993 he was William Wyse Professor of Social Anthropology at the University of Cambridge. He then moved to the new Central European University, Prague, where he became head of the Center for the Study of Nationalism. He died from a heart attack in Prague's airport.

Major Contributions

Gellner crosses the boundaries between three disciplines — sociology, philosophy and social anthropology. It was in the '60s that Gellner discovered his great love of social anthropology — the holistic study of

humanity. Some of the subjects he covered are the analysis of kinship; the social life of Middle Eastern cultures; the study of frameworks for understanding political order outside the state in tribal Morocco; syntheses of the theories of Émile Durkheim and Max Weber (see entries) in western social theory; and ethnicity and nationalism. He was not always popular because of his fierce criticism of people, ideas and practices — psychoanalysis, religion and the free market are examples. He strongly criticized nationalism and the right wing policies of the British Prime Minister Margaret Thatcher, and his scorn for western Marxism was unswerving.

Major Literature

Gellner, E.L. *Words and Things.* London, England: Taylor and Francis Books, Ltd, Routledge, 1959, 2005.
_____. *Thought and Change.* London, England: Orion Publishing Group, Weidenfeld and Nicolson, 1964.
_____. *Saints of the Atlas.* London, England: Orion Publishing Group, Weidenfeld and Nicolson, 1969. University of Michigan Library: ACLS History E-Book Project, 2001.
_____. *Nations and Nationalism.* Ames, Iowa: Blackwell Publishing, 1983.
_____. *The Psychoanalytic Movement: The Cunning of Unreason.* London: Paladin, 1985. Ames, Iowa: Blackwell Publishing, 2002.
_____. *Conditions of Liberty: Civil Society and Its Rivals.* London, England: Penguin Group, Hamish Hamilton, 1994.

Gershuny, Jonathan

SOCIAL CLASS

Jonathan Gershuny earned a B.Sc. degree in social sciences with joint honors in economics and politics at Loughborough University, Loughborough, Leicestershire, England (1971). His M.Sc. in research methods in political science was from Strathclyde University, Glasgow, Scotland (1972). He was research officer, Department of Transport

Technology, Loughborough University (1973–1974). At the Science Policy Research Unit (SPRU) at Sussex University, Brighton, Sussex, he was fellow (1974–1981) and senior fellow (1981–1984), and gained a D.Phil. in history and social studies (1977). His dissertation was titled "Rationality and Public Policy-making: An Approach to the Problems of Synopsis."

He was research fellow (part-time, on secondment from SPRU) at the Research Unit on Ethnic Relations, University of Bristol, Avon, England (1978–1979). At University of Bath, Avon, England, he was professor; head of Sociology and Social Policy Group (1984–1988); and head of the School of Social Sciences (1988–1989). He was visiting fellow or professor at Wissenschaftszentrum (International Institute of Management) in Berlin (1983); University of Frankfurt (1988); ZUMA, University of Mannheim, Germany (1990); European University Institute, Florence, Italy (1995); German Institute for Economic Research, Berlin. Germany (1996).

Since 1993 he has been professor of sociology and director of the Institute for Social and Economic Research, University of Essex, Colchester, Essex. His awards and honors include the German Marshall Fund of the USA, personal fellowship (1980–1982); honorary vice-president, British Association Section J. (1986); silver medalist of the Market Research Society (1987); faculty fellow of Nuffield College Oxford, England (1990–1993); and elected fellow, British Academy (2002).

Major Contributions

Gershuny's research shows that family background has had a bigger impact on the lives of the generation of Britons born in the late 1950s and 1960s than it did on previous generations. For women in particular, the increase in inequality in intergenerational life chances for women is dramatic. Key drivers of the rising inequality of life chances have been the growth in women's participation in paid work, the growing instability of marriages, increasing divorce, more partnerships and more multiple families. British men born in the fifties and sixties have gained just a little more from their parents' advantages than men from earlier birth cohorts.

Instead of class categories, Gershuny uses levels of marketable capabilities for work — the personal resources that give people material advantages or disadvantages, now and in the future — those skills and experiences that determine their earning capacity. One of the major influences in the leveling out of opportunities between males and females is education, though there is still evidence of disparity in earnings in certain fields.

Major Literature

Gershuny Jonathan. *After Industrial Society? The Emerging Self-Service Economy.* Atlantic Highlands, New Jersey: Humanities Press, 1978.
___. *Social Innovation and the Division of Labor.* Oxford, England: Oxford University Press, 1983.
___. *Seven Years in the Lives of British Families: Evidence on the Dynamics of Social Change from the British Household Panel Survey.* University of Bristol, Policy Press, new edition, 2001.
___. *Changing Times: Work and Leisure in Postindustrial Society.* Oxford, England: Oxford University Press, new edition, 2003.

Giddens, Anthony (1938–)

STRUCTURATION

Born and raised in Edmonton, London, Anthony Giddens graduated from Hull University with a master's degree from the London School of Economics and a Ph.D. from the University of Cambridge. From 1961 to 1969 he taught social psychology at the University of Leicester. From 1969 he worked at the University of Cambridge, where he later created the faculty of Social and Political Sciences and was promoted to professor of sociology and fellow of King's College, Cambridge. He co-founded Polity Press (1985), one of the world's leading social science publishers.

From 1997 to 2003 he was director of London School of Economics and a member of the advisory council of the Institute for Public Policy Research. He was an adviser to the British Prime Minister Tony Blair. In 2004 he was created a life peer as Baron Southgate in the London Borough of Enfield and sits in the House of Lords for Labor.

Giddens has been awarded 14 honorary degrees. He is a fellow of the American Academy of Arts and Sciences and a life fellow of King's College, Cambridge. He won the title of the "Best Lecturer in the World" from the University of Aarhus, Denmark. In 2002 he was awarded the Prince of Asturias Prize, known as "the Spanish Nobel Prize," for the social sciences. He was the 1999 BBC Reith Lecturer.

Major Contributions

Giddens developed the theory of structuration, which is the understanding of the relationship between individuals and the conditions around them. Giddens argues that to view social systems and what individuals do as separate entities is a mistake; neither can exist without the other. For example, the Lawn Tennis Association at Wimbledon, London, would not exist if there were no players to compete. The Chicago Cubs baseball team would not exist if there were no players or spectators. And within these two examples are rules, and it is upon these rules that the game is founded. Society should be viewed as a series of ongoing activities and practices that people carry on, but which reproduce larger institutions at the same time. Giddens has helped to popularize the idea of the "Third Way" a centrist (moderate) philosophy of government

that usually stands for deregulation, decentralization and lower taxes. This philosophy is embraced by former British Prime Minister Tony Blair, former President of the United States Bill Clinton, and several European heads of state. Giddens has been described as Britain's best known social scientist since Baron John Maynard Keynes (1883–1946).

Major Literature

Giddens, Anthony. *Modernity and Self-Identity: Self and Society in the Late Modern Age*. Cambridge, England: Polity Press, 1991.

___. *The Giddens: Constitution Society (Paper): Outline of the Theory of Structuration*. Berkeley, California: University of California Press, 1992.

___. *The Third Way and Its Critics*. Cambridge, England: Polity Press, 2000.

___, and Patrick Diamond. *The New Egalitarianism*. Cambridge, England: Polity Press, 2005.

Giddens, Anthony. *Sociology*. Cambridge, England: Polity Press, 2006.

Giddings, Franklin Henry (1855–1931)

CONSCIOUSNESS OF KIND

Born in Sherman, Connecticut, in 1873 Franklin Henry Giddings started studying civil engineering at Union College, Schenectady, New York. In 1875 he became the associate editor of the Winston *Herald* and taught school in Massachusetts and Connecticut. He was editor of the Berkshire *Courier* and the New Milford *Gazette*, and wrote for the Springfield *Republican* and the Springfield *Union*. He worked for a short time in 1885 with the Massachusetts Bureau of Labor Statistics and wrote on social science theory and practice. Giddings received his A.B. from Union College (1888).

His scholarly writings resulted in his being invited by the future President Woodrow Wilson to succeed him as lecturer in politics at Bryn Mawr College, Bryn Mawr, Pennsylvania (1888). By 1892 Giddings was full professor. He offered courses in political economy and methods and principles of administration, and taught a graduate seminar on theories of sociology in 1890. In 1894 Giddings became the chair and first full professor of sociology and the history of civilization at Columbia University, New York, the first full professor of sociology in the United States. He remained at Columbia until he retired in 1928. From 1892 to 1905 he was a vice president of the American Academy of Political and Social Science. He was the third president of the American Sociological Society (Association, 1959) (1910 and 1911).

Major Contributions

One of the founders of American sociology, Giddings built his reputation as a leading quantitative sociologist and one of the scholars responsible for transforming American sociology from a branch of philosophy into a research science utilizing statistical and analytic methodology. Giddings was noted for his doctrine of the "consciousness of kind," which he derived from Adam Smith's (1723–179) conception of "sympathy," or shared moral reactions. In Giddings's view, consciousness of kind — innate collective feelings of similarity and belonging — fosters a standardized society and results from the interaction of individuals and their exposure to common stimuli. Giddings believed that human nature is prone to be either progressive or conservative, either of which can be dominant depending on the time and social environment. He also held that emotion has played an integral part in the development of human society. In addition to Smith's concept of sympathy, Giddings's sociology was influenced by Auguste Comte's "positivism" and Herbert Spencer's "social Darwinism" (see entries). Giddings believed that inequality in society is inevitable and results from constitutional or genetic differences, forming the bases for class divisions. These divisions are natural and lead to permanent conflicts.

Major Literature

Giddings, Franklin Henry. *Principles of Sociology*. New York: Macmillan, 1896. Honolulu, Hawaii: University Press of the Pacific, 2002.
___. *Elements of Sociology*. New York: Macmillan 1898.
___. *Democracy and Empire*. New York: Macmillan, 1900.
___. *Inductive Sociology*. New York: Macmillan, 1901.
___. *The Mighty Medicine*. Macmillan, 1929. Whitefish, Montana: R.A. Kessinger Publishing Co., 2003.
___. *Civilization and Society: An Account of The Development and Behavior of Human Society*. New York: H. Holt & Co., 1932.

Gillette, John Morris (1866–1949)
RURAL SOCIOLOGY

Born near Maryville, Missouri, John Morris Gillette gained a B.A. at Park College, Parkville, Missouri (1892) and an M.A. from Princeton Theological Seminary, New Jersey (1895). He was then a Presbyterian minister in rural churches in Kansas and in the frontier town of Dodge City (1895). He gained a Ph.D. at the Chicago Theological Seminary, Chicago, Illinois (1898), and was president of Chadron, Nebraska, State Normal School (1898–1901). He gained a Ph.D. in sociology at the University of Chicago, Illinois (1901), and was principal of the Academy for Young Women in Jacksonville, Illinois (1901–1903), then at Valley City Normal School, North Dakota (1903–1907). At University of North Dakota, Grand Forks, Gillette was assistant professor in sociology and an instructor in history (1907), founder and chair of the Department of

Sociology (1908–1949) and retired in 1948. He was the 18th president of the American Sociological Society (Association, 1959) (1928). Park College awarded him an honorary doctor of humanities.

Major Contributions

By 1911, the Department of Sociology and University of North Dakota had grown to such a point that seventeen courses were part of the curriculum. The department was among the first on campus to offer graduate degrees; the university's first Ph.D. was granted to George R. Davies in 1914. A major milestone in Gillette's career was the publication of *Rural Sociology*. This book, the first formal textbook in the field, won Gillette nationwide acclaim as the founder of this branch of sociology. In 1914, Gillette and the Sociology Club established the University Settlement House. Sponsored jointly by Gillette and university President Frank McVey, the house cared for over eighty needy families.

In later years, Gillette led the Department of Sociology toward a great emphasis on statistics, while also reintroducing the study of anthropology, which had not been part of the curriculum since 1907. Gillette was also involved with an increased emphasis on the study of social work. He was especially interested in issues surrounding jails and poor farms. He recommended that poor farms be eliminated, while also calling for more inspections of jails and greater supervision of local and state charities.

He was an associate member of the International Institute of Sociology and an advisory member of the Academy of Agriculture of Czechoslovakia. He was also a member of the North Dakota State Welfare Commission; of the advisory committee of the National Child Labor Committee; of the National Committee on Prisons and Prison Labor; as well as of the advisory committee of the State Workmen's Compensation and Unemployment Insurance Division. Gillette

was often referred to as the dean of rural sociology because of his pioneering work in the field in the United States and other countries. The former chemistry building was re-dedicated in his honor on October 7, 1983.

Major Literature

Gillette, John M. *Problems of a Changing Social Order*. New York: American Book Co., 1905.
___. *Constructive Rural Sociology*. New York: Sturgis and Walton, 1913, revised, 1916.
___, and James M. Reinhardt. *Current Social Problems*. New York: American Book Co., 1933, revised, 1937.

Gillin, John Lewis (1871–1958)

CRIMINOLOGY AND PENOLOGY

John Lewis Gillin gained a B.Litt. at Upper Iowa University (1894), an A.B. Grinnell College, Grinnell, Iowa (1895), an A.M. from Columbia University, New York (1903), and a B.D at the Union Theological Seminary, New York (1904). On completion of his training at Union he became an ordained minister with the Church of the Brethren. He then earned a Ph.D. from Columbia (1906), after which he held important positions at Ashland College, Ashland, Ohio (where he was president for one year), and at the State University of Iowa, Ames, Ohio.

In 1912 he was appointed associate professor of sociology and secretary of the Department of General Information and Welfare at the University of Wisconsin, Madison, working under Edward A. Ross (see entry). Gillin spent the remaining 46 years of his professional career at Wisconsin, the last sixteen as emeritus professor. The dual character of this appointment involved him in teaching sociology part-time and applying himself to the Wisconsin Idea, which included both extension instruction and community and welfare programs in many parts of the state.

Gillin served as 16th president of the American Sociological Society (Association, 1959) in 1926. His presidential address was "The Development of Sociology in the United States." Gillin said sociology arose in the United States following the Civil War (1861–1865) because the war left America with many problems that challenged the attention of many people; it had rocked the social structure of the United States to its foundations; it had challenged thinking men to a reconsideration of the fundamental problems of government and social relationships. It was a time when social readjustment was necessary and new relationships had to be established. In 1865 the American Social Science Association was formed in Boston, Massachusetts, along the lines of the British Social Science Association founded a quarter of a century earlier.

Gillin's writings on criminology and penology were so extensive that his role as adviser, consultant, and administrator in Wisconsin perhaps remained obscure outside of the state, particularly his social reforms that touched the lives of many prisoners. Gillin's working philosophy seemed to be that human beings can control at least part of their destiny when goodwill is united with the demonstrable conclusions of social science.

Major Literature

Gillin, John Lewis. *Poverty and Dependency: Their Relief and Prevention*. New Jersey: Century Co., 1921.
___. *Social Problems*. New Jersey: Appleton-Century-Crofts, 1928.
___, and Frank Wilson Blackmar. *Outlines of Sociology*. New York: Macmillan, 1931.
Gillin, John Lewis. *Criminology and Penology*. New Jersey: Appleton-Century-Crofts, 1935. Whitefish, Montana: R.A. Kessinger Publishing Co., 2005.
___. *Taming the Criminal*. New York: Macmillan, 1931.

___. *Social Pathology*. New Jersey: Appleton-Century-Crofts, 1946.
___, and John Philip Gillin. *Cultural Sociology*. New York: Macmillan, 1948.

Gini, Corrado (1884–1965)
DEMOGRAPHY

Born at Motta di Livenza, near Treviso, Italy, Corrado Gini graduated in law at Bologna (1905) with a thesis titled "Gender from a Statistical Point of View" (published 1908). He was chair of statistics, University of Cagliari, Sardinia (1910); professor of statistics, Padua University (1913); founder and director of the statistical journal *Metron* (1920–1965); founder, the School of Statistics, Rome (1928); founder, the Faculty of Statistical, Demographic and Actuarial Sciences, Rome (1936); president of the independent Central Institute of Statistics (1926); founder of *La Vita Economica Italiana* (1926), shut down by the government in 1943; chair of statistics at Rome (1927), where he founded and directed a lecture course on sociology until he retired; and founder, the Italian Committee for the Study of Population Problems (1929).

He organized the first Population Congress in Rome (1931); was vice president of the International Sociological Institute (1933); founded the journal *Genus* as the medium of the Italian Committee for the Study of Population Problems (1934); was president, Italian Genetics and Eugenics Society (1934); was president, International Federation of Eugenics Societies in Latin-language Countries (1935); founded, directed, and was dean of the faculty of Statistical, Demographic, and Actuarial Sciences, Rome (1936–1954); was president of the Italian Sociological Society (1937); and was president of the Italian Statistical Society (1941).

He received the Gold Medal for outstanding service to the Italian School (1957) and was made national member of the Accademia dei Lincei (1962). He received honorary degrees in economics at Catholic University of the Sacred Heart, Milan (1932); sociology at the University of Geneva (1934); sciences at Harvard University, Cambridge, Massachusetts (1936); and social sciences, University of Cordoba, Argentina (1963).

Major Contributions

At Rome, Gini pioneered the teaching of sociology, treating the subject as a study of populations and their measurable characteristics, drawing on biological concepts for his view of social development. His statistical studies began with the relationship of probability to population statistics — e.g., determining the sex ratio at birth. Italian policy under Mussolini aimed at population increase; the role of women in that policy was as breeders (fattrici); Gini followed an independent line. His most widely known contribution, the Gini Coefficient, is his 1921 measure of the inequality of distribution of wealth (or any other variable). Between 1945 and 1956 Gini was involved in a number of different projects: the effect of migrations; measures of ability to produce offspring; measurement of differences between two populations; and wealth of nations. The concept of "human capital" was Gini's (see also Gary S. Becker). He distinguished stages in the growth of societies, and also distinguished normal from abnormal processes in societies.

Major Literature

Gini, Corrado. "Report on the Problem of Raw Materials and Foodstuffs." *Journal of the American Statistical Association* 18, No. 143 (1923): 936–937. London, England: Taylor and Francis, 1983.
___. "The Scientific Basis of Fascism." *Political Science Quarterly* 42, No. 1 (1927): 99–115.
___. *Population*. Chicago, Illinois: University of Chicago Press, 1930.

Ginsberg, Morris (1889–1970)
CULTURAL SOCIOLOGY

Born in Lithuania, Morris Ginsberg entered University College, London (UCL), in 1910 and made a successful transition from an entirely Yiddish-speaking Talmudic scholar into a member of the austere English middle class. He obtained a B.A. in philosophy and sociology with first class honors (1913), and an M.A. (1915) from the London School of Economics (LSE). At UCL he was as assistant to the philosopher Professor G. Dawes Hicks (1862–1941), but it is with sociology and the LSE that Ginsberg is mainly associated, from 1914 when he was first invited to be a part-time assistant to L.T. Hobhouse (see entry). He was at LSE from 1921 for more than forty years, as reader (1924), successor to Hobhouse in the Martin White chair of sociology (1929), and as an emeritus professor (1954) who undertook part-time teaching well into the 1960s.

Although prevented from active service by poor eyesight in World War II, he stood in for four of the regular teaching staff. His association with and devotion to Hobhouse began while he was at UCL, where he collaborated in a comparative anthropological study that became a classic (L.T. Hobhouse, G.C. Wheeler, and M. Ginsberg, *The Material Culture and Social Institutions of the Simpler Peoples*. London, England: Chapman and Hall, 1915).

Ginsberg devoted himself to the understanding of the evolution of mankind, materially, socially, culturally, and morally. He demonstrated his knowledge of philosophy and social history in a long series of books, essays, and lectures. After Hobhouse, Ginsberg was the major British sociologist between the wars, but after the war, attention shifted mainly to American empirical sociology; Ginsberg was more in harmony with

European sociologists Max Weber, Emile Durkheim and Vilfredo Pareto (see entries). The question of the relation between moral and social evolution remained important but no longer occupied center stage.

Ginsberg became a fellow of the British Academy in 1953; was awarded honorary degrees from London, Glasgow, and Nottingham, and was an honorary fellow of LSE. He was Frazer lecturer in 1944, Conway memorial lecturer in 1952, and Clarke Hall lecturer in 1953, the year in which he received the Huxley medal and gave the Huxley lecture. In 1958 he gave the Herbert Spencer lecture. In 1942–1943 he was president of the Aristotelian Society. He was the founding chairman of the British Sociological Association in 1951 and its first president in 1955. The Hebrew University has established the Ginsberg Postdoctoral Fellowship.

Major Literature

Ginsberg, Morris. *The Unity of Mankind*. London, England: Oxford University Press, 1935.
___. *The Psychology of Society*. London, England: Methuen and Co., Ltd., 1944.
___. *Moral Progress*. Glasgow, Scotland: Jackson, 1944.
___. *Reason and Unreason in Society*. Cambridge, Massachusetts: Harvard University Press, 1948.
___. *The Idea of Progress: A Revaluation*. London, England: Methuen, 1953. Westport, Connecticut: Greenwood Press, 1972.
___. *On the Diversity of Morals*. London, England: Heineman, 1953.
___. *On Justice in Society*. London, England: Heineman, 1965.

Glass, David Victor (1911–1978)

DEMOGRAPHY

Born in London, England, David Victor Glass graduated in economic and social geography from the London School of Economics (LSE) in 1931 and was appointed research assistant to Sir William (later Lord) Beveridge, the director of LSE. In 1936 Glass was appointed research secretary to the newly formed Population Investigation Committee (see also, Alexander Morris Carr-Saunders). Until 1941, Glass was engaged in full-time demographic research. His work was concerned with demographic trends and policies in European countries and culminated in the publication, early in 1940, of his doctoral thesis "Population, Policies and Movements in Europe."

During the World War II, Glass worked as deputy director of the British Petroleum Mission in Washington and for the Ministry of Supply in London. He became reader in demography at LSE (1945), was promoted to a chair of sociology (1948) and became Martin White professor (1961). Between 1944 and 1949 Glass served on the statistics committee of the Royal Commission On Population and on its biological and medical committee as well as directing the family census of 1946. In the family census he pioneered the use of the method, which has been widely adopted since, of cohort analysis for the study of fertility.

He was the U.K. delegate to the newly founded Population Commission of the United Nations. He organized a number of enquiries into social mobility, and his study *Social Mobility in Britain* not only provided new facts and insights into the subject, but pioneered methods that became standard. He was elected Fellow of the British Academy (1964) and achieved the rare distinction for a social scientist of election to the Royal Society (1971). Glass was a foreign associate of the United States National Academy of Sciences and received honorary degrees from a number of universities, and was president of the International Union for the Scientific Study of Population.

His emphasis on the need for quantitative information in the discussion of social problems and his suspicions of generalization were not universally shared by his fellow sociologists at the time and led him to stand somewhat apart from the profession. Nonetheless, his influence was considerable, not only in Britain but also in the less developed countries, and particularly in India, a country to which he became greatly attached and which he visited regularly during the later years of his life. Glass founded *Population Studies: A Journal of Demography* and *The British Journal of Sociology*.

Major Literature

Glass, David Victor. *Population Policies and Movements in Europe*. London: Oxford University Press, 1940. New York: Augustus M. Kelley Publishers, 1969.

___. *The Trend and Pattern of Fertility in Britain*. London, England: H.M. Stationery Office, 1954.

___. *Social Mobility in Britain*. London, England: Taylor and Francis Group, Routledge, 1954, 1998.

___. *Population in History*. London, England: Edward Arnold, 1965, 1974.

___. *Numbering the People*. Farnborough, England: Saxon House, 1973.

___. *London's Newcomers: West Indian Immigrants*. Cambridge, Massachusetts: Harvard University Press, 1974.

Goffman, Erving (1922–1982)

STIGMA

Born in Manville, Alberta Canada, Erving Goffman gained a B.A. at the University of Toronto, Ontario, Canada (1945). At University of Chicago, Illinois, he gained an M.A., (1949) and Ph.D. (1953) and was assistant and resident associated professor, Division of Social Sciences (1952–1954). From 1954 to 1957, he worked at the National Institute of Mental Health, Bethesda, Maryland. At University of California, Berkeley, he was visiting scientist (1958–1959); assistant professor (1959–1962); and associate professor (1962–1968). He was Benjamin Franklin Professor of Anthropology and Sociology at the University of Pennsylvania, Philadelphia (1968–1982).

Goffman was president of the American Sociological Association (1981–1982). His awards and honors: LL.D., University of Manitoba, Winnipeg (1976); Guggenheim fellowship (1977–1978); Doctor of Humane Letters, University of Chicago (1978); and Mead-Cooley Award in social psychology (1979).

Major Contributions

Goffman is known for his theories suggesting that routine social actions, such as gossip, gestures, and grunts, indicate that people naturally strive to formulate identities. Goffman relied less on formal scientific method than on observation to explain contemporary life. He will be remembered for his influential work on institutionalization.

His work focused on the individual self, in a world that at the same time creates and oppresses self. His work is intensely moral in character, marked by a passionate defense of the self against society. His work is intensely human rather than theoretical, and has taken him into the studies of role behavior, deviance and its effects on identity. His book *Asylums* studies the significance of social structure in producing conforming behavior, especially in environments such as mental asylums, prisons and military establishments, which he labeled "total institutions."

In *The Presentation of Self*, Goffman explores individual identity, group relations, the impact of environment, and the movement and interactive meaning of information, and provides new insight into the nature of social interaction and the psychology of the individual. In *Stigma* Goffman draws attention to how people who have different physical characteristics, suffer from mental illness, have different sexual orientation or are of a different religion are all considered "abnormal." It seems that they are judged by one part of themselves rather than as whole people. They are stigmatized and suffer from a spoiled identity. Although much has been done in recent years to remove stigma from people who are disabled, the fear of being stigmatized is deeply rooted in our psyches. Goffman was a prolific writer of books and articles and he contributed to many professional journals.

Major Literature

Goffman, Erving. *The Presentation of Self in Everyday Life*. New York: Doubleday, 1990. London: Penguin Books, Ltd., 1956.
___. *Asylums: Essays on the Social Situation of Mental Patients and Other Inmates*. New York: Anchor Books, 1961. New York: Doubleday, 1990.
___. *Stigma: Notes on the Management of Spoiled Identity*. New Jersey: Prentice-Hall, 1963. London: Penguin Books, Ltd., 1990.
___. *Behavior in Public Places: Notes on the Social Organization of Gatherings*. New York: The Free Press, 1963. London: Greenwood Press, 1980.
___. *Interaction Ritual: Essays on Face-to-Face Behavior*. New York: Doubleday, 1967. Los Angeles: Aldine Books, 2005.

Goode, William Josiah (1917–2003)

SOCIOLOGY OF MARRIAGE

Born in Houston, Texas, William Josiah Goode gained a B.A. (1938) and M.A. in philosophy (1939) at the University of Texas, Austin, and a Ph.D. in sociology at Pennsylvania State University, Philadelphia (1945). He enlisted in the Navy as a radar man, then was assistant professor in sociology at Wayne State University, Detroit, Michigan (1946–1950). At Columbia University, New York, he collaborated with Robert K. Merton (see entry) on a project analyzing the professions in American society (1950) and was associate professor (1952); professor of sociology (1956); Franklin H.

Giddings professor of sociology (1975); chair of the Department of Sociology for several periods in the 1960s and 1970s, and also served as the associate director of the Bureau of Applied Social Research and was on its Board of Governors (1956–1970).

He was professor of sociology (1977–1986) and emeritus professor (1986) at Stanford University, California, and from 1986 to 1993 at Harvard University, Cambridge, Massachusetts, Department of Sociology. He was affiliated with the Sociology Department, George Mason University, Washington, D.C. (1994). He was the 63rd president of the American Sociological Association (1972). He was visiting professor and lecturer at Free University, Berlin (1954); Wolfson College, Oxford University, England (1980); Chinese Academy of Science, China (1986); and Hebrew University, Jerusalem (1992).

His awards and honors include being named fellow, American Academy of Arts and Sciences; an honorary doctorate of science, Upsala College, New Jersey (closed 1978); Merit Award for a Lifetime of Scholarship, Eastern Sociological Association; two Guggenheim fellowships; and National Institute of Mental Health Senior Scientist Career Award.

Major Contributions

Goode's presidential address for the American Sociological Association—"The Place of Force in Human Society"—was published in *American Sociological Review* (37, No. 5 [1972]: 507–519). During his years at Columbia, he was a supporter of the budding women's movement, both intellectually and personally, working with Betty Friedan when she was writing *The Feminine Mystique*, and with Cynthia Fuchs Epstein on a jointly edited book, *The Other Half: Roads to Women's Equality*.

Always something of nonconformist (at 16 he was expelled from Rice Institute, Houston,

Texas, for wearing tennis shorts to class), he encouraged and promoted the careers of his women graduate students, although he was no soft touch. He was best known for his pioneering cross-cultural analysis of marriage and divorce, although his work covered basic issues in sociological theory, focusing on social control systems of prestige, force and force threat, and love.

Major Literature

Goode, William Josiah. *Religion Among the Primitives.* Glencoe, Illinois: The Free Press, 1951, 1964.

___, and Paul Hatt. *Methods in Social Research.* Columbus, Ohio: McGraw-Hill Education, 1952.

Goode, William Josiah. *World Revolution and Family Patterns.* Glencoe, Illinois: The Free Press, 1963, 1971.

___, and Cynthia Fuchs Epstein. *The Other Half: Roads to Women's Equality.* Englewood Cliffs, New Jersey: Prentice-Hall, 1971.

Goode, William Josiah. *Explorations in Social Theory.* New York: Oxford University Press Inc., 1973.

___. *Principles of Sociology.* Columbus, Ohio: McGraw-Hill Education, 1977.

___. *World Changes in Divorce Patterns.* New Haven, Connecticut: Yale University Press, 1993.

Gramsci, Antonio (1891–1937)

CULTURAL HEGEMONY

Atonio Gramsci was born in Ales, Italy, on the island of Sardinia, though he was brought up in Ghilarza. A childhood accident left him with a deformed spine and he suffered from constant poor health. In 1911 Gramsci won a scholarship to the University of Turin, where he read literature and took a keen interest in linguistics. Gramsci was closely involvement with the industrialization taking place in Turin. Trade unions were being established and the first industrial social conflicts started to emerge. Gramsci joined the Italian Socialist Party in late 1913.

By 1915, financial problems and poor health, as well as his growing political commitment, forced Gramsci to abandon his education. From 1914 onward Gramsci's writings for socialist newspapers such as *Il Grido del Popolo* earned him a reputation as a notable journalist, and in 1916 he became co-editor of the Piedmont edition of *Avanti!*, the Socialist Party official organ, and proved an articulate and prolific writer of political theory. He was also involved in the education and organization of Turin workers.

Following the arrest of Socialist Party leaders that followed the revolutionary riots of August 1917, Gramsci became one of Turin's leading socialists when he was both elected to the party's Provisional Committee and made editor of *Il Grido del Popolo*. In April 1919 he helped set up the weekly newspaper *L'Ordine Nuovo*. In 1921, in the town of Livorno, the Communist Party of Italy was founded, with Gramsci as its leader, and in 1922 he traveled to Russia as a representative of the new party. The party was outlawed by the fascist government of Benito Mussolini in 1926; Gramsci was arrested and spent 11 years in prison and died soon after being released.

Gramsci wrote more than 30 notebooks and 3000 pages of history and analysis during his imprisonment. These writings, known as the *Prison Notebooks*, contain Gramsci's tracing of Italian history and nationalism. They also contain his ideas on Marxist theory, critical theory and educational theory. He also wrote on cultural hegemony as a means of maintaining the capitalist state, and the need for popular workers' education to encourage development of intellectuals from the working class.

Gramsci stated that, in the West, bourgeois cultural values were tied to Christianity, and therefore much of his opposition to cultural hegemony was aimed at religious norms and values. Gramsci argued that the domination of the capitalist class could not be secured by economic factors alone but required political force and, much more importantly, an ideological apparatus that secured the consent of the dominated classes. The class struggle is very largely a struggle between intellectual groups, one beholden to the capitalist class and the other to the workers. Gramsci was one of the most important Marxist thinkers of the twentieth century.

Major Literature

Gramsci, Antonio, and Geoffrey Nowell-Smith (Editor). Hoare Quintin (Introduction). *Prison Notebooks: Selections.* London, England: Lawrence and Wishart Ltd., 1973.

Granovetter, Mark (1943–)

SOCIAL NETWORKS

Mark Granovetter gained an A.B. in American and modern European history at Princeton University, New Jersey (1965), and a Ph.D. in sociology at Harvard University, Cambridge, Massachusetts (1970). He was assistant professor of social relations, Johns Hopkins University, Baltimore, Maryland (1970–1973); assistant to associate professor and director of the undergraduate program in sociology, Harvard (1973–1977); distinguished visiting professor of research, Graduate School of Business, Stanford University (1986–1987); and visiting research professor at the Social Science Research Center in Berlin (1989). At State University of New York, Stony Brook, he was associate professor, (1987–1992) and chair, Department of Sociology (1989–1992).

At Northwestern University, Evanston, Illinois, he was professor of sociology; professor of organization behavior, Kellogg Graduate School of Management (by courtesy) (1992–1995); and director of the program in

business institutions, College of Arts and Sciences (1994–1995). At Stanford University, California, he was professor of sociology (1995); Joan Butler Ford Professor in the School of Humanities and Sciences (1997); and chair, Department of Sociology (2002–2005).

His awards and honors: National Science Foundation Science Faculty Professional Development Award (1982–1983); elected to Johns Hopkins University Society of Scholars (1995); honorary doctor of philosophy, Stockholm University, Sweden (1996); and honorary doctor of philosophy at Institut d'Études Politiques de Paris (2006). He was editor, *Structural Analysis in the Social Sciences* series (Cambridge University Press, New York, 1996) and on the editorial board of the *Journal of Consumer Culture* (since 1999).

Major Contributions

Granovetter's main teaching interests are economic sociology, social stratification and sociological theory. He is best known for social network theory and economic sociology, particularly his theory on the spread of information in a community. In his sociology paper "The Strength of Weak Ties," Granovetter's basic argument is that our relationship to family members and close friends ("strong ties") will not supply us with as much diversity of knowledge as our relationship to acquaintances, distant friends, and the like ("weak ties"). Our acquaintances are less likely to be socially involved with one another than are our close friends. Thus the set of people made up of any individual and his or her acquaintances comprises a low-density network (one in which many of the possible relational lines are absent), whereas the set consisting of the same individual and his or her close friends will be densely knit (many of the possible lines are present), and social systems lacking in weak ties will be fragmented and incoherent. New ideas will spread slowly, scientific endeavors will be handicapped, and subgroups separated by race, ethnicity, geography, or other characteristics will have difficulty reaching a satisfactory way of life.

Major Literature

Granovetter, Mark. "The Strength of Weak Ties," *American Journal of Sociology* 78, 6 (1973): 1360–1380.

___. *Getting a Job: Study of Contacts and Careers.* University of Chicago Press; 2nd revised edition, 1995.

Wasserman, Stanley, Katherine Faust, Dawn Iacobucci, and Mark Granovetter. *Social Network Analysis: Methods and Applications.* New York: Cambridge University Press, 1994.

Carrington, Peter, John Scott, Stanley Wasserman, and Mark Granovetter (Eds.). *Models and Methods in Social Network Analysis.* New York: Cambridge University Press, 2005.

Gumplowicz, Ludwig (1838–1909)

SOCIOLOGY OF CONFLICT

Born in, Kraków, Poland, Ludwig Gumplowicz studied law in Kraków, then became a lawyer and publicist there. From 1875 to 1909 he was on the faculty of Graz University, Austria; in 1882 he became an associate professor and in 1893 a full professor. In 1909, ill with cancer, he and his wife committed suicide.

Gumplowicz was known for his disbelief in the permanence of social progress and for his theory that the state originates through inevitable conflict rather than through cooperation or divine inspiration. For him, social development rose out of conflict, first among races, then among states, then among other social groups.

In his view, human beings have an innate tendency to form groups and develop a feeling of unity, a process he called "syngenism." Initially, conflict arises between pre-political

racial groups. When one racial group has prevailed, it forms a state that becomes an amalgam of victor and vanquished. Wars then take place between states, and the process of conquest and assimilation occurs again, on a larger scale. Finally, each state creates by coercion a system of division of labor; as a result, social classes are formed, and they also engage in conflict.

Gumplowicz saw the state as an institution that served various controlling elites at different times. He leaned toward macrosociology (the study of large-scale society), predicting that if the minorities of a state became socially integrated, they would break out in war. In his 1909 publication *Der Rassenkampf* (*Struggle of the Races*) he foresaw world war. Considering history a cyclical process, Gumplowicz refuted the idea that social planning and welfare measures can save societies from ultimate collapse.

His political beliefs and his polemic character attracted many Polish and Italian students, making his theories important in Poland, Italy and other crown states (today Croatia, Czech Republic). But the fact that he published his works in German meant that he was also an important figure in German-speaking countries. Émile Durkheim (see entry) was one of the social scientists who elaborated Gumplowicz' view of political parties as interest groups. Central to his work of are the following important propositions:

1. Social phenomena are subject to the general law of causation as much as other classes of phenomena which have been successfully treated by the scientific method.

2. Human acts, whether individual or social, are the product of natural forces and they excite reflection. The function of the mind or soul is secondary in point of time.

3. Society, the social group, the sociological unit, is an organism or organization

entirely different from any other. The nature of the individual will be influenced by the group.

4. Every political organization, and hence every developing civilization, begins at the moment when one group permanently exercises control over another.

Major Literature

Gumplowicz, Ludwig. *The Outlines of Sociology*, 1899. Republished, New Jersey: Transaction Publishers, 1980.

Habermas, Jürgen (1929–)
COMMUNICATIVE REASON

Born in Düsseldorf, Germany, Jürgen Habermas gained his Ph.D. from the University of Bonn (1954) with a dissertation on the philosopher Friedrick von Schelling (1775–1854). Shortly thereafter he moved to the University of Frankfurt where, until 1959, he was assistant to professor Theodor Adorno (see entry), who was associated with the Institute for Social Research Frankfurt School. Habermas took his habilitation in political science at the University of Marburg under the Marxist Wolfgang Abendroth (1906–1985). In 1961, he became a *privatdozent* in Marburg, and was called to an "extraordinary professorship" (professor without chair) of philosophy at the University of Heidelberg. In 1964 Habermas took over the chair in philosophy and sociology from Max Horkheimer (see entry) and became the successor to Frankfurt School tradition.

From 1971 to 1983 Habermas was director of the Max Planck Institute in Starnberg, near Munich, then returned to his chair at Frankfurt and the directorship of the Institute for Social Research. In 1986, he received the Gottfried Wilhelm Leibniz Prize of the Deutsche Forschungsgemeinschaft, which is the highest honor awarded in German research. He is also a permanent visiting professor at Northwestern University in Evanston, Illinois. In 1988 he was elected as a member of Serbian Academy of Sciences and Arts. In 2005 he received the Holberg International Memorial Prize.

Major Contributions

The Frankfurt School crossed the traditional boundaries that separate literary criticism, philosophy, psychoanalysis, and social science, and attempted to understand the various elements comprising modern society. Habermas is a philosopher and sociologist in the tradition of critical theory and pragmatism, best known for his concept of the public sphere based in his theory and pragmatics of communicative reason or communicative rationality (rational communication for the purpose of cooperative solidarity). His work, sometimes labeled as "neo-Marxist," focuses on the foundations of social theory and epistemology or the theory of knowledge; the analysis of advanced capitalist industrial society and of democracy; the rule of law in a critical social-evolutionary context; and contemporary, especially German, politics. He developed a theoretical system devoted to revealing the possibility of reason, emancipation and rational-critical communication rooted in modern liberal institutions and in the human capabilities to communicate, deliberate and pursue rational interests.

Within sociology, Habermas's major contribution is the development of a comprehensive theory of how societies evolve and modernize. Within that he focuses on the difference between communicative rationality and rationalization on the one hand and strategic/instrumental rationality and rationalization on the other. Habermas sees the rationalization, humanization, and democratization of society as evidence of the potential for rationality that is unique to the human species.

Related Literature

Calhoun, Craig J. (Ed.). *Habermas and the Public Sphere.* Cambridge, Massachusetts: MIT Press, 1993.

Rosenfeld, Michel, and Andrew Arato (Eds.). *Habermas on Law and Democracy: Critical Exchanges.* Berkeley, California: University of California Press, 1998.

Eriksen, Erik, and Oddvar Jarle Weigard. *Understanding Habermas: Communicative Action and Deliberative Democracy.* London, England: Continuum International Publishing Group, 2003.

Hallinan, Maureen T. (1940–)

SOCIOLOGY OF EDUCATION

Born in New York City, Maureen T. Hallinan gained a B.A. in mathematics and science at Marymount College, Tarrytown, New York (1961), and an M.S. in mathematics, University of Notre Dame, Indiana (1968). At University of Chicago, Illinois, she gained a Ph.D. in sociology and education (1972) and was visiting instructor, Department of Education (1973). At Stanford University, California, she was visiting assistant professor, Department of Sociology/School of Education (1975–1976) and visiting associate professor, Department of Sociology (1976–1978). At the University of Wisconsin, Madison, she was assistant professor of sociology (1972–1976); associate professor (1976–1980); and professor of sociology (1980–1984).

At the University of Notre Dame, Indiana, she was William P. and Hazel B. White Professor of Sociology (1984–); director of the Institute for Educational Initiatives (1997–1998); and director of the Center for Research on Educational Opportunity (since 1999). At the American Sociological Association she was chair, Sociology of Education Section (1991–1992) and 87th president (1996). From 1995 to 1996 she was on the advisory board at the Institute for High Intelligence Education, Hong Kong. Her honors and awards include member (1993) and president (1996) of Alpha Kappa Delta; Pi Lambda Theta member (1970) and president (1996); University of Notre Dame, Presidential Award Citation (1997); Research Achievement Award (2003) and Faculty Award (2006); president, Sociological Research Association (2000); and American Sociological Association, Willard Waller Award (2004).

Major Contributions

Hallinan's research is primarily in the sociology of education. She studies the determinants and consequences of the organization of students for instruction; for example, how students are assigned to ability groups and what the effects of ability group level are on student learning opportunities. She also examines the effects of school characteristics on student achievement and social development. Her work includes studies of the formation and duration of students' cross-race friendships in middle and secondary schools.

As director of the Center for Research on Educational Opportunity, Hallinan is the principal investigator of the "Comparative Analysis of Best Practices in Public and Private Elementary and Secondary Schools" project, a five-year study funded by the U.S. Department of Education to determine the best practices adopted by educators to promote student learning and social development.

Major Literature

Hallinan, Maureen T. *Restructuring Schools.* Notre Dame, Indiana: Kluwer Academic Publishers, 1995.

___. "The Sociological Study of Social Change." Presidential Address. *American Sociological Review*, 62 (1) (1996): 1–11.

___. "Should Your School Eliminate Tracking? The History of Tracking and Detracking in America's Schools." *Education Matters* (2005): 1–2.

___(Ed.). *School Sector and Student Outcomes*. Notre Dame, Indiana: University of Notre Dame Press, 2006.

___. "Present Status of Sociology in the United States." *Journal of Applied Sociology*, 48 (2006): 1–17.

___. *Handbook of the Sociology of Education*. New York: Springer-Verlag Inc.; new edition, 2006.

___, and B.J. Ellison. "The Practice of Ability Grouping: Sector Differences in Implementation." In M.T. Hallinan (Ed.), *School Sector Effects on Educational Outcomes*. Notre Dame, Indiana: University of Notre Dame Press, 2006.

Halsey, Albert Henry (1923–)

EDUCATIONAL EQUALITY

Albert Henry Halsey gained a B.Sc. in economics, an M.A. at the University of Oxford, and a Ph.D. at the University of London. He worked at the London School of Economics (1947–1952), then worked in research at the University of Liverpool (1952–1954). He was lecturer and senior lecturer, University of Birmingham (1954–1962); fellow, Center for Advanced Study in the Behavioral Sciences, Palo Alto, California (1956–1957); visiting professor of sociology, University of Chicago, Illinois (1959–1960); professorial fellow, Nuffield College, Oxford (1962–1990); adviser to Labor Education Secretary of State for Education Anthony Crossland (1965–1968); professorial fellow, Nuffield College, Oxford (1962–1990); professor, social and administrative studies, University of Oxford (1978–1990); and emeritus professor (from 1990).

His awards and honors include being a foreign associate, American Academy of Education (1973); honorary doctorate in social sciences, University of Birmingham (1987); foreign member, American Academy of Arts and Sciences (1988); honorary doctorate, Open University (U.K.) (1990); honorary fellowship, Goldsmiths College, London (1992); member of Academia Europaea (1992); honorary fellow, London School of Economics (1993); D.Litt, University of Glamorgan, Wales (1995); D.Litt, University of Leicester (1995); D.Litt, University of Warwick (1995); and senior fellow, British Academy (1995).

Major Contributions

Born to working class parents, Halsey grew up convinced that intelligence did not depend on class. "Chelly," as he was universally known, won a scholarship to grammar school but started his career inauspiciously as a sanitary inspector's apprentice. He served in the Royal Air Force (1942–1947), trained as a fighter pilot and perfected the "aerial handbrake turn" that would keep him out of the way of the Japanese kamikaze pilots. He made a name for himself at London School of Economics in the rapidly expanding discipline of sociology, and for some 40 years has held a professorship at Nuffield College, Oxford.

Halsey has focused primarily on the relationships between education and social class, family, and social mobility. He has been particularly interested in identifying social conditions under which equality, liberty, and fraternity might be possible in any society, as well as the social forces that leave them largely unrealized today. He was especially influential in efforts after World War II to reform the British school system to promote equality of opportunity.

A History of Sociology in Britain (Oxford, England: Oxford University Press, 2004) is the first-ever critical history of sociology in Britain, and presents a vivid and authoritative picture of the neglect, expansion, fragmentation, and explosion of the discipline during the past century. The book examines the literary and scientific contributions to the origin of the discipline, and the challenges faced by the discipline at the dawn of a new century.

Major Literature

Lauder, Hugh, Phillip Brown, Amy Stuart Wells, and A.H. Halsey. *Education: Culture, Economy and Society*. Oxford, England: Oxford University Press, 1997.

Halsey, A.H., and Josephine Webb (Eds.). *Twentieth-century British Social Trends*. New York: Palgrave Macmillan, 2000.

Halsey, A.H., and W.G. Runciman. *British Sociology Seen from Without and Within*. Oxford, England: Oxford University Press, 2005.

Lauder, Hugh, Phillip Brown, Jo-Anne Dillabough and A.H. Halsey (Eds.). *Education, Globalization and Social Change*. Oxford, England: Oxford University Press, 2006.

Hankins, Frank Hamilton (1877–1970)

SCIENTIfiC SOCIOLOGY

Born in Wilkshire, Ohio, Frank Hamilton Hankins grew up in Kansas and received an A.B. from Baker University, Baldwin City, Kansas (1901). He served as superintendent of schools in Waverly, Kansas, and gained his Ph.D. (1908) from Columbia University, New York. His doctoral dissertation, "Adolphe Quetelet as Statitician" (1908), was an important contribution to the development of empirical sociology (see entry, Adolphe Quételet). Hankins was on the faculty of Clark University, Worcester, Massachusetts, from 1906 to 1922, and head of the Department of Political and Social Science from 1908. Clark University, at the time, was under the leadership of the influential psychologist G. Stanley Hall (1844–1924).

From 1922 to 1946, Hankins was professor of sociology at Smith College, Northampton, Massachusetts, and for many years he served as department chairman. In 1930, Hankins was elected the first president of the American Sociological Society (Association, 1959) and in 1945, was president of the American Population Association. Hankins contributed numerous articles to scholarly journals, lectured frequently at other universities, studied social conditions in Europe before and after World War I, and taught at the École Libre des Sciences Politique in Paris in 1921.

He served on the faculties of Amherst College, Massachusetts; Columbia, New York; Berkeley, California; the Army Center at Biarritz, France, and, following his retirement from Smith College, the University of Pennsylvania, Philadelphia. In 1936, he studied social conditions in Nazi Germany. He was the 28th president of the American Sociological Association (1938); his presidential address was "Social Science and Social Action." Hankins contributed to the *Encyclopedia of the Social Sciences*.

Major Contributions

His ground-breaking study, *The Racial Basis of Civilization: A Critique of the Nordic Doctrine*, was published in 1926. In 1928, he published *An Introduction to the Study of Society*, in which he presented his principal theoretical and practical concerns and convictions. On the one hand, Hankins had a keen interest in the role of biological factors in social life and history and, on the other, he was interested in the role of such processes as urbanization, education, persecution, and war in the determination of population quantity and quality. He argued in favor of birth control, more for the lower classes and less for the privileged. He condemned authoritarian institutions and practices and supported the maximization of opportunity for all. He also denounced racist policies and believed that racially mixed populations were physically and socially beneficial.

In 1958 Hankins carried out a survey of the question "How Many Jews Were Eliminated by the Nazis?" Hankins's effort was an attempt to review and explore this situation, approaching it objectively as a demographer, minus the standard starting assumption that, six million (or more) Jews having perished, therefore any analysis of the problem must fit the data to this assumption rather than the other way around. Hankins restricted himself purely to a study of the possible numbers involved, and a critique of previous explanations and methods of arriving at conclusions. The study can be reviewed at http://www.ihr.org/jhr/v04/v04p-61_Hankins.html.

Haraway, Donna J. (1944–)

CYBORG THEORY

Born in Denver, Colorado, Donna J. Haraway earned a degree in zoology and philosophy at Colorado College and received the Boettcher Foundation scholarship. She studied philosophies of evolution in Paris for a year on a Fulbright scholarship and completed her Ph.D. from the Biology Department of Yale University, New Haven, Connecticut (1972). Her dissertation was titled "The Functions of Metaphor in Shaping Research in Developmental Biology in the Twentieth Century." After teaching Women's Studies and General Science at the University of Hawaii, she went on to Johns Hopkins University, Baltimore, Maryland, and is currently a professor and former chair of the History of Consciousness Program at the University of California, Santa Cruz. She also teaches feminist theory and technoscience at the European Graduate School in Saas-Fee, Switzerland.

In 2000, Haraway was awarded the highest honor given by the Society for Social Studies of Science — the J.D. Bernal Award, for lifetime contributions to the field. Her influential work *Simians, Cyborgs, and Women* has become the authoritative text in theorizing the politics of the post-human, the cyborg, the techno-mythological ideal and its promised utopia(s).

Major Contributions

Haraway is a leading thinker about people's love and hate relationship with machines. Her ideas have sparked an explosion of debate in areas as diverse as primatology, philosophy, and developmental biology. She uses the metaphor of the cyborg to discuss the relationships of science, technology, and "socialist-feminism." She holds that high-tech culture challenges and breaks down the old dualisms of Western thinking like the mind-body split, self-other, male-female, reality-appearance, and truth-illusion.

She holds that we are no longer able to think of ourselves in these terms, or even strictly speaking, as biological entities. Instead, we have become cyborgs, mixtures of human and machine, where the biological side and the mechanical and electrical side become so inextricably entwined that they cannot be split. Haraway's ideal "cyborg world" consists of people living together, unafraid of their joint kinship with animals and machines. She has identified a social and cultural movement from an organic, industrial society toward a system of information that exists in many different forms, which she has charted as a series of transformations that restructure webs of power created by the politics of science and technology. Some of these transformations:

From	To
Small group	Subsystem
Eugenics	Population control
Hygiene	Stress management
Nature/culture	Fields of difference
Sex	Genetic engineering
Physiology	Communications engineering
Organic division of labor	Ergonomics/cybernetics of labor

Major Literature

Haraway, Donna, J. *Simians, Cyborgs and Women: The Reinvention of Nature*. London, England: Free Association Books, Ltd., 1991.

___. *Primate Visions: Gender, Race and Nature in the World of Modern Science*. London, England: Verso Books, 1992.

___. *Modest Witness: Feminism and Technoscience*. London, England: Taylor and Francis Books, Ltd., Routledge, 1997.

___. *Cyborg Babies: From Techno-sex to Techno-tots*. London, England: Taylor and Francis Books, Ltd., Routledge, 1998.

___. *The Haraway Reader*. London, England: Taylor and Francis Books, Ltd., Routledge, 2003.

Hauser, Philip Morris (1909–1994)

URBAN STUDIES

Born in Chicago, Philip Morris Hauser gained all his degrees from the University of Chicago, Illinois: Ph.B. (1929), M.A. (1933), and Ph.D. in sociology (1938). From 1932 to 1938 Hauser was instructor in sociology and a researcher with the Federal Emergency Relief Administration from 1934 to 1937. He was professor of sociology at the University of Chicago from 1947; associate dean of the Division of Social Sciences (1949 to 1952); chairman of the Department of Sociology (1956–1965); and named Lucy Flower Professor of Urban Sociology in 1974. When he retired in 1977, Hauser had spent nearly 50 years at the University of Chicago.

Major Contributions

Hauser served as the 58th president of the American Sociological Association (1968); his presidential address, "The Chaotic Society: Product of the Social Morphological Revolution," was published in the *American Sociological Review* (34, No. 1 [1969]: 1–19). He was president of the Population Association of America and the American Statistical Association. He founded the University of Chicago's Population Research Center and directed it for thirty years, during which time he trained approximately 100 Ph.D. students and many other M.A. students. About half of these students were from other countries. Hauser served as U.S. representative to the Population Commission for the United Nations (1947-1951) and was a statistical advisor to the governments of Burma and Thailand during the 1950s.

Major Contributions

Hauser was especially concerned with the consequences of racial segregation and over-population. In 1963 he became chairman of the Advisory Panel for the Desegregation of the Chicago Public Schools. His interests included the relationships between population characteristics and development, factors affecting fertility and mortality rates, and the study of racial segregation and many other aspects of urbanization. During the 1960s, he studied mortality figures and found very large differentials based on income and social status, with college-educated people living longer than less-educated people. He was the author of a report in 1964 on desegregation of the Chicago public schools.

In the early 1980s, he assembled a team of experts to study the remapping of city wards. Using the 1980 U.S. Census of Chicago, Hauser testified in U.S. District Court that the map had diluted the voting strengths of minority groups, especially African-Americans and Hispanics. A dynamic speaker, he was often called upon to explain and interpret population data to a wide variety of audiences, including government panels, academic conferences, business groups, and for television and radio programs.

Major Literature

Hauser, Philip Morris. *Government Statistics for Business Use*. New Jersey: John Wiley and Sons, Inc., 1956.

___. *Urbanization in Asia and the Far East.* UNESCO, 1958.

___. *The Study of Population: An Inventory and Appraisal.* Chicago, Illinois: University of Chicago Press, 1959.

___. *Population Perspectives.* Piscataway, New Jersey: Rutgers University Press, 1961.

___. *Urbanization in Latin America.* New York: Columbia University Press, 1967.

___. *Handbook For Social Research in Urban Areas.* UNESCO, 1967.

___. *World Population and Development: Challenges and Perspectives.* New York: Syracuse University Press, 1979, 2006.

Hauser, Robert Mason (1942–)

SOCIOLOGY OF AGING

Robert Mason Hauser gained a B.A. in economics at the University of Chicago, Illinois (1963), and at the University of Michigan, Ann Arbor. He was Metropolitan Community Research Fellow (1963–1964) and National Institutes of Mental Health Fellow in Social Organization and Human Ecology (1965–1967). He gained an M.A. in sociology (1966) and a Ph.D. in sociology (1968). He was assistant professor of research, Department of Sociology and Anthropology, Brown University, Providence, Rhode Island (1967–1969).

At the University of Wisconsin, Madison, Hauser was assistant professor (1969–1971); associate professor (1973–1981); professor, Department of Sociology (from 1981); Samuel A. Stouffer Professor of Sociology (from 1981); Hilldale Professor of Sociology (1983–1987); director, Center for Demography and Ecology, (1985–1989); Vilas Research Professor of Sociology (from 1987); director, Institute for Research on Poverty (1991–1994); and director, Center for Demography of Health and Aging (1999–present).

He was fellow, Center for Advanced Studies in the Behavioral Sciences, Palo Alto, California (1977–1978); visiting professor, Institute for Advanced Study, Vienna, Austria (1980); visiting professor, Department of Sociology, University of Bergen, Norway (1983–1984); member, National Academy of Sciences; fellow, American Academy of Arts and Sciences (1984); and member, American Philosophical Society (2005). He received the Paul F. Lazarsfeld Award, Methodology Section, and the Award for Distinguished Contributions to the Teaching of Sociology, both from the American Sociological Association.

Major Contributions

Hauser's doctoral dissertation was "Family, School, and Neighborhood Factors in Educational Performances in a Metropolitan School System." Hauser collaborated on two major projects of national importance. One was the "Occupational Changes in a Generation Survey" (1973), with David L. Featherman of Wisconsin University, a replication and extension of an earlier study by Otis Dudley Duncan and Peter Michael Blau (see entries). The second was the Wisconsin Longitudinal Study with William H. Sewell (see entry). Hauser has led the study since 1980.

In recent years, Hauser has combined work on the Wisconsin Longitudinal Study with studies of trends and differentials in educational attainment and of the role of achievement testing in American society. His classroom teaching repertoire includes social stratification, research methods, and introductory and advanced courses in statistics, including structural equation models and discrete multivariate analysis. He has pursued connections between social science and social policy through his work with the National Research Council.

Major Literature

Featherman, David L., and Robert M. Hauser. *Opportunity and Change.* New York: Academic Press, 1978.

Hauser, Robert M., David Mechanic, Archibald O. Haller, and Taissa S. Hauser (Eds.). *Social Structure and Behavior: Essays in Honor of William H. Sewell.* New York: Academic Press, 1982.

Hauser, Robert M., Brett V. Brown and William Prosser (Eds.). *Indicators of Children's Well-Being.* New York: Russell Sage Foundation, 1997.

Hauser, Robert M., Christopher F. Edley, Jr., Judith Anderson Koenig, and Stuart W. Elliott (Eds.). National Research Council. *Measuring Literacy: Performance Levels for Adults.* Washington, D.C.: National Academy Press, 2005.

Haveman, Heather A.

INDUSTRIAL SOCIOLOGY

Heather A. Haveman gained a B.A. in history (1982) and an M.B.A. (1985) from the University of Toronto, Ontario, Canada, and a Ph.D. in organizational behavior and industrial relations at the University of California, Berkeley, Graduate School of Business Administration (1990). She was assistant professor to associate professor, Duke University, Durham, North Carolina, Fuqua School of Business, Department of Sociology (1990–1994); associate professor to professor, Cornell University, Ithaca, New York, Johnson Graduate School of Management; member, Cornell University Graduate Field of Sociology (1994–1999); professor, Graduate School of Business, Columbia University, New York, Department of Sociology (1998); professor, University of California, Berkeley, Department of Sociology; and Haas School of Business (since 2006).

She is on the editorial board of *American Sociological Review* and *Administrative Science Quarterly.* Haveman teaches Ph.D. organizational theory, careers and social mobility, and research design; M.B.A. organizational design and change, entrepreneurship, managing innovation, managing growth, and women in management; and to undergraduates, organizational theory, research

methods, gender at work, and entrepreneurship. Her honors and awards include the Lou Pondy Award, Organization and Management Theory Division of the Academy of Management (best paper from a dissertation) (1990); Clifford H. Whitcomb Faculty Fellow, Cornell University (1997–1998); and the Max Weber Award, Organizations, Occupations, and Work Section of the American Sociological Association (best paper published in the last three years, for Haveman and Cohen, 1994, *American Journal of Sociology*) (1997).

Major Contributions

Haveman's research areas are organizational theory (ecology and institutionalism), economic sociology, historical sociology, entrepreneurship, organizational demography, gender, careers and social mobility. In her research, Haveman investigates the stability and change in systems of firms: How strong are the forces that impel or inhibit change in organizational structures and activities? What are the consequences of such change? Her research focuses on three related phenomena:

1. firms' responses to shifting industry conditions and the impact of organizational change on firm performance and survival
2. the evolving structures and activity patterns of entire industries
3. the consequences of organizational founding, failure and change processes for the careers of employees and the composition of firms' workforces.

Haveman is currently studying the early magazine industry in America from its inception in 1741 to 1861. She aims to tell the story of how magazines built a coherent, distinctively American society and, at the same time, sustained many separate and often opposing communities. Her focus is both on how forces in American society supported and constrained magazines, and how the growing number and variety of magazines promoted community-building. A second area of research is the U.S. wine industry from 1940 to the present.

Major Literature

Haveman, Heather A. "The Future of Organizational Sociology: Forging Ties Between Paradigms." *Contemporary Sociology,* 29 (2000): 476–486.

Sine, Wesley D., Heather A. Haveman, and Pamela S. Tolbert. "Risky Business? Entrepreneurship in the New Independent-power Sector." *Administrative Science Quarterly* 50 (2005): 200–232.

Haveman, Heather A., and Hayagreeva Rao. "Hybrid Forms and the Evolution of Thrifts." *American Behavioral Scientist,* 49 (2006): 974–986.

Hayes, Edward Cary (1868–1928)

SOCIAL PROCESS

Born in Lewiston, Maine, Edward Cary Hayes graduated from Bates College in Lewiston (1887) and graduated as a minister from its Cobb Divinity School (1893). He was a pastor in Augusta, Maine, until 1896, at which point he began to find that his beliefs clashed with most of the congregation's. He taught philosophy and served as dean at Keuka College, New York (1897–1899). In 1899 Hayes enrolled at the University of Chicago, Illinois, to acquire a doctorate degree in philosophy but, influenced by A.W. Small (see entry), he studied sociology. He gained a doctor of philosophy in 1902 from Chicago, with a dissertation titled "The Sociologist's Object of Attention."

Between 1899 and 1902, Hayes studied at the University of Berlin with Georg Simmel (see entry). From 1902 to 1907 he was professor of sociology and economics in Miami University, Oxford, Ohio. In 1907 Hayes became professor of sociology and head of the new department of sociology Chicago. In spite of opposition from his academic colleagues, the department grew steadily, until in 1928 seven men were employed in sociology and the registration was more than 2,000 a year. In addition to his regular teaching work, Hayes taught in summer sessions in many other universities in America.

He was present at the meeting in December 1905 in which the American Sociological Society was started (Association, 1959) and thus became a charter member. He was a member of the Committee of Ten appointed by the society to outline the subject matter of the fundamental course in sociology; represented the society on the Joint Commission on Presentation of Social Studies in the Schools; was second vice-president of the society (1919), first vice-president (1920); and president (1921).

He was secretary of the Social Psychology Section of the World's Congress of Science in the St. Louis Exposition (1904). He was advisory editor of the *American Journal of Sociology,* cooperating editor of the *Journal of Applied Sociology,* and editor of the Lippincott series in sociology, the first volume of which appeared in 1922. He was a member of the German Sociological Society, a member of the Institut Internationale de Sociologie (Paris), and a member and former vice-president of the Instituto Internazionale di Sociologia (Rome).

Major Contributions

His works mostly consisted of attempts to define sociology and to analyze the general problems facing sociologists. His main contribution is his elaboration of his primary thesis, the social process, in which sociologists direct their attention to interrelated social activities rather than to the social organism, the group, or the person. Hayes argued that sociology must be a synthesis of the knowledge of all the conditions in which social activities occur, that social activities are essentially psychic, and that the purpose and essential part of sociology is ethics.

Major Literature

Hayes, Edward Cary. *Introduction to the Study of Sociology.* New Jersey: Appleton-Century-Crofts, 1915.

___. *Sociology and Ethics.* New Jersey: Appleton-Century-Crofts, 1921.

Hobhouse, Leonard Trelawny (1864–1929)

POLITICAL SOCIOLOGY

Born at St. Ives, near Liskeard, Cornwall, England, Leonard Trelawny Hobhouse gained first classes in classical moderations (1884) and classics (1887), Corpus Christi College, Oxford, and in 1887 obtained a prize fellowship at Merton College, Oxford. In 1890 he was appointed assistant tutor at Corpus, and in 1894 was elected a fellow of that college. In 1889 he took up the cause of the movement known as the "New Unionism." This brought him in contact with the world of labor, which led him into the study of sociology. From 1897 to 1902 he was on the staff of the Manchester *Guardian* newspaper, became a director of the paper in 1911, contributing frequently to it, especially from 1915 to 1925, and in 1921 acted as deputy editor.

In 1903 he was active in forming the Sociological Society, and from then on, sociology was his chief preoccupation, though he continued his journalistic work. From 1903 to 1905 he was secretary of the Free Trade Union, and he acted for some time as the editor of its organ, the *Sociological Review.* For eighteen months (1906–1907) he was political editor of *The Tribune.* From 1907 to 1929 he was the first professor of sociology in London University. He was opposed to the Boer War and had reservations about the First World War. He was chairman of several trade boards and had taken a keen interest from their first formation.

His sociological works were more appreciated in America than in England, and he had many requests to lecture in American universities. He received honorary degrees from the universities of St. Andrews, Scotland (1919) and Durham (1913). The Hobhouse Memorial Trust, which provides for an annual lecture to be delivered in rotation at the London School of Economics, University College, King's College, and Bedford College, and also for a memorial prize to be awarded annually to a student who shows conspicuous merit in sociology, was founded in 1930. Hobhouse held out hope that Liberals and what would now be called the social democrat tendency in the rising Labour party could form a grand progressive coalition.

Major Literature

Hobhouse, Leonard T. *The Labor Movement.* London, England: T. Fisher Unwin, 1893. New York: Barnes and Noble, 1974.

___. *The Theory of Knowledge.* London, England: Methuen and Co., 1896. Whitefish, Montana: R.A. Kessinger Publishing Co., 2005

___. *Development and Purpose.* London, England: Macmillan, 1913. Honolulu, Hawaii: University Press of the Pacific, 2004.

___. *The Metaphysical Theory of the State.* London, England: George Allen and Unwin, 1918. Honolulu, Hawaii: University Press of the Pacific, 2004.

___. *The Rational Good.* New York: Henry Holt and Company, Inc., 1921. Honolulu, Hawaii: University Press of the Pacific, 2004.

___. *The Elements of Social Justice.* New York: Henry Holt and Company, Inc., 1922. London, England: George Allen and Unwin, 1992.

___. *Social Development.* New York, 1924. London, England: George Allen and Unwin, 1967.

Homans, George Casper (1910–1989)

EXCHANGE THEORY

Born in Boston, Massachusetts, from 1928 George Casper Homans studied English and American literature at Harvard University, Cambridge, Massachusetts. From 1934 to 1939 he was a junior fellow of the newly formed Society of Fellows at Harvard, studying sociology, psychology and history. From 1939 until he retired he was a Harvard faculty member, teaching both sociology and medieval history. In 1964 he was elected 54th president of the American Sociological Association.

Major Contributions

Within sociology and social psychology, Homans is regarded as one of the major sociological theorists in the period from the 1950s to the 1970s, although his ideas about theoretical principles in sociology were much debated and often rejected. Homans put forward the argument that social life is solely a product of individual psychology and the economic principles of exchange, rather than social systems and social facts. He was best-known for his social exchange theory (see also, Peter Blau). Social exchange theories use principles from learning theory and economics to analyze the structure and functions of interaction, where individuals are driven by goals, the outcome of which will be to their benefit. Individuals are likely to apply exchange rules that have proved to benefit them in the past rather than seek new ones. Homans' approach to theory developed in two phases, usually interpreted by commentators as inductive reasoning (based on observation and measurement) and deductive (based on definitions and premises) respectively.

By 1958 Homans, influenced by the logical philosophers of that period, had decided that theory should be expressed as a deductive system. Essentially, he argued that satisfactory explanations in the social sciences are based upon "propositions" — principles — about individual behavior that are drawn from the behavioral psychology of the time. For instance, the choice of a behavior is one out of all the choices that is more likely to result in a more favorable net reward.

Homans' approach is an example of methodological individualism in social science, an approach also favored by some more recent influential social theorists, particularly those who have adopted some form of rational choice theory (see entry, James S. Coleman). By 1974 Homans' theory rested upon two major claims:

1. the basic principles of social science must be true of individuals as members of the human species, not as members of particular groups or cultures
2. any other generalizations or facts about human social life will be derivable from these principles (and suitable initial conditions).

Major Literature

Homans, George Casper. *The Nature of Social Science*. London, England: Thomson Learning, 1967.
___. *Social Behavior: Its Elementary Forms*. Orlando, Florida: Harcourt Brace, 1974.
___. *English Villagers of the Thirteenth Century*. New York: W.W. Norton and Co., Ltd., 1980.
___. *Coming to My Senses: Autobiography of a Sociologist*. New Jersey: Transaction Publishers, 1985.
___. *Sentiments and Activities: Essays in Social Science*. New Jersey: Transaction Publishers, 1988.
___. *Witch-hazel: Poems of a Lifetime*. New Jersey: Transaction Publishers, 1988.
___. *The Human Group*. New Jersey: Transaction Publishers, 1992

Horkheimer, Max (1895–1973)
CRITICAL THEORY

Born in Stuttgart, Germany, Max Horkheimer received his Ph.D. in philosophy at the University of Frankfurt (1922). He was habilitated (1925) with a dissertation titled "Kant's Critique of Judgment as Mediation Between Practical and Theoretical Philosophy," and was appointed as *privatdozent* (1926). Horkheimer is known especially as the founder and guiding thinker of the Frankfurt School of critical theory and was director of the Frankfurt Institute for Social Research (1930–1958). Following the defeat of the German Revolution (1917–1923), Horkheimer argued that culture and consciousness are partly independent of economics; his ideas about liberation and consumer society continue to influence contemporary empirical sociologists. The institute's journal *Zeitschrift für Sozialforschung* (*Journal for Social Research*) was begun in 1931 with Horkheimer as its editor.

When the Nazis came to power in 1933, they revoked the institute's license; Horkheimer immigrated to Switzerland, then to the U.S. in 1934. Columbia University, New York City, offered to host the institute in exile, which allowed for the continued publication of the journal. In 1940 Horkheimer received American citizenship. He directed the institute until 1941, when it was dissolved owing to financial difficulties, and he moved to Pacific Palisades, Los Angeles, California.

In 1949, Horkheimer returned to Frankfurt and re-established the institute (1950). Between 1951 and 1953 he was rector of the University of Frankfurt; he retired to Switzerland in 1958.

Major Contributions

Horkheimer states that we have moved from objective to subjective reasoning. Objective reason deals with universal truths that dictate that an action is either right or wrong. Subjective reason takes into account the situation and social norms. Actions that produce the best situation for the individual are "reasonable" according to subjective reason. The movement from one type of reason to the other occurred when thought could no longer accommodate these objective truths or when it judged them to be delusions. Under subjective reason, concepts lose their meaning. All concepts must be strictly functional to be reasonable. Because subjective reason rules, the ideals of a society, for example democratic ideals, become dependent on the "interests" of the people instead of being dependent on objective truths.

Writing in 1946, Horkheimer outlined how the Nazis had been able to make their agenda appear "reasonable," but also issued a warning about the possibility of this happening again. Horkheimer believed that the ills of modern society are caused by the misuse and misunderstanding of reason: if people use true reason to critique their societies, they will be able to identify and solve their problems.

Major Literature (In English; many more are in German)

Adorno, Theodor W., and Max Horkheimer. *Dialectic of Enlightenment*. Amsterdam: Querido Verlag, 1947. London, England: Verso Books, 1997.

Horkheimer, Max. *Critique of Instrumental Reason*. New York: Continuum Publishing Group, 1993.

___. *Critical Theory*. New York: Continuum Publishing Group, 1997.

___. *Eclipse of Reason*. New York: Continuum Publishing Group, 1997.

Huber, Joan (1925–)
SOCIOLOGY OF THE FAMILY

Born in Bluffton, Ohio, Joan Huber gained a B.A. in German (1945) at Pennsylvania

State University, Lewistown, Pennsylvania, and was instructor in German (1945–1947). She gained an M.A. in sociology (1963) at Western Michigan University, Kalamazoo, and a Ph.D. in social stratification at Michigan State University, East Lansing, Michigan (1967). She was assistant professor of sociology at the University of Notre Dame, Notre Dame, Indiana (1967–1971). At the University of Illinois, Urbana, Champaign, Huber was professor of sociology (1971–1983); director, Women's Studies (1978–1980); and head, Department of Sociology (1979–1983).

She was president of the Sociologists for Women in Society (1972–1974) and the Midwest Sociological Society (1979–1980). At Ohio State University, Athens, she was dean, College of Social and Behavioral Sciences (1984–1992); professor, sociology (1984–1993); senior vice president for academic affairs and provost (1992–1993); professor of sociology emeritus (since 1994). She received the Jessie Bernard Award, American Sociological Association (1985).

Major Contributions

Huber (see also, William Form) studies the effects of technology and demographic factors on gender stratification over time, within the overall study of social stratification. She has done this primarily by linking women's involvement in the family and labor force with changes in technology and birth rates. Although her approach is essentially sociological, it also draws upon history, demography, economics, anthropology, and political science. Huber is also prominent for her leadership in expanding sociology in the United States to include women. She served as the 79th president of the American Sociological Association; her presidential address, "Macro-micro Links in Gender Stratification," was published in the *American Sociological Review* (55, No. 1 [1990]: 1–9).

Huber argues that in all societies producers have more power than consumers; those who control the distribution of valued goods beyond the family have the most power. Historically, the requirements of population replacement, coupled with technology of the time, have shaped the distribution of power and prestige as well as gender. Evidence comes from hunter gatherer, agricultural and advanced industrial societies. Upon her retirement in 1993, Huber donated her professional papers to the archives at Pennsylvania State University, which may be accessed online at http://www.libraries.psu.edu/speccolls/FindingAids/huber.html.

Major Literature

Huber, Joan. *Changing Women in a Changing Society*. Chicago, Illinois: University of Chicago Press, 1973.
___, and William H. Form. *Income and Ideology*. New York: The Free Press, 1974.
Huber, Joan, and Glenna Spitze. *Sex Stratification: Children, Housework and Jobs*. Burlington, Massachusetts: Academic Press, Inc., 1983.
Huber, Joan, and Beth E. Schneider (Eds.) *The Social Context of AIDS*. Thousand Oaks, California: Sage, 1991.
Huber, Joan (Ed.). *Macro-micro Linkages in Sociology*. Thousand Oaks, California: Sage, 1991.
Huber, Joan. *On the Origins of Gender Inequality*. Boulder, Colorado: Paradigm Publishers, 2007.

Hughes, Everett Cherrington (1897–1983)

RACE RELATIONS

Born in Ohio, Everett C. Hughes gained a B.A. at Ohio Wesleyan College, Delaware (1918), taught English at Wisconsin Steel Works, Chicago (1918–1920) and worked for the Upper Peninsula Industrial Relations Association, Escanaba, Michigan (1920–1922).

The Methodist Church awarded a Centenary Fund grant for Hughes to study the community of Pullman, Illinois, (1922–1923). In 1923 Hughes studied sociology and anthropology at University of Chicago, Illinois, and did his sociological research as director of Mark White Square Park for the South Park Commission, then moved to McGill University, Montreal, Quebec, Canada, which at that time was the only university in Canada to offer a program in sociology in 1927. He gained a Ph.D. in sociology (1928); his dissertation, "The Growth of an Institution: The Chicago Real Estate Board," was published by the Society of Social Research of the University of Chicago (1931).

He was awarded Social Science Research Council fellowship to study the Catholic labor movement in Rhineland, Germany (1931–1932). At the University of Chicago, Hughes was assistant professor (1938); associate professor (1943); professor (1949); and chairman of the Department of Sociology (1952–1961). Then he was at Brandeis University, Waltham, Massachusetts (1961). He was 53rd president of the American Sociological Association (1963); member of the American Medical Association's Citizens Commission on Graduate Medical Education (1963–1967) and emeritus professor of Boston College, Chestnut Hill, Massachusetts (1968).

Major Contributions

In the late 1930s he and his wife carried out a study of the change in a French Canadian town as it industrialized under English Canadian management. During World War II, Hughes was a member of the Committee on Human Relations in Industry, a business and academic partnership to study industrial society. He was also a member of the Committee on Education, Training, and Research in Race Relations. He participated in the efforts to aid German universities after the war through the University of Chicago's Committee for Aid to German and Austrian Scholars. He held visiting professorships at Frankfurt University through the exchange program in the years 1948, 1953, and 1958.

In the 1950s Hughes became a member of the Committee on Human Development and began to take a more active interest in the sociology of education. His presidential address, "Race Relations and the Sociological Imagination," was published in *American Sociological Review* (28, No. 6 [1963]: 879–890). His research interests were in the fields of race and ethnic relations, industrialization, and occupations.

Major Literature

Hughes, Everett Cherrington, Helen MacGill Hughes and Irwin Deutscher. *Twenty Thousand Nurses Tell Their Story: A Report on Studies of Nursing Functions Sponsored by the American Nurses' Association.* Philadelphia, Pennsylvania: Lippincott, 1958.

Hughes, Everett Cherrington, and Helen MacGill Hughes. *Where Peoples Meet: Racial and Ethnic Frontiers.* Westport, Connecticut: Greenwood Press, 1981.

___. *Men and Their Work.* Westport, Connecticut: Greenwood Press, 1981.

Hughes, Everett Cherrington. *French Canada in Transition.* Chicago, Illinois: University of Chicago Press, 1983.

Becker, Howard S., Blanche Geer and Everett Cherrington Hughes. *Making the Grade: The Academic Side of College Life.* New Brunswick, New Jersey: Transaction Publishers, 1995.

Humphreys, Laud
(1930–1988)
SOCIOLOGY OF HOMOSEXUALITY

Robert Allan Humphreys was born in Oklahoma. On being ordained an Episcopal priest at Seabury-Western Theological Seminary in Evanston, Illinois, in 1955, he adopted the name "Laud" from William Laud, a seventeenth-century Archbishop of

Canterbury. Humphreys worked in several Oklahoma parishes and in Wichita, Kansas, where he annoyed powerful members of each of the congregations with outspoken attacks on privilege, including racial privilege, which led to his dismissal from the Wichita post.

He gained his Ph.D. from Washington University in Saint Louis (1968) for his sociological dissertation on male-male sex in St. Louis-area public restrooms, known in gay slang as "tearooms." The university chancellor was outraged and sought to have Humphreys' degree revoked on the grounds that the observations of sexual felonies were also felonies, and demanded that Humphreys not be employed by the university. Humphreys's dissertation research was published as *Tearoom Trade: Impersonal Sex in Public Places.* The book won the C. Wright Mills Award of the Society for the Study of Social Problems, but was frequently denounced as covert research and condemned for its invasion of the privacy of those having sex in a public place.

He was appointed to Southern Illinois University in Carbondale. On May 5, 1970, he led an anti-war demonstration that invaded a draft board office, where he destroyed a picture of President Richard Nixon. He was subsequently convicted of destroying government property and served three months of a one-year prison sentence in the summer of 1972. While in jail he was hired by Pitzer College, Claremont, California, where he became a full professor of sociology in 1975.

When Humphreys was twenty-three he discovered that his father — who had just died — made regular trips to New Orleans to have sex with men, providing an example of secret homosexuals donning what Humphreys would later label the "breastplate of righteousness." Around the late 1970s, Humphreys declared himself to be gay; he helped found the Sociologists' Gay Caucus (an interest group based in Saint Cloud, Minnesota). In 1980, he left his wife and children to establish a gay relationship.

Humphreys earned California certification as a psychotherapist in 1980 and established a private counseling practice. He largely abandoned research to focus on counseling. In his final years, Humphreys also served as a consultant to police forces and frequently provided expert testimony in court cases. He retained his position at Pitzer College through 1986. Although his study *Out of the Closets* has been largely ignored, his research on straight-identified and gay-identified males who have sex with males in secluded public places is of continuing relevance. Especially interesting are his findings about hyper conformity in politics and other aspects of their lives by the married men who were the subjects of *Tearoom Trade.*

Major Literature

Humphreys, Laud. *Out of the Closets: Sociology of Sexual Liberation.* New Jersey: Prentice-Hall, 1972.
___. *Tearoom Trade: Impersonal Sex in Public Places.* Los Angeles: Aldine Books, 1975.

Ibn Khaldun (1332–1406)

HISTORICAL SOCIOLOGY

Abd al-Rahman Ibn Mohammad is generally known as Ibn Khaldun after a remote ancestor. His parents, originally Yemenite Arabs, had settled in Spain, but after the fall of Seville migrated to Tunisia. He was born in Tunisia, where he received his early education and where, still in his teens, he entered the service of the Egyptian ruler Sultan Barquq. Ibn Khaldun held various offices under the rulers of Tunis and Morocco and served (1363) as ambassador of the Moorish king of Granada to Peter the Cruel of Castile. In 1382 he sailed to Cairo, where he spent most of the rest of his life as a teacher and lecturer. In 1400 he accompanied the Egyptians in their campaign against Timur, and he was sent to arrange for the capitulation of Damascus to Timur.

Ibn Khaldun is generally considered the greatest of the Arab historical thinkers. He sought to write a world history, the first volume of which aimed at an analysis of historical events. This volume, commonly known as *Muqaddimah* or *Prolegomena*, was based on Ibn Khaldun's unique approach and original contribution and became a masterpiece in literature on philosophy of history and sociology. His contribution to history is marked by the fact that, unlike most earlier writers interpreting history largely in a political context, he emphasized environmental, sociological, psychological and economic factors governing the apparent events. This revolutionized the science of history and also laid the foundation of *Umraniyat* (sociology).

He wrote an autobiography, completed in 1394, but expanded a few months before he died. His theory of degeneration (which can be applied to nations) is that successive generations inevitably are inferior to the first. He predicts that a family will degenerate within four generations; each preceding generation is inferior to the last. Successive generations will lapse more and more into a life of ease and as a result, the life of the progenitor will be lost forever.

He wrote that those who die in famines are victims of their previous habitual state of satiation, not of the hunger that now afflicts them for the first time. Applied to nations, those weakened in the same way as an individual family will be swallowed up by younger and more virile nations, and the process will start over again. Although Ibn Khaldun was talking of nomads, and in the 14th century, his theory has relevance in the 21st century, as life becomes easier, we lose some intrinsic value.

Major Literature

Abd al-Rahman ibn Muhammad Ibn Khaldun, and C. Issawi (Translator). *An Arab Philosophy of History: Selections from the Prolegomena of Ibn Khaldun of Tunis*. Princeton, New Jersey: Darwin Press, 1987. The American University in Cairo Press, 1998.

___, N.J. Dawood (Ed.), and Franz Rosenthal (Translator). *The Muqaddimah: An Introduction to History*. New Jersey: Princeton University Press, 2004.

Janowitz, Morris (1919–1988)
MILITARY SOCIOLOGY

Born in Paterson, New Jersey, of Polish immigrant parents, Morris Janowitz gained a B.A. in economics at Washington Square College, New York University (1941), and until 1943 he was research assistant for war community research at the Library of Congress. He was senior propaganda analyst of the Organization and Propaganda Section at the U.S. Department of Justice Special War Policies Unit. He analyzed German radio broadcasts at the Supreme Headquarters of the Allied Expeditionary Forces in London, England. At the University of Chicago, Illinois, Janowitz was instructor in sociology (1947); earned a Ph.D. in sociology (1948); assistant professor (1948); chair of the department of sociology (1961–1972); visiting professor in the Graduate School of Business (1961); and Kimpton Distinguished-Service Professor, department of sociology (1972–1973).

At the University of Michigan, Ann Arbor, he was assistant professor (1951); associate professor (1953); full professor (1957) and Pitt Professor and Distinguished Professor at the University of Cambridge, England (1972–1973). His awards and honors include a Guggenheim Foundation fellowship (1976); Decoration for Distinguished Civilian Service (1977); honorary doctorate, University of Toulouse, France (1977); and Distinguished Scholarship Award, American Sociological Association (1984). Janowitz was the first scholar to hold the S.L.A. Marshall chair at the U.S. Army Research Institute for the Behavioral and Social Sciences in Alexandria, Virginia (1986).

Major Contributions

An innovative sociologist and political scientist, Janowitz made major contributions to sociological theory and to the study of prejudice, urban issues, and patriotism. His work in political science concentrated mainly on civil-military affairs. His sociological studies of the military, mass communications, and propaganda were ultimately rooted in the interests he developed and the early training he received during the war.

He cooperated with the psychologist Bruno Bettelheim (1903–1990) in writing *The Dynamics of Prejudice*, a psychological and sociological study of racial and ethnic prejudice. *The Professional Soldier* spurred increased interest in civil-military relations. In 1974, he founded *Armed Forces and Society*, a journal closely linked to the Inter-University Seminar, and served as its editor for almost 10 years. *The Last Half-Century: Societal Change and Politics in America*, won the Laing Prize, the highest honor for books written by University of Chicago faculty.

Major Literature

Janowitz, Morris. *Sociology and the Military Establishment*. New York: Russell Sage Foundation, 1959, revised 1965.

___. *The Professional Soldier*. New York: The Free Press, 1960.

___, and Bruno Bettelheim. *Social Change and Prejudice*. Glencoe, Illinois: The Free Press, 1964.

Janowitz, Morris. *The New Military — Changing Patterns of Organization*. New York: Russell Sage Foundation, 1967.

___. *Institution Building in Urban Education*. New York: Russell Sage Foundation, 1971.

Blackwell, James, and Morris Janowitz (Eds.). *Black Sociologists: Historical and Contemporary Perspectives*. Chicago, Illinois: University of Chicago Press, 1975.

Janowitz, Morris. *The Last Half-Century: Societal Change and Politics in America*. Chicago, Illinois: University of Chicago Press, 1978.

___. *The Reconstruction of Patriotism: Education for Civic Consciousness*. Chicago, Illinois: University of Chicago Press, 1985.

Kanter, Rosabeth Moss (1943–)
SOCIOLOGY OF MANAGEMENT

Born in Cleveland, Ohio, Rosabeth Moss Kanter graduated with honors from Bryn Mawr College, Bryn Mawr, Pennsylvania (1964), and gained an M.A. in sociology (1965) and a Ph.D. (1967) at the University of Michigan, Ann Arbor. She did her postdoctoral studies at Harvard University, Cambridge, Massachusetts (1975–1976) and taught sociology at the University of Michigan, Brandeis University, Harvard, and Yale (1967–1986). Since 1986 she has been Ernest L. Arbuckle Professor at the Harvard Business School, where she specializes in strategy, innovation, and leadership for change.

Kanter was editor of *Harvard Business Review* (1989–1992). Her awards and honors include the Academy of Management's Distinguished Career Award for scholarly contributions to management knowledge (2001); being named "Intelligent Community Visionary of the Year" by the World Teleport Association (2002); receiving 22 honorary doctoral degrees; and numerous leadership awards and prizes for her books and articles. She co-founded Goodmeasure, Inc., a consulting firm based in Cambridge, Massachusetts (1977).

Major Contributions

Kanter's strategic and practical insights have guided leaders of large and small organizations worldwide for over 25 years, through teaching, writing, and direct consultation to major corporations and governments. Her current work focuses on the transformation of major institutions such as global corporations, health care delivery systems, and other organizations seeking innovative new models. Her many books, including several bestsellers and award winners, have been translated into several languages. *Confidence: How Winning Streaks and Losing Streaks Begin and End* describes the culture and dynamics of high-performance organizations as compared with those in decline, and shows how to lead turnarounds, whether in businesses, hospitals, schools, sports teams, community organizations, or countries.

Her latest initiative involves the development and creation of an innovative institute for advanced leadership, to ensure that successful leaders at the top of their professions can apply their skills not only to managing their own enterprises but also to helping solve the most challenging national and global problems. She is an adviser to the chief executive officers (CEOs) of large and small companies, serves on numerous boards and national commissions, wrote (from 2004 to 2006) a bi-weekly national "Business of America" column for the *Miami Herald* and *Knight-Ridder/Tribune*; speaks widely, often sharing the platform with presidents, prime ministers, and CEOs worldwide at national and international events, such as the World Economic Forum in Davos, Switzerland.

Kanter was named by the *Times* of London to be among the 50 most powerful women in the world.

Major Literature

Kanter, Rosabeth Moss. *When Giants Learn to Dance: Mastering the Challenges of Strategy Management and Careers in the 1990s.* London, England: Thomson Learning, 1998.

___. *Evolve! Succeeding in the Digital Culture of Tomorrow.* Boston, Massachusetts: Harvard Business School Press, 2001.

___. *Rosabeth Moss Kanter on the Frontiers of Management.* Boston, Massachusetts: Harvard Business School Press, 2003.

___. *Challenge of Organizational Change: How Companies Experience It and Leaders Guide It.* New York: The Free Press, 2003.

___. *Confidence: How Winning Streaks and Losing Streaks Begin and End.* London, England: Random House Group, Random House Business Books, 2005.

Kaufman, Jason Andrew
POLITICAL SOCIOLOGY

From 1988 to 1989 Jason Andrew Kaufman did orchestral studies (trumpet) at the Curtis Institute of Music in Philadelphia, Pennsylvania. He earned an A.B. degree in social studies, with honors from Harvard College, Cambridge, Massachusetts (1993). At Princeton University, New Jersey, he gained an M.A. (1996) and Ph.D. in sociology (1999) and was lecturer, Department of Sociology (1998–1999). At Harvard University, Cambridge, Massachusetts, he was assistant professor, (1999–2003) and John L. Loeb Associate Professor of the Social Sciences (since 2003).

His awards and honors include Innovation Award for Teaching (funding for preparation of a new course called "Media and the American Mind") (2000), and the George Kahrl Award in Sociology "in recognition of outstanding commitment to undergraduate education, enthusiasm for students, and scholarly guidance" (2001).

Major Contributions

Kaufman's research areas and teaching interests are comparative and historical sociology, political sociology, sociology of culture, and sociology of law. At the Curtis Institute of Music, Kaufman was one of four scholarship students of Frank Kaderabek, principal trumpeter of the Philadelphia Orchestra. While at Harvard, Kaufman served as music director of the Harvard-Radcliffe Gilbert and Sullivan Players in his freshman year. For his senior honors essay he wrote on the political potential of rap music. More recently, he has joined Gamelan Galak Tika, a Balinese percussion ensemble. He retains an abiding intellectual interest in music, the arts, and the sociological study thereof. Kaufman's doctoral dissertation examined patterns of local political development in the United States through the Progressive Era, focusing on the impact of new information networks on early American political behavior.

Kaufman is currently working on six projects:

1. A major comparative history of the United States and Canada (1763–1939).
2. A study of the path to political polarization in modern-day Vermont and New Hampshire, both of which were once considered the "most Republican" states in the Union.
3. A study of the historical origins of the American business corporation as seen through the lens of legal restrictions on the right of incorporation.
4. A project with two graduate students on the relationship between high schools arts and music training and post-secondary educational attainment.
5. A study of the question, "Are American evangelicals more politically conservative than Canadian evangelicals, or are there simply more of them in the United States?"
6. A quantitative study of social networks and cultural preferences using data collected from college students' Facebook.com profiles.

Major Literature

Kaufman, Jason Andrew. "Municipal Government and Civic Associational Activity in Late 19th Century America." Paper presented to the Urban History Group Conference, University of Sussex, Brighton, England, 1997.

___. *For The Common Good? American Civic Life and the Golden Age of Fraternity*. New York: Oxford University Press, 2003.

___. "Endogenous Explanation in the Sociology of Culture." *Annual Review of Sociology* 30 (2004): 335–357.

___, and David Weintraub. "Social Capital Formation and American Fraternal Association: New Empirical Evidence." *Journal of Interdisciplinary History*, 35 (1) (2004): 1–36.

Kaufman, Jason Andrew, and Orlando Patterson. "Cross-National Cultural Diffusion: The Global Spread of Cricket." *American Sociological Review*, 70 (2005): 82–110.

Kaufman, Jason Andrew, and Jay Gabler. "Chess, Cheerleading, and Chopin: What Matters and Why." *Contexts*, 5 (2) (2006): 45–49.

Kay, Tamara

POLITICAL SOCIOLOGY

Born in Harrison, New York, Tamara Kay gained a B.A. in sociology with art theory and practice at Northwestern University, Evanston, Illinois, earning highest distinction (1993) and Phi Beta Kappa honors. At the University of California, Berkeley, she gained an M.A. in sociology (1998); her thesis was "Bypassing the State: The Effects of Legal and Political Contexts on Union Organizing Strategies." She earned a Ph.D. in sociology in 2004; her dissertation was "North American Free Trade Agreement (NAFTA) and the Politics of Labor Transnationalism".

Kay was teaching assistant, Women, Society, and the Law, Northwestern University (1993). At the University of California, Berkeley, she was teaching assistant, history of social theory (2001–2002); teaching assistant, social movements (2003, 2004/2005); instructor, photography and sociology (2004/2005); and instructor, law and social movements, University of California, San Diego (2005). She is currently assistant professor of sociology at Harvard University, Cambridge, Massachusetts.

Other professional experience: research assistant, American Bar Foundation (1993–1994); legislative assistant, American Civil Liberties Union, Washington, D.C. (1994–1995); volunteer HIV/AIDS educator, Guadalajara, Mexico (1995); Planning Committee, Living Wage Working Summit, Berkeley (1998); researcher and consultant, United Farm Workers of America, Watsonville, California (1999–2001); fellow, John F. Henning Center for International Labor Relations, Berkeley (1999–2001); consultant, International Labor Organization, Regional Office for Latin America and the Caribbean, Lima, Peru (2002–2003); consultant, American Center for International Labor Solidarity, Washington, D.C. (2003–2004); and editor, *The Labor Center Reporter*, Center for Labor Research and Education, Berkeley (1998–1999).

Her awards and honors include a National Science Foundation graduate fellowship (1996–1999); Center for Culture, Organizations and Politics research grant, Berkeley (1999); Andrew W. Mellon Foundation fellowship in Latin American sociology (1999–2002); Outstanding Graduate Student Instructor Award, Berkeley (2004).

Major Contributions

Kay's research and teaching fields include political sociology, social movements, sociology of work and labor, law and society, economic development and modernization, Latin America, globalization and international trade, and social theory. Her work centers on the political and legal implications of regional economic integration, transnationalism, and global governance. Her research agenda stems from a commitment to better articulate how regional economic integration affects workers and labor movements. In particular, she is concerned with how labor movements respond to changes in the global political economy and to the creation and development of global

governance institutions and international legal structures. She is also interested in how these changes in the international arena affect the relationship between social movements and nation-states.

Major Literature

Kay, Tamara. "The Agricultural Labor Relations Board: A Captured Political Process." *Labor Center Reporter*, Institute of Industrial Relations, University of California, Berkeley. Issue 305, 1998.

——. "Even Labor Unions Can Gain from Free Trade." Yale Center for the Study of Globalization, *Yale Global Online*, 2003.

Beisel, Nicola, and Tamara Kay. "Abortion, Race, and Gender in Nineteenth-Century America." *American Sociological Review*, 69 (4) (2004): 498–518.

Kay, Tamara. "Labor Transnationalism and Global Governance: The Impact of NAFTA on Transnational Labor Relationships in North America." *American Journal of Sociology* 111 (3) (2005): 715–756.

Keyfitz, Nathan (1913–)
DEMOGRAPHY

Born in Montreal, Quebec, Canada, Nathan Keyfitz graduated in mathematics at McGill University, Montreal (1934), and was research statistician, Dominion Bureau of Statistics, Ottawa, Canada (1936–1959). He was elected to the International Union for the Scientific Study of Population, a leading international professional association for individuals interested in population studies (1950), and was census advisor (three months) to the Burmese Statistical Office, Rangoon, Burma, where he helped develop a trial census and procedures for editing schedules, punching cards, and taking tabulations (1951).

At the University of Chicago, Illinois, he gained a Ph.D. in sociology (1952). His dissertation was on the study of the fertility of the Canadian population as reported by the

1941 census. He taught general sociology at the University of Toronto, Ontario, Canada (1959–1962), and was a faculty member, University of Montreal, teaching sociology and learning French (1962–1963). He was at the University of California, Berkeley, Department of Demography from 1968 until the department was disbanded in 1972. He was Andelot Professor of Demography and Sociology at Harvard University, Cambridge, Massachusetts (1972–1983).

Keyfitz founded the International Institute for Applied Systems Analysis in Vienna, Austria (1972), and was director (1983) and first president (1998). He was professor in social demography at Ohio State University (1981); serving both at Harvard and Ohio until retirement from teaching in 1983. Between 1973 and 1993 he was awarded seven honorary doctorates and won the International Union for the Scientific Study of Population Award (1997).

Major Contributions

Keyfitz is a leader in the field of mathematical demography and a pioneer in the application of mathematical tools to the study of population characteristics where vital statistics and census data are incomplete. He has written extensively on a wide range of topics that include population theory, historical demography, mortality, urbanization, forecasting, social security and retirement, poverty, democracy, and the interaction between people and their environment. At Harvard, he was associated with the Department of Sociology, the Department of Population Sciences in the School of Public Health, and the Center for Population Studies.

During his eleven years at Harvard, Keyfitz acted as a demographic consultant for the Indonesian government (1972) and a lecturer on population mathematics in Rome (1974), India (1975), Russia (1978), and China (1982). He has taught population

and planning in Ceylon and Argentina, lectured at the Indian Statistical Institute in Calcutta, and advised the United States Bureau of the Census and the Social Security Administration.

Major Literature

Keyfitz, Nathan, and Hal Caswell. *Applied Mathematical Demography*. New Jersey: John Wiley and Sons, Inc., 1977. New York: Springer-Verlag, 3rd edition, 2005.
Keyfitz, Nathan. *Urban Influence on Farm Family Size*. Manchester, New Hampshire: Ayer Co. Publishers, 1980.
___. *Demography Through Problems*. New York: Springer-Verlag, 1984, 1990.
___. *Population Change and Social Policy*. Lanham, Maryland: Rowman and Littlefield Publishers, Inc., 1982.
___. *World Population and Growth and Aging: Demographic Trends in the Late Twentieth Century*. Chicago, Illinois: University of Chicago Press, 1990.

Kidd, Benjamin (1858–1916)
SOCIAL EVOLUTION

Benjamin Kidd was born in County Clare, Ireland, the son of a constable with the Royal Irish Constabulary. Without much education, Kidd worked from 1877 to 1894 in the Inland Revenue Department of the Civil Service. He devoted his spare time to study and in 1894 published *Social Evolution*, which brought him financial success and international fame. The main theme of *Social Evolution* is the conflict between private interest and social welfare, the struggle that eliminates the unfit being the condition of progress. A secondary theme of this controversial book was that religion is the hub of humanity. For Kidd, reason is selfish and short-sighted and is of no help to mankind in the important crises of life. Religion has been the chief agency in promoting philanthropy and the political enfranchisement of the masses. Superior intelligence is not really a quality conducive either to virtue in the individual or to survival in the race.

Critics of the book stated that the style was more suited to sensational journalism than to the exposition of philosophical ideas. The book contained a strong attack on socialism, a fact that commended it to the reactionary section of the public and ensured its success. It was translated into ten languages, including Arabic, Chinese, Czechoslovakian, French, German and Swedish.

The success of his work allowed Kidd to retire from the Civil Service and between 1898 and 1902 he traveled extensively throughout America and Canada and in South Africa. These travels resulted in a series of articles commissioned by *The Times* (London) and later published under the title *The Control of the Tropics*. The subject matter of *The Principles of Western Civilization* was similar to his first book but was not as well received, being described as long, verbose and obscure.

The last twelve years of his life Kidd spent in ever increasing seclusion. In 1903 he left London and lived first at Tonbridge, Kent, and later at Ditchling, Sussex. In May 1908, Kidd delivered the Herbert Spencer Lecture to Oxford University, titled "Individualism and After." In 1910 he started work on his book *The Science of Power* in which he reiterated his ideas on religion and humanity. He also expressed the view that woman was the great power in creating the "enthusiasm of the ideal." This book, published posthumously, was a success. Kidd wrote the article "Sociology" for the 1911 edition of *Encyclopedia Britannica*. A number of papers on natural history were also published posthumously by his son under the title *A Philosopher with Nature* (London, England: Methuen, 1921).

Major Literature

Kidd, Benjamin. *Social Evolution*. London, England: Macmillan, 1894. Boston, Massachusetts: Adamant Media Corporation, 2002.

___. *The Principles of Western Civilization*. London, England: Macmillan, 1905.
___. *The Control of the Tropics*. New York: MacMillan, 1905.
___. *The Science of Power*. New York, G.P. Putnam's Sons, 1918. Boston, Massachusetts: Adamant Media Corporation, 2000.

Kimmerling, Baruch (1939–)

POLITICAL SOCIOLOGY

Born in Rumania, Baruch Kimmerling immigrated to Israel in 1952. At the Hebrew University, Jerusalem, Israel, he gained a B.A. in sociology and political science (1965), an M.A. in sociology with honors (1969), and a Ph.D. in sociology (1975). His dissertation was titled "The Territorial Factors in Israeli Nation-Building Process." At Jerusalem he held junior research and teaching positions (1965–1978) and in the Department of Sociology, lecturer (1978–1982) and senior lecturer (1983); associate professor, Department of Sociology and Anthropology (1989–1997); and full professor (1997). He was research fellow (1978–1979) and visiting associate professor (1987–1988) at the Center of International Studies, Massachusetts Institute of Technology (MIT), Cambridge, Massachusetts; then visiting professor at Henry Jackson School for International Studies, University of Washington, Seattle (1991–1992).

From 2002 to 2004 he was distinguished visiting professor of sociology, Department of Sociology, University of Toronto, Ontario, Canada. He was George A. Wise Professor of Sociology, Hebrew University of Jerusalem (2003) and professor emeritus (2006). Kimmerling was editor-in-chief of the "Eshkolot" books series of the Hebrew University Press, Jerusalem (1994). His memberships include the American Sociological Association, International Sociological Association, American Political Science

Association, Israel Sociological Society, Inter-University Seminar on Armed Forces and Society (elected), and Middle Eastern Studies Association.

Major Contributions

Professor Kimmerling is a sociologist of politics in the wider sense of the term, interested in both the institutional and cultural dynamics of the political foundations of social life, in its historical backgrounds. The original foci of his research and theoretical, as well as intellectual, interests were mainly on the impact of the Jewish-Arab (and Israeli-Palestinian) conflict on the Israeli society. Later he focused on the development of the Palestinian collective consciousness and emerging nationalism. He has analyzed how the Jewish-Arab conflict penetrated most of the Israeli state and society's institutional spheres, such as the economy, stratification, ethnicity and ideology (including religion). *The Interrupted System* provides an analytical and experimental study of direct and indirect impact of wars on Israeli civilian society.

During the 1990s Kimmerling revisited and revised his own and others' research in this field, which led him to characterize the Israeli state as a special (but not unique) type of militaristic society.

Major Literature

Kimmerling, Baruch. *A Conceptual Framework for the Analysis of Behavior in a Territorial Conflict: The Generalization of the Israeli Case.* Hebrew University of Jerusalem, Leonard Davis Institute for International Relations, 1979.

___. *Zionism and Territory: The Socio-Territorial Dimensions of Zionist Politics.* Berkeley: University of California, Institute of International Studies, 1983.

___. *Zionism and the Economy.* Cambridge, Massachusetts: Schenkman Publishing Company, 1983.

___. *The Interrupted System: The Israeli Civilians in War and Routine Times.* New Jersey: Transaction Publishers, 1985.

___, and Joel Samuel Migdal. *The Palestinian People: A History.* Cambridge, Massachusetts: Harvard University Press, 2003.

Kimmerling, Baruch. *The Invention and Decline of Israeliness: State, Society, and the Military.* Berkeley, California: University of California Press; new edition, 2005.

___. *Politicide: The Real Legacy of Ariel Sharon.* London, England: Verso Books, 2006.

Kollontai, Alexandra (1872–1952)

RIGHTS OF WOMEN

Alexandra Mikhailovna Kollontai was born in St. Petersburg, Russia. In 1903 she joined the Mensheviks, but after a period of exile in Scandinavia and America, for her earlier political activities, she joined the Bolsheviks in 1914 and returned to Russia. After the Bolshevik revolution in October 1917, she became people's commissar for social welfare. She was the most prominent woman in the Soviet administration and was best known for founding the Zhenotdel in 1919, the first government women's department in the world. This organization worked to improve the conditions of women's lives in the Soviet Union, fighting illiteracy and educating women about the new marriage, education, and working laws put in place by the Revolution. The Zhenotdel was closed in 1930. In 1923, she was appointed Soviet ambassador to Norway, becoming the world's first female ambassador, and later served as ambassador to Mexico and Sweden. She was also a member of the Soviet delegation to the League of Nations.

While Kollontai promoted free love, she did not advocate casual sexual encounters; indeed, she believed that due to the inequality between men and women that persisted under socialism, such encounters would lead to women being exploited and left to raise children alone. She believed that true socialism could not be achieved without a radical change in attitudes toward gender, particularly related to property. Her ideas influenced Soviet social policy, and many welfare benefits for mothers and children were introduced that were well in advance of those of every other European country.

In several of her writings Kollontai explored the connection between social change and personal relationships. She recognized how the most intimate of personal relations are shaped by economic and social structures, and that social inequality is reflected in sexual relations. Women were socialized under capitalism into believing that their identity depended on their role as a wife and mother. Men on the other hand were conditioned to believe that their role was to be dominant and in control in personal relationships.

"Over and over again the man always tries to impose his ego upon us and adapt us fully to his purpose," she wrote in *The Autobiography of a Sexually Emancipated Communist Woman* (1917). It was important, she argued, that men should be interested in women as intellectual equals and not just as sexual objects. "A man would only see in me the feminine element, which he tried to mould into a willing sounding board to his ego."

Many of the gains women had secured in the post-revolutionary period were rolled back by the Stalinist regime in order to defend the bureaucracy's own interests. Those who are still fighting for an end to women's oppression have much to gain from a study of Kollontai's writings and activities.

Major Literature

Kollontai, Alexandra. *Selected Writings of Alexandra Kollontai*. New York: W.W. Norton and Co., Ltd., 1980.

Komarovsky, Mirra (1906–1999)

SOCIOLOGY OF THE FAMILY

Mirra Komarovsky was born in Akkerman, Russia. When she was a child, the ardent Jewish Zionist family was driven from their land and home by the czar's police, and finally settled in Baku, on the Caspian Sea, where her father was a banker. Her privileged world collapsed after the Revolution in 1921, amidst growing anti–Semitism, dwindling food rations, and Bolshevik persecution of the middle class. The Komarovsky family fled to Wichita, Kansas, where several relatives already lived. After a short stay at Wichita, the family moved to Brooklyn, where her father supported them as an accountant, translator, and writer.

Komarovsky studied economics, sociology, and anthropology at Barnard College, New York. She graduated and was admitted to Phi Beta Kappa (1926) and gained an M.A. (1927) from Columbia University, New York City. Following two years teaching at Skidmore College, New York, she completed the course work for her Ph.D., which was awarded in 1940. Until she joined New York's Institute for Social Research (1935), she worked at various research jobs.

At Barnard, Komarovsky became a part-time lecturer (1935); instructor (1938); assistant professor (1947); associate professor (1948); full professor (1954); and professor emeritus (1970). Working with Paul Lazarsfeld (see entry), she wrote *The Unemployed Man and His Family* (1940), an intensive study of fifty-nine families, modeled on work Lazarsfeld had just completed in Europe. Komarovsky based all her subsequent work on Ogburn's theory of "cultural lag," according to which cultural attitudes lag behind technological change. For example, some unemployed men during the Depression said they would rather starve than let their wives work. In *Blue-Collar Marriage* (1964) she found that white, working-class, Protestant couples suffered a particularly severe form of cultural lag; men were prepared for their wives to work, provided work did not interfere with the traditional role of wife and mother.

At a time when Talcott Parsons dominated American sociology with his functionalist faith in social equilibrium, Komarovsky emphasized dysfunction, conflict, and change. In *Women in the Modern World,* she challenged Parsons's belief in the naturalness of conventional gender roles, pointing out that young women then did not fit his stereotype. She urged that all students be prepared for careers, that good nursery schools be made universally available, and that men accept their fair share of domestic work. Komarovsky was the second woman elected to serve as the president (64th) of the American Sociological Association (1973).

Major Literature

Komarovsky, Mirra. *Sociology and Public Policy: The Case of Presidential Commissions.* Burlington, Massachusetts: Elsevier Science, 1975.
____. *The Unemployed Man and His Family: The Effect of Unemployment Upon the Status of the Man in Fifty-Nine Families.* Lanham, Maryland: Rowman and Littlefield Publishers, Inc., AltaMira Press, 2004.
____. *Dilemmas of Masculinity: A Study of College Youth.* Lanham, Maryland: Rowman and Littlefield Publishers, Inc., AltaMira Press, 2004.
____. *Women in the Modern World: Their Education and Their Dilemmas.* Lanham, Maryland: Rowman and Littlefield Publishers, Inc., AltaMira Press, 2004.

Lamont, Michèle (1957–)
RACE AND CULTURE

Born in Toronto, Canada, Michèle Lamont gained a B.A. in political science (1978), an M.A. in political science (1979) Ottawa University, Ottawa, Ontario, Canada. She earned a DEA (pre-doctoral degree) (1979) and a Ph.D. in sociology (1983) at the Université de Paris. She was post-doctoral research fellow, Department of Sociology, Stanford University, California (1983–1985), and assistant professor, Department of Sociology, University of Texas, Austin (1985–1987). In the Princeton University, New Jersey, Department of Sociology she was assistant professor (1987–1993); associate professor (1993–2000); and full professor (2000–2003).

Lamont was chair, Culture Section, American Sociological Association (1994–1995), and fellow and program director, Canadian Institute for Advanced Research (2002). At Harvard University, Cambridge, Massachusetts, she was professor, Department of Sociology, and faculty associate, Center for European Studies (2003). Lamont was also director, European Inequality Network, Multidisciplinary Program in Inequality and Social Policy, Kennedy School of Government (2004), professor of African and African American Studies (2005), and Robert I. Goldman Professor of European Studies (since 2006). Lamont has been visiting professor at the universities of Paris, Oslo, and Tel Aviv, and was scholar-in-residence at Schomburg Center for Research in Black Culture, New York Public Library, in 1993.

She is a fellow and project co-director of the Successful Societies program, Canadian Institute for Advanced Research, and a member of the Sociological Research Association. She was chair, Theory Section, American Sociological Association (2003–2004), and she won the C. Wright Mills Prize of the Society for the Study of Social Problems, for *The Dignity of Working Men* (2001).

Major Contributions

Lamont has done extensive research on racial and class boundaries in France and the

United States, and has published widely in the fields of inequality, culture, race, immigration, qualitative methods, and comparative sociology. Her prime focus is on how culture is used to create and maintain boundaries between categories of people and how these symbolic boundaries generate and perpetuate social and economic inequality. *The Dignity of Working Men* explored how black and white workers in the United States, and white workers and North African immigrants in France, think about similarities and differences between various categories of people. She has also analyzed how marketing specialists understand the use of consumption by African-Americans as a means to gain cultural membership. *Rethinking Comparative Cultural Sociology* is the result of a five-year collaboration of teams of French and American sociologists who analyzed how different modes of justifications and evaluation are unevenly noticeable in France and the United States.

Major Literature

Lamont, Michèle, and Marcel Fournier. *Cultivating Differences: Symbolic Boundaries and the Making of Inequality*. Chicago, Illinois: University of Chicago Press, 1992.

Lamont, Michèle. *Money, Morals, and Manners: The Culture of the French and the American Upper-Middle Class*. Chicago, Illinois: University of Chicago Press, 1992.

___. *The Cultural Territories of Race: Black and White Boundaries*. Chicago, Illinois: University of Chicago Press, 1999.

___. *The Dignity of Working Men: Morality and the Boundaries of Race, Class, and Immigration*. Harvard University Press, 2000, 2002.

___, and Laurent Thévenot (Eds.). *Rethinking Comparative Cultural Sociology: Repertoires of Evaluation in France and the United States*. New York: Cambridge University Press, 2000.

Lasswell, Harold Dwight (1902–1978)

POLITICAL SOCIOLOGY

Born in Donnellson, Illinois, Harold Dwight Lasswell gained a B.A. in philosophy and economics (1922), a Ph.D. (1926), and taught political science (1922–1938) at the University of Chicago, Illinois. From 1938 to 1939 he worked at the Washington School of Psychiatry and from 1939 to 1945 was director of war communications research and chief of the Experimental Division for the Study of War Time Communications at the Library of Congress. At Yale University, New Haven, Connecticut, he was professor of law and of political science; he was a Ford Foundation professor of law and social sciences. At Bramford College (1945 into the 1970s) he was emeritus professor. He was professor of law at John Jay College of the City University of New York and at Temple University, Philadelphia, Pennsylvania, and a visiting lecturer at campuses throughout the world. Lasswell was also a consultant to numerous U.S. government agencies.

Major Contributions

A member of the Chicago School of sociology, Lasswell was a political scientist known for his influential studies of power relations and of personality and politics and for other major contributions to contemporary behavioral political science. He defined values as desired goals and power as the ability to participate in decisions, and he conceived political power as the ability to produce intended effects on other people. Lasswell argued that democracies needed propaganda to keep the uninformed citizenry in agreement with what the specialized class had determined was in their best interests, as he wrote in his entry on propaganda for the 1954 edition of the *Encyclopedia of the Social Sciences*.

Much of his thinking on motives and propaganda and communication in general was influenced by his study of psychoanalytic theory. He believed that the social and biological sciences had a duty to develop a science of social policy that would serve the democratic will for justice. In other words, they should not be mere observers but be active participants in change. Systems theory, functional and role analysis, and content analysis can be traced to Lasswell's theory. His work was important in the post–World War II development of behavioralism (not behaviorism).

Lasswell developed a model of communication which implies that more than one channel can carry a message. The model is shown by finding the answers to this simple question: Who says what, in which channel, to whom, with what effect? He also defined the functions of the media in three parts: surveillance of the environment; the correlation of the parts of society in responding to the environment; and the transmission of the social heritage from one generation to the next.

Major Literature

Lasswell, Harold D., and Daniel Lerner. *World Revolutionary Elites: Studies in Coercive Ideological Movements*. Cambridge, Massachusetts: MIT Press, 1965.

Lasswell, Harold D. *Power and Personality*. Westport, Connecticut: Greenwood Press, 1976.

___, and Merritt B. Fox. *The Signature of Power: Buildings, Communication and Policy*. New Jersey: Transaction Publishers, 1979.

Lasswell, Harold D. *On Political Sociology*. Chicago, Illinois: University of Chicago Press, 1980.

___. *Propaganda and Communication in World History*. Honolulu, Hawaii: University of Hawaii Press, 1986.

Lazarsfeld, Paul Felix (1901–1976)

COMMUNICATION THEORY

Born and educated in Vienna, Austria, Paul Felix Lazarsfeld gained a doctorate in mathematics, then taught research methodology in the Department of Psychology in Vienna. In 1925, Lazarsfeld founded the Research Center for Economic Psychology, which engaged in market research, to provide jobs for his unemployed Socialist party friends. He participated in several early quantitative studies, including what was possibly the first scientific survey of radio listeners (1930–1931).

From 1933 to 1935, finding promotion at the University of Vienna blocked by anti-Semitism, Lazarsfeld traveled to American research universities on a Rockefeller Foundation fellowship and settled in America. In 1937, he founded and became the director of the Research Center of the University of Newark (now the Newark campus of Rutgers University, New Jersey), mainly conducting research on the unemployment of youth. He deployed a battery of social-scientific investigative methods — mass market surveys, statistical analysis of data, focus group work, etc.— to solve specific problems for specific clients. Funding came not only from the university, but also from commercial clients who contracted out research projects.

The Rockefeller Foundation funded the Radio Research Project on the effects of radio at Princeton University, with Lazarsfeld directing from his base at Newark. In 1939, he moved with the Radio Research Project to Columbia University, where he became a faculty member in the Department of Sociology, and where he joined forces with Robert Merton (see entry). The Rockefeller Foundation project on radio effects became the Bureau of Applied Social Research in 1944.

Among the most noted of the studies conducted by the bureau was the Erie County

(Ohio) investigation of the role of the mass media and of opinion leaders in the "two-step flow of communication". His studies indicated that voters follow informal media-wise leaders among family and friends rather than the media itself. Lazarsfeld was one of the forefathers of market research and one of four main forefathers of communication study, along with the political scientist Harold Lasswell (see entry) and the social psychologists Kurt Lewin and Carl Hovland.

From 1949 to 1969 Lazarsfeld taught at Columbia University, New York City, and made major contributions to mathematical sociology, methodology, and the study of mass communications and voting behavior.

Major Literature

Lazarsfeld, Paul F., Bernard Berelson, and Hazel Gaudet. *The People's Choice: How the Voter Makes Up His Mind in a Presidential Campaign.* New York: Duell, Sloan and Pearce, 1944.

Katz, Elihu, and Paul F. Lazarsfeld. *Personal Influence: The Part Played by People in the Flow of Mass Communication.* Glencoe, Illinois: Free Press, 1955. New Jersey: Transaction Publishers, 2005.

Jahoda, Marie, Paul F. Lazarsfeld, and Hans Zeisel. *Marienthal: The Sociography of an Unemployed Community.* Chicago, Illinois: Aldine, Atherton, 1971. New Jersey: Transaction Publishers, 2002.

Lazarsfeld, Paul F. *Main Trends in Sociology.* London, England: George Allen and Unwin, 1973.
___. *On Social Research and Its Language.* Chicago, Illinois: University of Chicago Press, 1993.

Lee, Alfred McClung (1906–1992)

HUMANIST SOCIOLOGY

Born in Oakmont, Pennsylvania, Alfred McClung Lee gained a B.A. at the University of Pittsburgh, Pennsylvania, and a Ph.D. at Yale University, New Haven, Connecticut.

Between 1934 and 1971 he was a professor at the University of Kansas, Lawrence; lecturer and professor at New York University; chairman of the sociology and anthropology departments, Wayne University, Detroit, Michigan (now Wayne State University); chairman of the sociology and anthropology departments at Brooklyn College, New York, and professor emeritus. He was also a visiting scholar at Drew University in Madison, New Jersey, until he died.

He was linked to many different public affairs organizations, such as the Federal Communications Commission, Department of Justice, and the American Civil Liberties Union. He was director and professor for the Center for Sociological Research (a part of UNESCO) in Milan (1957–1958), and president of the National Committee on Fraternities in Education (1953–1960). Lee founded and was president of the Association for Humanist Sociology. He was 67th president of the American Sociological Association (1976–1977). His presidential address — "Sociology for Whom?" — was published in the *American Sociological Review* (41, No. 6 [December 1976]: 925–936).

Major Contributions

Lee pressed for greater press freedom, for more popular understanding of communication processes, for greater equality of opportunity for all racial and religious groups, and ways to help make life more livable for people. By becoming a leader of many sociological movements, he tried to democratize these organizations and focus their attention on contemporary problems. The Society for the Study of Social Problems established the Lee Founders Award in 1981 in recognition of significant achievements that, over a distinguished career, have demonstrated continuing devotion to the ideals of the founders of the society and especially to the humanist tradition of Alfred McClung Lee and his wife, Elizabeth Briant Lee.

Major Literature

Lee, Alfred McClung. *The Daily Newspaper in America: The Evolution of a Social Instrument.* New York: Macmillan, 1937. New York: Taylor and Francis Group, Routledge, 2000.

___. *The Fine Art of Propaganda.* New York: Harcourt, Brace and Co., 1939.

___. *Race Riot.* Fort Worth, Texas: Dryden Press, Inc., 1943.

___. *Principles of Sociology.* New York: Barnes and Noble, 1946. New York: Harper and Row, 1961.

___. *How To Understand Propaganda.* New York: Rinehart and Company, 1952.

___. *Social Problems in America.* New York: Henry Holt and Company, 1955.

___. *Fraternities Without Brotherhood.* Boston, Massachusetts: Beacon Press, 1955.

___. *Marriage and the Family.* New York: Barnes and Noble, 1964, 1970.

___. *Sociology for Whom?* New York: Oxford University Press, 1976.

___. *Terrorism in Northern Ireland.* New York: General Hall, Inc., 1983.

___. "The Services of Clinical Sociology." *American Behavioral Scientist* 22 (1979): 487–511.

___. *Sociology for People.* New York: Syracuse University Press, 1990.

Lieberson, Stanley (1933–)

ETHNIC RELATIONS

Born in Montreal, Canada, Stanley Lieberson grew up in Brooklyn, New York, and gained an M.A. (1958) and Ph.D. (1960) in sociology at the University of Chicago, Illinois. He was instructor to assistant professor of sociology, University of Iowa, Ames, Ohio (1959–1961); assistant professor to professor of sociology, University of Wisconsin, Madison (1961–1967); professor of sociology, Washington University, St. Louis, Missouri (1967–1971); professor of sociology, Chicago (1971–1974); professor of sociology, University of Arizona, Tucson (1974–1983); Claude Bissell Distinguished Visiting Professor, Stanford University, California (1974–1983); University of Toronto, Ontario, Canada (1979–1980); and professor of sociology, University of California, Berkeley (1983–1988). At Harvard University, Cambridge, Massachusetts, he was professor of sociology (1988) and Abbott Lawrence Lowell Professor (1991). He was 82nd president of the American Sociological Association (1991) and Sackler Fellow, Institute of Advanced Studies, Tel Aviv University, Israel (1999).

His awards and honors include an honorary M.A., Harvard (1988); National Academy of Sciences (1992); doctor of humane letters, University of Arizona (1993); co-recipient, Best Book in the Sociology of Culture, Culture Section, American Sociological Association for *A Matter of Taste* (2001); and Book Award, Eastern Sociological Society, for *A Matter of Taste* (2002). Since 1965 Lieberson has done editorial work on eleven major journals and served on several societies and committees, including as president of the Sociological Research Association (1980–1981), and president, Pacific Sociological Association (1987–1988).

Major Contributions

Lieberson's presidential address — "Einstein, Renoir, Greeley: Some Thoughts About Evidence in Sociology" — was published in the *American Sociological Review* (57, No. 1 [1992]: 1–15). Much of his career has involved work on race and ethnic relations in the United States and elsewhere. His doctoral dissertation won the university's Colver-Rosenberger Prize, and was later revised and published by the Free Press, New York, 1962, as *Ethnic Patterns in American Cities*. He has written a number of other books dealing with race and ethnic relations, along with numerous papers on this topic in the leading journals. One of these books, *A Piece of the Pie*, received the Distinguished Contribution to Scholarship Award of the American Sociological Association.

An interest in language use in multi-ethnic nations led Lieberson to study bilingualism, language conflict, comparative diversity, economic issues and the like, thus crossing into the rapidly developing interdisciplinary field of sociolinguistics.

Major Literature

Lieberson, Stanley. "Societal Theory of Race and Ethnic Relations." *American Sociological Review,* 26 (1961): 902–910.

___. "Suburbs and Ethnic Residential Patterns." *American Journal of Sociology,* 67 (1962): 673–681.

___. *A Piece of the Pie: Blacks and White Immigrants Since 1880.* Berkeley, California: University of California Press, 1981.

___. *Making It Count: The Improvement of Social Research and Theory.* Berkeley, California: University of California Press; new edition, 1987.

___, and Waters, Mary C. *From Many Strands: Ethnic and Racial Groups in Contemporary America (Population of the United States in the 1980s).* New York: Russell Sage Foundation, 1988.

Lieberson, Stanley, and Freda Lynn. "Barking Up the Wrong Branch: Scientific Alternatives to the Current Model of Sociological Science." *Annual Review of Sociology,* 28 (2002): 1–19.

Lipset, Seymour Martin (1922–2006)

POLITICAL SOCIOLOGY

Born in New York of Russian Jewish immigrant parents, Seymour Martin Lipset gained a B.S. at City College of New York (1943) and was lecturer, University of Toronto (1946–1948) and assistant professor, University of California, Berkeley (1948–1950). At Columbia University, New York City, he gained a Ph.D. (1949), was lecturer (1950–1956), and was assistant director of the Bureau of Applied Social Research (see entry, Paul Lazarsfeld) (1954–1956). At the University of California, Berkeley, he was professor of sociology (1956–1966) and director of the Institute of International Studies (1962–1966). From 1966 to 1990 he was professor of

government and sociology at Harvard University, Cambridge, Massachusetts; Caroline S.G. Munro Professor of Political Science and Sociology, Hoover Institute, Stanford University, California; and Hazel Professor of Public Policy, George Mason University in Washington, D.C. He was president, American Sociological Association (1992–1993); president, American Political Science Association (1979–1980); past director of the United States Institute of Peace; and past president of the National Academy of Arts and Sciences, the International Society of Political Psychology, the Sociological Research Association, the World Association for Public Opinion Research, the Society for Comparative Research, the Paul F. Lazarsfeld Society in Vienna, and American Professors for Peace in the Middle East.

For the last five years of his life, Lipset was largely incapacitated by a massive stroke. He received many awards, including Leon Epstein Prize in Comparative Politics by the American Political Science Association, the Marshall Sklare Award for distinction in Jewish studies, and the Helen Dinnerman Prize by the World Association for Public Opinion Research.

Major Contributions

Lipset's principal work is in the fields of political sociology, trade union organization, social stratification, public opinion, and the sociology of intellectual life. In an interview with David Gergen, March 11, 1996, about his book *American Exceptionalism,* Lipset highlights going metric as one of the differences between America and Canada — Canada did, America didn't. He said, "Canadians respect the state, are obedient. They're ... the country which preserved the monarchy. The United States is the country which overthrew the state and which is anti-statist and disobedient and, and much more lawless" (http://www.pbs.org/newshour/gergen/lipset.html).

In an interview with Metta Spencer of *Peace Magazine* (July–September 2000, p. 15 http://www.peacemagazine.org/archive/v16n3p15.htm), speaking of democracy, Lipset drew attention to a significant fact: in presidential elections in the United States and Switzerland, two of the world's richest nations, turnout runs at about 50 percent. It would appear that the richer the nation, the less interested people are in the democratic process.

Major Literature

Lipset, Seymour Martin. *Continental Divide: The Values and Institutions of the United States and Canada.* New York: Taylor and Francis Group, Routledge, 1990.

____. *The Encyclopedia of Democracy.* Washington, D.C.: CQ Press, 1995.

____. *American Exceptionalism: A Double-Edged Sword* (about the dynamics of the American national character). New York: W.W. Norton and Co., Ltd., 1996.

____, and Earl Raab. *Jews and the New American Scene.* Cambridge, Massachusetts: Harvard University Press, 1996.

Loomis, Charles Price (1905–1995)

RURAL SOCIOLOGY

Born in Broomfield, Colorado, Charles Price Loomis gained a B.S. at the New Mexico School of Agriculture and Mechanical Arts (New Mexico State University, Las Cruces, New Mexico) (1928). At North Carolina State University, Raleigh, he gained an M.S. in sociology and economics (1929). His master's thesis was "The History of the North Carolina Farmers' Union" at Raleigh; he was also instructor in sociology (1930–1931) at N.C. State. At Harvard University, Cambridge, Massachusetts, he was research fellow in sociology (1932) and gained a Ph.D. in sociology and economics (1933);

his dissertation was "Family Composition and Socio-Economic Activities of the White Farmers in Wake County, North Carolina."

From 1933 to 1934 Loomis was a research fellow, Social Science Research Council, Universities of Heidelberg and Koenigsberg, Germany. He was agricultural economist and social scientist in the Division of Farm Population and Rural Life for the U.S. Department of Agriculture (USDA) in Washington, D.C. (1935–1942); head of the Division Extension and Training in the Office of Foreign Agricultural Relations at USDA (1943); and head of the Department of Sociology and Anthropology, Michigan State University, East Lansing, Michigan (1944–1957).

He was also president, Rural Sociological Association (1948); president, American Society for Applied Anthropology (1948); senior social scientist for USDA in Costa Rica while on sabbatical from Michigan State (1949–1950); research professor, Department of Sociology, Michigan State (1957–1971); and 57th president of the American Sociological Association (1967). His presidential address, "In Praise of Conflict and its Resolution," was published in the *American Sociological Review* (32, No. 6 [1967]: 875–890). He was professor emeritus of sociology at M.D. Anderson Cancer Center in Houston, Texas (1971–1979).

Major Contributions

Loomis was advisory editor of the *Journal of International Sociometry* of the *European Journal for Cooperation*. His article "Developing a Permanent and Stable Supply of Needed Agricultural Materials" (*Human Organization*, Vol. 2 [1942–1943], 15–17) focused on the need to develop and sustain food supplies following Pearl Harbor (1941). As a result of the shortage, the United States Department of Agriculture, assisted by land grant colleges, established Complimentary Products Projects in Latin America for the production of strategic agricultural materials. The most important of these materials included rubber, bark from which quinine is derived, rope and fiber crops, unique woods and a variety of plants that were used to produce insecticides.

After the war, Loomis continued his work with the USDA in Latin American countries, focusing on experimentation, extension work, and resident teaching. Loomis argued that anthropologists and sociologists both would have a part to play in the redevelopment of Latin American countries.

Major Literature

Loomis, Charles Price. *Rural Sociology: The Strategy of Change.* New Jersey: Prentice-Hall, 1905, 1957.

___. *Studies in Applied and Theoretical Social Science at Michigan State College.* Michigan State College Press, 1905.

___. *Rural Social Systems: A Textbook in Rural Sociology and Anthropology.* New Jersey: Prentice-Hall, 1950.

___. *Modern Social Theories: Selected American Writers.* New York: Van Nostrand Reinhold, 1965.

___, and Joseph Allan Beegle. *A Strategy for Rural Change.* New Jersey: John Wiley and Sons, Inc., 1975.

Lowenthal, Leo (1900–1993)

SOCIOLOGY OF LITERATURE

Leo Lowenthal was born in Frankfurt, the son of a Jewish physician, and he came of age during the turbulent early years of the Weimar Republic. He joined the newly formed Frankfurt School in 1926 and quickly became its leading expert on the sociology of literature and mass culture, as well as the managing editor of *Zeitschrift für Sozialforschung* (*Journal for Social Research*) launched in 1932. With others of the School, Lowenthal fled to America in 1933 where they established the school at Columbia University, New York. During the war Lowenthal worked with the Office of War Information in Washington, D.C.

After the war, while others returned to reestablish the school in Frankfurt, Lowenthal remained in America. He worked as research director of the radio station Voice of America, then at the Stanford Center for the Advanced Study of the Behavioral Sciences. In 1956, he joined the Speech Department at University of California, Berkeley, then the Department of Sociology.

Though he retired in 1968, Lowenthal remained active in departmental and university affairs until virtually the end of his life. From 1968 to 1972, he served on the Budget Committee, and in 1973–1974, chaired the Sociology Department at Berkeley. From 1970 through 1992, he conducted a private seminar with graduate students interested in the sociology of literature.

Lowenthal played a leading role both in the institutional and intellectual life of the campus as a whole. An early supporter of the Free Speech Movement, but troubled by the excesses that followed, he was a leading member of the faculty committee chaired by Charles Muscatine that produced the report published as "Education at Berkeley." As the final survivor of the Frankfurt School's inner circle, Lowenthal achieved international recognition as an icon of its remarkable collective achievement. In the last decade of his life, Lowenthal was honored on both sides of the Atlantic. Awarded the Berkeley Citation and the Federal Republic of Germany's Distinguished Merit Cross in 1985, he also received honorary doctorates from the German universities of Siegen, the Free University of Berlin, and the University of Hamburg. He was given the city of Frankfurt's Goethe Medal and Adorno Prize, as well as a year at the Berlin Institute for Advanced Study. Lowenthal died in Berkeley.

Major Literature

Lowenthal, Leo, and Norbert Guterman. *Prophets of Deceit*. Gold Coast, Queensland, Australia: Pacific Book House, 1949, 1970.

Lowenthal, Leo. *Literature and the Image of Man*. Manchester, New Hampshire: Ayer Co. Publishers, 1957. New Jersey: Transaction Publishers, 1986.

___. *Literature, Popular Culture, and Society*. New Jersey: Englewood Cliffs, 1961. Gold Coast, Queensland, Australia: Pacific Book House, 1985.

___. *Literature and Mass Culture: Communication in Society*, Volume 1. Transcribed, Andy Blunden. New Jersey: Transaction Publishers, 1984, 2006.

___. *An Unmastered Past: The Autobiographical Reflections of Leo Lowenthal*. Edited with an Introduction by Martin Jay. Berkeley, California: University of California Press, 1987.

Luhmann, Niklas (1927–1998)

SYSTEMS THEORY

Born in Lüneburg, Germany, Niklas Luhmann was in the German army from 1944 and was a short-term prisoner of war. From 1946 to 1949 he studied law at the University of Freiburg, where he obtained a J.D. degree, and then began a career in public administration, first at the Court of Administration at Lüneburg (1954), then at the State Ministry of Culture and Education in Hannover. In 1961, he studied the sociology of Talcott Parsons (see entry) at Harvard University, Cambridge, Massachusetts. At that time Parsons was the world's most influential social systems theorist. In later years, Luhmann dismissed Parsons' theory, developing a rivaling approach of his own — the theory of autopoietic systems, developed from the work of the Chilean biologists Francisco Varela and Humberto Maturana in 1973.

From 1962 to 1965 Luhmann lectured at the University for Administrative Sciences in Speyer, Germany. In 1965 he moved to the University of Munster, working with Helmut Schelsky (see entry). He gained his Ph.D. on the merit of two earlier books and habilitation at the University of Münster in 1966, qualifying him for a university professorship. After a brief spell as lecturer at the University of Frankfurt, from 1969–1993 he was professor of sociology at the then newly founded University of Bielefeld, Germany. His sociological theories — popular in Germany, Japan and Eastern Europe, and Russia — are less well-known in English-speaking countries, because of the difficulty of translating his complex theories.

The core element of Luhmann's autopoietic theory is communication. Social systems are systems of communication, and society is the most encompassing social system. Today's society is a global society; boundaries exist to protect that which is within from the information that is available outside. This process is called "reduction of complexity." Each system has a distinctive identity that is constantly reproduced in its communication and depends on what is considered meaningful and what is not. If a system fails to maintain that identity, it ceases to exist as a system and dissolves back into the environment from which it emerged. Luhmann called this process of reproduction from elements previously filtered from an over-complex environment *autopoiesis* (pronounced "auto-poy-E-sis"; literally: self-creation). A major difference between Parsons and Luhmann is that Luhmann states that each system works independently of all other systems; for example, the economic system is independent of the moral system. Luhmann himself said that he was more interested in systems than in people.

Major Literature

Luhmann, Niklas. *Luhmann: The Differentiation of Society*. New York: Columbia University Press, 1984.

___. *Religious Dogmatics and the Evolution of Societies.* Peter Beyer (Translator). Lewiston, New York: Edwin Mellen Press, Ltd., 1984.

___. *The Reality of the Mass Media.* Cambridge, England: Polity Press, 2000.

___. *Art as a Social System.* Eva M. Knodt (Translator). Palo Alto, California: Stanford University Press, 2000.

___. *Race and Ethnicity in the United States: Our Differences and Our Roots.* London, England: Thomson Learning, 2001.

___. *Risk: A Sociological Theory.* Rhodes Barrett (Translator). Los Angeles: Aldine Books, 2005.

Maciver, Robert Morrison (1882–1970)

THE NATURE OF AUTHORITY

Born in Stornoway, Isle of Lewis, Outer Hebrides, Scotland, Robert Morrison MacIver gained an M.A. in classics (1903), a D.Phil. (1905) at the University of Edinburgh, a B.A. in classics at the University of Oxford (1907), and a Ph.D. at the University of Edinburgh (1915). At University of Aberdeen, he was lecturer on political science (1907–1911) and on sociology (1911–1915). He was professor of political science at the University of Toronto, Canada (1915–1927); vice-chairman of the Canadian War Labor Board (1917–1919); professor and head of the department of economics and sociology, Barnard College, New York (1927–1936); Lieber Professor of political philosophy and sociology, Columbia University, New York (1929–1950); and president, American Sociological Society (Association, 1959) (1940).

MacIver served in a variety of public service positions, including the City of New York Juvenile Delinquency Evaluation Project (1956–1963). He was president of the New School for Social Research, New York (1963–1965), and chancellor (1965–1966). He was a fellow of the American Academy of Arts and Sciences, the American Philosophical Society, and the British Academy; he received eight honorary degrees from major universities.

Major Contributions

MacIver's theories tended to be modeled on classical scholars like Plato and Aristotle, and sociologists like Émile Durkheim and Georg Simmel (see entries). He upheld the idea that societies evolve from highly communal states to ones in which individual functions and group affiliations are extremely specialized. However, he rejected the growing trend in sociology toward professionalism, specialization, measurement, behaviorism, and experimentation. Instead he focused on ethical issues and on making sociology more human.

MacIver sought to define an integrated social science that could understand people in their economic, political, and social aspects simultaneously. He believed that sociologists must avoid imposing their own values on social fact. He also stressed that social evolution is not necessarily equivalent to social progress, which he believed could only be measured by personal judgment. He also expressed the belief that it is possible for individualism and social organization to coexist. His distinctions between state and community led to new theories of democracy, of multi-group coexistence, and of the nature of authority.

MacIver once said, "When you educate a man you educate an individual; when you educate a woman you educate a whole family."

Major Literature

MacIver, Robert Morrison. *Elements of Social Science.* New York: Macmillan, 1905. London, England: Methuen Publishing, Ltd., 1921.

___. *Community: A Sociological Study.* Manchester, New Hampshire: Ayer Co. Publishers, 1917. London, England: Frank Cass Publishers, 1970.

___. *Society: Its Structure and Changes.* New York: Ray Long and Richard R. Smith, Inc., 1931.

___. *The Web of Government.* New York: The Free Press, 1947.

___. *The More Perfect Union: A Program for the Control of Inter-group Discrimination in the United States.* New York: Macmillan, 1948.

___. *The Nations and the United Nations.* London, England: Greenwood Press, 1959.

___. *As a Tale That is Told: The Autobiography of P.M. MacIver.* Chicago, Illinois: University of Chicago Press, 1968.

___. *Politics and Society.* New York: Atherton Press, 1969. Los Angeles: Aldine Books, 2005.

Mannheim, Karl (1893–1947)

SOCIOLOGY OF KNOWLEDGE

Born in Budapest, Hungary, of Jewish parents, Karl Mannheim was one of the founding fathers of classical sociology and a founder of the sociology of knowledge. From 1922 to 1925 he worked under Alfred Weber at Heidelberg University and from 1926 to 1933, Mannheim taught sociology at the Universities of Heidelberg and Frankfurt am Main. He fled Germany and from 1933 to 1945 he lectured on sociology at the London School of Economics, University of London, and was professor of philosophy and sociology of education at London University's Institute of Education from 1945 to 1947.

Major Contributions

Mannheim's sociology of knowledge broadened Karl Marx's notion that the lower class proletariat and the middle-class bourgeoisie develop different belief systems. In Mannheim's view, social conflict is caused by the diversity in thoughts and beliefs (ideologies) among major sections of society, influenced by differences in a particular society's culture and structure. He also saw capitalism contributing to a lack of cohesion and meaning in modern life. Ideas and beliefs are rooted in larger thought systems. He elaborated on these concepts in *Ideology and Utopia.*

In the posthumously published *Freedom, Power, and Democratic Planning*, Mannheim tried to reconcile his dislike of totalitarianism with his growing belief in the need for social planning. His ambitious attempt to promote a comprehensive sociological analysis of the structures of knowledge was treated with suspicion by Marxists and neo–Marxists of the Frankfurt School. They saw the rising popularity of the sociology of knowledge as a neutralization and a betrayal of Marxist inspiration. Prior to 1933 there was fierce rivalry at Frankfurt between Mannheim's approach and that of Max Horkheimer (see entry) and the Frankfurt School of the Institute for Social Research.

While in Britain, Mannheim attempted a comprehensive analysis of the structure of modern society by way of democratic social planning and education. His work was admired more by educators, social workers, and religious thinkers than by the small community of British sociologists. However, his books on planning had a profound influence on the political debates of the immediate post-war years, both in the United States and in several European countries. Mannheim's sociological theorizing has been the subject of numerous book-length studies, evidence of an international interest in his principal themes.

Major Literature

Mannheim, Karl. *Ideology and Utopia.* London: Routledge and Kegan Paul, 1936.

___. *Man and Society in an Age of Reconstruction.* London: Routledge and Kegan Paul, 1940.

___. *Diagnosis of Our Time.* London: Routledge and Kegan Paul, 1943.

___. *Freedom, Power and Democratic Planning.* London: Routledge and Kegan Paul, 1950.

___. *Essays on the Sociology of Knowledge.* London: Routledge and Kegan Paul, 1952.

___. *Essays on Sociology and Social Psychology.* London: Routledge and Kegan Paul, 1953.
___. *Essays on the Sociology of Culture.* London: Routledge and Kegan Paul, 1956. London, England: Taylor and Francis Books, Ltd., Routledge, 1969.

Marchak, Patricia (1936–)
POLITICAL SOCIOLOGY

Patricia Russell Marchak was born in Lethbridge, Alberta, Canada. At the University of British Columbia, Vancouver, she gained a B.A. (1958) and Ph.D. (1970) and was part-time lecturer and instructor (1965–1972); full-time (1973); chair of the Board of B.C. Buildings Corporation (crown corporation) (1992–1995); professor, Department of Anthropology and Sociology and associate of the Institute for Resources and Environment; and faculty representative on the Board of Governors. She was president of the Canadian Sociology and Anthropology Association (1977–1978); fellow of the Royal Society of Canada (1987); invited to lecture as the Shastri Indo-Canadian Institute Canadian Professor in India (1987); and president of the Academy of Humanities and Social Sciences (1998–1990).

She won the John Porter Memorial Award (1983) for *Green Gold* and the Governor General's Commemorative Medal for "significant contributions to Canada" (1993). Marchak has served on the executive board of numerous Canadian and international associations, in the fields of sociology, forestry and ecology, and on the British Columbia Rhodes Scholarship Selection Committee, the Open Learning Institute, and University Hospital as member of the B.C. Forest Appeals Commission. She had been on the editorial boards of various journals, including *Canadian Review of Sociology and Anthropology, Canadian Journal of Sociology, BC Studies,* and *Current Sociology.*

Major Contributions

Marchak has conducted extensive research in two major areas: political sociology and environmental issues/resource industries. She researched state terrorism during the 1970s in Argentina and Chile. In collaboration with her husband, William Marchak, she adopts the definition of state terrorism that was developed by Hannah Arendt (German political theorist, 1906–1975) from her work on the Nazi regime in Germany. According to this definition, terrorism is an instrument designed to terrify people, not simply to eliminate political opponents. The authors assert that state terrorism is a process, not just an event, and that the process begins when a majority of the population believes that the state's actions are necessary to bring stability and order to the society. *Reigns of Terror* (2003) is a study of states that have committed gross human rights crimes against their own citizens.

Major Literature

Marchak, Patricia. *Ideological Perspectives on Canada.* New York: McGraw-Hill Education, three editions: 1975, 1981, 1987.
___. *Green Gold: The Forest Industry in British Columbia.* Montreal, Quebec: McGill-Queen's University Press, 1983.
___. *Uncommon Property: The Fishing and Fish Processing Industries in British Columbia* (with co-authors/editors Neil Guppy and John McMullan). Montreal, Quebec: McGill-Queen's University Press, 1987.
___. *The Integrated Circus: The New Right and the Restructuring of Global Markets.* Montreal, Quebec: McGill-Queen's University Press, 1991.
___. *Logging the Globe.* Montreal, Quebec: McGill-Queen's University Press, 1995.
___. *Sexism, Racism and the University.* Montreal, Quebec: McGill-Queen's University Press, 1996.
___. *Falldown: Forest Policy in British Columbia.* Vancouver, British Columbia: David Suzuki Foundation, 1999.
___*God's Assassins: State Terrorism in Argentina in the 1970s.* Montreal, Quebec: McGill-Queen's University Press, 1999.

___. *Reigns of Terror.* Montreal, Quebec: McGill-Queen's University Press, 2003.

Marcuse, Herbert
(1898–1979)

POLITICAL THEORY

Born in Berlin to a Jewish family, during World War I Herbert Marcuse served in the German Army. He completed his Ph.D. thesis at the University of Freiburg in 1922, then worked in publishing in Berlin until 1929, when he returned to Freiburg to write his habilitation. Martin Heidegger, who was close to the Nazis, refused the completed manuscript, which was published in 1932 as *Hegel's Ontology and Theory of Historicity.* Finding his academic career blocked, Marcuse joined the Frankfurt Institute for Social Research in 1933. He emigrated from Germany in 1933, first to Switzerland, then with others of the Frankfurt School to the United States, where he became an American citizen in 1940.

During World War II Marcuse worked for the U.S. Office of War Information on anti–Nazi propaganda projects, then in 1943, transferred to the Office of Strategic Services (OSS). His work for the OSS involved research on Nazi Germany and de–Nazification. After the dissolution of the OSS in 1945, Marcuse was employed by the U.S. Department of State as head of the Central European section until 1951, when he retired. From 1952 to 1958 he taught political theory at Columbia University, New York and Harvard University, Cambridge, Massachusetts. He was professor of philosophy and politics at Brandeis University, Waltham, Massachusetts, from 1958 to 1965, then at the University of California, San Diego.

In the post-war period, Marcuse was the most explicitly political left-wing member of the Frankfurt School, continuing to iden-tify himself as a Marxist, a socialist, and a disciple of the German philosopher Georg Wilhelm Friedrich Hegel (1770–1831). Marcuse was a willing speaker at student protests and became known as "the father of the New Left," a term he disliked and rejected. His work heavily influenced intellectual discussion on popular culture and scholarly popular culture studies. He had many speaking engagements in the U.S. and Europe in the late 1960s and early 1970s.

Marcuse was severely critical of capitalist societies, claiming that capitalist democracies can have totalitarian aspects. Marcuse argues that genuine tolerance does not tolerate support for repression, since doing so ensures that marginalized voices will remain unheard. He characterizes tolerance of repressive speech as "inauthentic." Instead, he advocates a discriminating tolerance that does not allow repressive intolerance to be voiced.

Major Literature

Marcuse, Herbert. *Reason and Revolution.* New York: Oxford University Press, 1941. Boston: Beacon Press, 1960.

___. *Eros and Civilization.* Boston: Beacon Press, 1955. London, England: Taylor and Francis Books, Ltd., Routledge, 1998.

___. *Soviet Marxism.* New York: Columbia University Press, 1958. Second edition, 1988.

___. *One Dimensional Man.* Boston: Beacon Press, 1964. London, England: Taylor and Francis Books, Ltd., Routledge, 2002.

___. *An Essay on Liberation.* Boston: Beacon Press, 1969, 1991.

___. *Counterrevolution and Revolt.* Boston: Beacon Press, 1972.

___. *Studies in Critical Philosophy.* Boston: Beacon Press, 1973.

___. *The Aesthetic Dimension.* Boston: Beacon Press, 1978.

Marshall, Thomas Humphrey (1893–1981)

SOCIAL POLICY

Born in London, Thomas Humphrey Marshall graduated from Trinity College, Cambridge, in 1914. He spent the next four years as a civilian prisoner of war in Germany. Upon his return to Cambridge in 1919, he was elected to a fellowship in history at Trinity. In 1925 he became an assistant lecturer in the social science department at the London School of Economics (LSE), which by that time was already an established center of teaching and research in theoretical sociology and social policy. Initially engaged to teach social work students, in 1929 Marshall transferred to the sociology department under Morris Ginsberg (see entry). He was made reader in 1930 and he helped launch the *British Journal of Sociology*. He was an essential part of the pioneering work on social class and population studies that was carried out at the LSE after 1945.

During World War II, Marshall was head of the German Section, Research Department of Foreign Office, until 1944, when he rejoined the LSE as professor of social institutions and head of the social science department. From 1949 to 1950, he was seconded as educational adviser to the British High Commission in Germany and to succeed to the Martin White chair of sociology in 1954. From 1956 to 1960 he was director of the social sciences department at UNESCO.

Major Contributions

Marshall's first collection of essays, *Citizenship and Social Class* (Cambridge, England: Cambridge University Press, 1950), later reprinted in an extended edition as *Sociology at the Crossroads* (London, England: Longmans, Green and Co., 1963), became an influential text in the history of British sociology. These essays are a brilliant analysis of the changing relationship between the institutions of citizenship and social class, set in historical and comparative perspective. They also put forward Marshall's distinctive view of sociology as a discipline that brings together not only theoretical issues but a wide range of practical applications in the field of social policy.

He perceived society as a social system of interrelated activities that maintains social behavior and identity while allowing individual freedom of choice. Marshall believed that conflict builds up resilience and democracy is strengthened by conflict and competition. On the topic of poverty, he believed that certain inequalities are in themselves the spur to improvement, provided that the right to a basic level of social services is guaranteed by the state. Marshall's honors were: Companion Order of St. Michael and St. George (1947): presidency of the International Sociological Association (1959–1962); honorary fellowship, LSE; honorary D.Sc. (1969), Southampton; honorary D.Litt. (1970), Leicester; honorary D.Univ. (1971), York; honorary Litt.D. (1978), Cambridge.

Major Literature

Marshall, Thomas Humphrey. *International Comprehension In and Through Social Science.* London University: Athlone Press, 1959.
___. *Social Policy in the Twentieth Century.* London, England: Hutchinson, 1967.
___. *The Right to Welfare.* London, England: William Heinemann, 1981.

Related Literature

Anthony, Martin, Martin Bulmer, and Anthon Rees (Eds.). *Citizenship Today: Contemporary Relevance of T.H. Marshall.* London, England: Taylor and Francis Books, Ltd., Routledge, 1996.

Martineau, Harriet (1802–1876)

EARLY SOCIOLOGIST

Called by William Davenport Adams (British journalist, 1851–1904) "the first of the notable women of the nineteenth century," Harriet Martineau was born in Norwich, England. Clearly highly intelligent, Martineau suffered from multiple sensory defects and had to use an ear trumpet when she was quite young. In 1821 she began to write anonymously for the *Monthly Repository*, a Unitarian periodical, and in 1823 she published *Devotional Exercises and Addresses, Prayers and Hymns*. After her father died, leaving the family financially impoverished, in 1826, precluded by deafness from teaching, she took up writing in earnest.

For *Traditions of Palestine* (London: Longman, Rees, Orme, Brown, and Green, 1830)—a collection of stories—she won three essay-prizes of the Unitarian Association. *Illustrations of Political Economy* (1831) was a runaway success and her literary future was secured. In *Poor Laws and Paupers Illustrated* (4 volumes, 1833–1834), her support for the Whig Poor Law reforms were praised by the Whigs (Liberals) and ridiculed by Tories (Conservatives) who claimed she discounted the charity and provision for the poor that they were introducing. *Illustrations of Taxation* was published in 1834.

From 1834 to 1836, Martineau visited the United States. Her open support for the Abolitionist Party, then small and very unpopular, gave great offense, which was deepened by the publication, soon after her return to England, of *Society in America* and a *Retrospect of Western Travel* (1838). Although generally impressed by American democracy, in *Society in America* Martineau expressed disappointment in the free enterprise system for the tendency that allowed "a sordid love of gain, to trample the rights of others." On the position of women, she believed that, given America's expressed values, the position of woman ought to have been far better than it actually was, that the condition of American women differed from that of slaves only in that they were treated with more indulgence. She maintained that if the principles of the Declaration of Independence excluded half of the human race, then it was worthless.

An article in the *Westminster Review*, "The Martyr Age of the United States," introduced English readers to the struggles for the abolition of slavery. *Letters on Mesmerism* (London: Edward Moxon, 1845) describes her return to health through mesmerism (Franz Anton Mesmer [1734–1815] developed mesmerism, the forerunner of hypnotism). Her translation of Auguste Comte made the sociological theories of this French sociologist available to the English-speaking world.

Major Literature

Martineau, Harriet. *Society in America*. New York: Ams Press, Inc., 1976.

___, and Gayle Graham Yates. *On Women*. Rutgers University Press, 1986.

Martineau, Harriet. *Positive Philosophy of Auguste Comte*, Volumes 1 and 2 (1855). Whitefish, Montana: R.A. Kessinger Publishing Co., 2003.

___, and Deborah Anna Logan. *Illustrations of Political Economy: Selected Tales*. Peterborough, Ontario: Broadview Press, Ltd., 2004.

___. *Harriet Martineau's Autobiography Parts One and Two*. Whitefish, Montana: R.A. Kessinger Publishing Co., 2005.

Martineau, Harriet. *The Collected Letters of Harriet Martineau*. London, England: Pickering and Chatto, 2007.

Marx, Karl Heinrich (1818–1883)

CLASS CONFLICTS

Although Karl Marx was a philosopher, political economist, and socialist revolutionary, he is credited with being a major contributor to sociological thinking. He is most famous for his analysis of history in terms of class struggles, summed up in the opening line of the introduction to *The Communist Manifesto* (1848), written with his close friend, Friedrich Engels (see entry): "The history of all hitherto existing society is the history of class struggles."

Marx was born in Trier, Rhine province, Prussia (Germany). Although his family was Jewish, they converted to Christianity so that his father could pursue his career as a lawyer in the face of Prussia's anti–Jewish laws. Marx studied law in Bonn and Berlin, and then wrote a Ph.D. thesis in philosophy, comparing the views of Democritus and Epicurus. Although he hoped for an academic career on gaining his doctorate in 1841 from the Friedrich Schiller University of Jena, his views were too radical, so he became a journalist. He quickly became involved in political and social issues, and soon found himself considering communist theory.

His radical ideas led to successive exiles which forced him to Paris, Brussels, and finally to London in 1849, where he became a British citizen. Marx spent years reading, researching, and writing in the British Museum, supported by Engels. His association with Engels concluded with the three-volume *Das Kapital*, the last two volumes of which Engels completed from Marx's rough notes and manuscripts. Other works by Marx were not published until the twentieth century. When Marx was buried at Highgate Cemetery in London, only eleven people attended his funeral.

Major Contributions

Although Marx turned away from philosophy in his mid-twenties, toward economics and politics, his later writings have many points of contact with contemporary philosophical debates, especially in the philosophy of history, the social sciences, and in moral and political philosophy. Historical materialism, Marx's theory of history, is centered around the idea that as societies rise, they impede the development of human productive power. Marx sees the historical process as proceeding through a necessary series of modes of production, culminating in communism. His economic analysis of capitalism is based on his version of the labor theory of value, and includes the analysis of capitalist profit as the extraction of surplus value from the exploited proletariat. The analysis of history and economics come together in Marx's prediction of the inevitable breakdown of capitalism for economic reasons, to be replaced by communism.

Major Literature (Modern editions)

Marx, Karl, and Friedrich Engels. *The German Ideology: Introduction to a Critique of Political Economy*. London, England: Lawrence and Wishart, Ltd., 1970.

Marx, Karl. *Capital: Critique of Political Economy* (3 volumes). London, England: Penguin Books, Ltd., 1993.

Marx, Karl, and Friedrich Engels. *The Communist Manifesto*. Oxford, England: Oxford University Press, Oxford Paperbacks, 1998.

Marx, Karl. *Capital: An Abridged Edition*. Oxford, England: Oxford University Press, 1999.

___. *Selected Writings*. Oxford, England: Oxford University Press, 2004.

Massey, Douglas S. (1952–)

INTERNATIONAL MIGRATION

Born in Olympia, Washington, Douglas S. Massey gained a B.A. in sociology, psychology, and Spanish at Western Washington University, Bellingham, Washington (1974). At Princeton University, Princeton, New Jersey, he gained an M.A. (1977) and Ph.D. in sociology (1978) and was research associate, Office of Population Research (1978–1979), and lecturer, Woodrow Wilson

School of Public and International Affairs (1979). He was a National Science Foundation postdoctoral fellow, Graduate Group in Demography, University of California, Berkeley (1979–1980).

At the University of Pennsylvania, Philadelphia, Massey was assistant professor, Department of Sociology and Graduate Group in Demography (1980–1985), and associate professor, Department of Sociology and Graduate Group in Demography (1985–1987). At University of Chicago he was professor, Department of Sociology (1987–1994); professor, Irving B. Harris School of Public Policy Studies (1990–1994); and Dorothy Swaine Thomas Professor, Department of Sociology, Graduate Group in Demography, and Lauder Program in International Studies (1994–2003). He was professor of sociology and public policy, Princeton (2003–2005), and has been Henry G. Bryant Professor of Sociology and Public Affairs, Princeton University, since 2005.

He was president, Population Association of America (1996); member of the National Academy of Sciences (1998); and 92nd president of the American Sociological Association (2001). His presidential address, "Emotion and the History of Human Society," was published in the *American Sociological Review* (67, No. 1 [February 2002]: 1–29).

Major Contributions

Massey has written for all the major journals: *American Journal of Sociology, American Sociological Review, Demography, International Migration Review, Population and Development Review, Social Forces, Social Science Quarterly, Social Science Research,* and *Sociology and Social Research.* Most of his books and articles deal with Mexican or international migration and with segregation and stratification. *Miracles on the Border: Retablos of Mexican Migrants to the United States* (with Jorge Durand) deals with a form of Mexican folk art, which Massey almost

single-handedly introduced to non–Latin America. It won the Southwest Book Award from the Border Regional Library Association.

Major Literature

Massey, Douglas S., and Nancy A. Denton. *American Apartheid: Segregation and the Making of the Underclass.* Cambridge, Massachusetts: Harvard University Press, 1998.

Massey, Douglas S., et al. *Worlds in Motion: International Migration at the End of the Millennium.* Oxford, England: Oxford University Press, 1998, 2005.

Massey, Douglas S., Camille Charles, Garvey Lundy, and Mary J. Fischer. *The Source of the River: The Origins, Aspirations, and Values of Freshmen at America's Elite Colleges and Universities.* Princeton, New Jersey: Princeton University Press, 2001, 2006.

Massey, Douglas S., Jorge Durand, and Nolan Malone. *Smoke and Mirrors: U.S. Immigration Policy in the Age of Globalization.* New York: Russell Sage Foundation, 2001, 2003.

Massey, Douglas S., and Elijah Anderson (Eds.). *Problem of the Century: Racial Stratification in the United States at Century's End.* New York: Russell Sage Foundation, 2001, 2004.

Durand, Jorge, and Douglas S. Massey (Eds.). *Crossing the Border: Research from the Mexican Migration Project.* New York: Russell Sage Foundation, 2004.

Sanchez, Magaly, Jere R. Behrman, and Douglas S. Massey (Eds.). *Chronicle of a Myth Foretold: The Washington Consensus in Latin America.* London, England: Sage Publications, Ltd., 2006.

Mauss, Marcel (1872–1950)
COMPARATIVE RELIGION

Born into a Jewish family from Épinal, France, Marcel Mauss assisted his uncle, Émile Durkheim (see entry), in the preparation of a number of works, notably *Le Suicide* (1897), and succeeded Durkheim as editor of the journal *L'Année Sociologique* (*The Sociological Year*). Mauss studied philosophy and the history of religion and graduated from the University of Bordeaux — where Émile Durkheim was teaching — and agrégated in 1893. He then studied comparative religion and Sanskrit in Paris.

His "Essay on the Nature and the Function of the Sacrifice" (1896) marked the beginning of a prolific career that would produce several landmarks in sociological literature. In 1902 he was appointed professor of primitive religion at the École Pratique des Hautes Études (Practical School of Higher Studies), Paris. He was a co-founder of the Ethnology Institute of the University of Paris (1925) and also taught at the Collège de France (1931–1939). A political activist for many years, he supported Alfred Dreyfus in his famed court battle, and helped edit the left-wing papers *le Populaire*, *l'Humanite* and *le Mouvement Socialiste*, and cofounded the socialist daily *L'Humanité* (1904).

An advocate of a close relationship between anthropology and psychology, Mauss sought to practice Durkheim's rules of sociological method by identifying how groups are socially organized. His most influential work is thought to be *Essai sur le don* (1925; *The Gift*), concentrating on the forms of exchange and contract in Melanesia, Polynesia, and northwestern North America. The work explores the religious, legal, economic, mythological, and other aspects of giving, receiving, and repaying, which although they appear to be voluntary and disinterested, they are in fact obligatory and very interested. He also wrote on magic, the concept of self, mourning rites, and other topics. *Sociology and Anthropology* (1950) is a collection of essays he published between 1904 and 1938.

Although Mauss never did fieldwork, he turned the attention of French sociologists, philosophers and psychologists towards ethnology Post-war World War I France was a difficult period for Mauss; Durkheim had died, and many of the changes Durkheim had made to school curricula across France

were not now popular. Mauss founded *l'Institut Français de Sociologie* (1924) and *l'Institut d'Ethnologie* (1926) in honor of his uncle. In 1931 Mauss took up the chair of sociology at the Collège de France, Paris. He actively fought against anti–Semitism and racial politics both before and after World War II.

Major Literature

Durkheim, Emile, Marcel Mauss, and Rodney Needham (Translator). *Primitive Classification*. London, England: Taylor and Francis Books, Ltd., Routledge, 1970.

Halls, W.D., Marcel Mauss and Henri Hubert. *Sacrifice: Its Nature and Function*. Chicago, Illinois: University of Chicago Press, 1981.

Mauss, Marcel, and W.D. Halls (Translator). *The Gift*. London, England: Taylor and Francis Books, Ltd., Routledge, 1990.

Mauss, Marcel. *A General Theory of Magic*. London, England: Taylor and Francis Books, Ltd., Routledge, 2001.

___, and James J. Fox (Translator). *Seasonal Variations of the Eskimo: A Study in Social Morphology*. London, England: Taylor and Francis Books, Ltd., Routledge, 2004.

Mead, George Herbert (1863–1931)
Symbolic Interactionism

Born in South Hadley, Massachusetts, George Herbert Mead graduated with a B.A. degree from Oberlin College, Ohio (1883), and a B.A. from Harvard University, Cambridge, Massachusetts (1888). From 1888 to 1891 he studied philosophy in Germany as well as psychology with Wilhelm Wundt. He taught philosophy and psychology at the University of Michigan, Ann Arbor (1891–1894), with John Dewey (psychologist) and Charles Horton Cooley (see entry). In 1894, Mead moved to the University of Chicago, Illinois, where he taught for the rest of his life.

Major Contributions

Mead is one of the people who straddles both social psychology and sociology, and was one of several distinguished pragmatists. His main contribution was to show how the human self arises in the process of social interaction, and how spoken language plays a central role in this development. Through language the child can take the role of other persons and guide his behavior in terms of the effect his contemplated behavior will have upon others. Mead traces the genesis of the self through the play and game stages of childhood. The self has two phases-the "I," which is the unpredictable and creative aspect of the self, and the "me," which is the organized set of attitudes of others assumed by the actor. An extremely important aspect of Mead's theory is "The Act." It consists of stages:

- *Impulse*— The actor's reaction to stimulation
- *Perception*— The actor searches for, and reacts to, stimuli that relate to the impulse
- *Manipulation*— The actor takes action with regard of the object
- *Consummation*— Taking action to satisfy the original impulse.

While non-human animals do manipulate objects (i.e., interact) humans are unique in that they are capable of considering a different perspective. For example, in buying and selling, only with a mutual perspective (agreement) between buyer and seller can the economic exchange occur. Mead's theory of how the mind and self emerge from the social process of communication by signs founded the symbolic interactionist school of sociology and social psychology. He also made significant contributions to the philosophies of nature, science, and history, to philosophical anthropology, and to process philosophy.

Although Mead published about 100 scholarly articles, reviews, and incidental pieces, he never published any books. Six books have been put together from his unpublished manuscripts and from stenographic records of his lectures. (See The Mead Project at http://spartan.ac.brocku.ca/~lward/.)

Major Literature (Posthumous)

Mead, G.H. *The Philosophy of the Present.* Loughton, Essex, England: Prometheus Books, 1932.

___. *Mind, Self, and Society.* C.W. Morris (Ed.). Chicago, Illinois: University of Chicago Press, 1934.

___. *The Philosophy of the Act.* C.W. Morris, et al. (Eds.). Chicago, Illinois: University of Chicago Press, 1938.

___. *Selected Writings.* A.J. Reck (Ed.). Chicago, Illinois: University Chicago Press, 1964.

___. *The Individual and the Social Self: Unpublished Essays by G.H. Mead.* David L. Miller (Ed.). Chicago, Illinois: University of Chicago Press, 1982.

___. *Essays in Social Psychology.* Ed. by M.J. Deegan. New Jersey: Transaction Publishers, 2001.

Merton, Robert King (1919–2003)

SOCIOLOGY OF SCIENCE

Robert King Merton (born Meyer Robert Schkolnick) was the son of Jewish Eastern European immigrant parents, born in Philadelphia, Pennsylvania. He gained an MA and Ph.D. at Harvard University, Cambridge, Massachusetts, then joined the faculty and was professor and chairman of the Department of Sociology at Tulane University in New Orleans (1939–1941). He was a lecturer at Columbia University, New York (1941–1946); professor (1947); Giddings Professor of Sociology (1963); university professor (1974); special service professor upon his retirement (1979), a title reserved by the trustees for emeritus faculty who "render special services to the University."

Merton was adjunct faculty member at Rockefeller University, New York; first foundation scholar at the Russell Sage Foundation, New York, and retired from teaching in 1984. Merton received more than 20 honorary degrees from universities in America and around the world and was awarded the National Medal of Science, the first sociologist so awarded (1994). In 1990, Columbia University established the Robert K. Merton Professorship in the Social Sciences.

Major Contributions

Merton was associate director of Columbia's Bureau of Applied Social Research (1942–1971), which had opened under the direction of Paul Lazarsfeld (see entry), though the bureau did not assume that title until 1944. The two men's work was complementary: Lazarsfeld combined quantitative and qualitative research methodologies, along with his logic of concept clarification, and thereby influenced Merton's orientation to historical studies. Merton's gift for theory influenced Lazarsfeld's philosophical grasp of sociology. Their academic collaboration, from 1941 to 1976, strengthened the standards of training for the social sciences.

While at the bureau, Merton began using focused interviews with groups to obtain reactions to such things as films and written materials. This technique gave rise to focus groups, which have become critical tools for marketers and politicians. Merton coined terms such as "self-fulfilling prophecy," "role model," and "unintended consequences," and he wrote at length on the concept of serendipity.

Merton analyzes society with reference to whether cultural and social structures are well or badly integrated. He believes that shared values are central in explaining how societies and institutions work. Merton

carried out extensive research into the sociology of science, developing the Merton Thesis explaining some of the causes of the scientific revolution, and the "Mertonian norms" of science. His son, Robert C. Merton, won a Nobel Prize for economics in 1997.

Major Literature

Merton, Robert K. *Science, Technology and Society in Seventeenth Century England* (1938). New York: Howard Fertig, 2002.

___. *The Sociology of Science.* Chicago, Illinois: University of Chicago Press, 1979.

___, Marjorie Fiske, and Patricia L. Kendall. *The Focused Interview: A Manual of Problems and Procedures.* New York: The Free Press, 1990.

Merton, Robert K. *On the Shoulders of Giants.* Chicago, Illinois: University of Chicago Press, 1993.

___. *Advances in Criminological Theory: The Legacy of Anomie* v. 6. New Jersey: Transaction Publishers, 1999.

___, and Elinor G. Barber. *The Travels and Adventures of Serendipity: A Study in Sociological Semantics and the Sociology of Science.* New Jersey: Princeton University Press, 2006.

Michels, Robert (1876–1936)

IRON LAW OF OLIGARCHY

Born in Cologne, Germany, of French, Italian and German background, Robert Michels studied in England, Munich, Leipzig, and Halle, and was a professor of sociology at Brussels, Paris, and Florence. He became a Socialist while teaching at the University of Marburg, Germany, and when he became active in the radical wing of the Social Democratic Party of Germany (SDP), established in 1875, he was barred from academic jobs in Germany. He left the SDP in 1907 and ended as one of Mussolini's professors of fascist political science.

At the University of Turin, he taught economics, political science, and sociology. From 1914 to 1926 he was professor of economics at the University of Basel, Switzerland. His last years were spent in Italy teaching economics and the history of doctrines at the University of Perugia.

Major Contributions

Michels's involvement in revolutionary causes gave him insights into trade unions, party congresses, demagogues, and the role of the intellectual in politics. His widely translated book *Political Parties* (1911) is an analysis of pre-war socialism in Germany, with examples also drawn from political protest movements in France, Italy, England, and the United States. He became a revolutionary syndicalist, and formulated the "iron law of oligarchy." The law states that political parties and other large, complex organizations inevitably tend toward oligarchy (government by a small elite group), authoritarianism, and bureaucracy as they become more interested in preserving their own power than in furthering the original goals of the group. Syndicalists argued that participation in Parliamentary politics will not achieve socialism. Winning elections requires too much compromise. The best way is militant trade union action, culminating in a general strike, which would transfer control of the factories not to the state but to the workers themselves.

In his later writings Michels came to view this elitist rule as not only inevitable but also desirable, and he did not oppose the rise of fascism in Italy. Michels compared working-class societies in Germany, Italy, and France and wrote about the political culture of Italy. He analyzed the Tripolitan War (1911–1912) (between Turkey and Italy, over disputed Libya) in terms of the suffering it caused and the impact of war propaganda. He believed that Italian imperialism resulted from demographic pressure and from the social and cultural loss caused by overseas migration. His writings in the 1920s and 1930s dealt with nationalism, Italian socialism and fascism,

elites and social mobility, the role of intellectuals, and the history of the social sciences. Michels was a protégé of Max Weber, whose views on bureaucracy strongly influenced Michels, who is ranked as a foremost thinker in classical political sociology.

Major Literature (Modern editions)

Michels, Robert. *Political Parties: Sociological Study the Oligarchical Tendencies of Modern Democracy*. Magnolia, Massachusetts: Peter Smith, Inc., 1960.
___. *Political Parties*. New York: Macmillan, 1968.
___. *First Lecture in Political Sociology*. Manchester, New Hampshire: Ayer Co. Publishers, 1974.

Mills, Charles Wright (1916–1962)

STRUCTURE OF POWER

Born at Waco, Texas, Charles Wright Mills gained his bachelor's and master's degrees in philosophy (1939) from the University of Texas, Austin, and a Ph.D. (1941) from the University of Wisconsin, Madison. Mills developed an approach to sociology based largely upon the pragmatism of John Dewey and George Herbert Mead (see entries). His first academic position was at the University of Maryland, College Park, in 1941. From 1945 to 1948 he was on the faculty of the Columbia University Labor Research Division of the Bureau of Applied Social Research, New York. In 1946 he was promoted to assistant professor at Columbia and in 1956 to full professor. He was a member of the American Sociological Society and served as its vice president (1947–1948).

Major Contributions

Mills synthesizes the social behaviorism or personality formation of the pragmatists with the emphasis upon social structure of

Max Weber (see entry) and the German sociologists. The basic concept in Mills' working model is that of role. Roles by definition are interpersonal; that is, they are oriented to our expectations of others. The concept of role through its relationship to institutions provides a link between the psychology of the individual and the controls of a society. Mills' model shows the type of person selected, how these roles are performed, and how the chosen roles are internalized. Roles make up the social person as well as organizing society and have a profound effect on one's self-esteem.

Five major institutional orders make up the skeletal structure of the total society:

1. The *political* order; institutions within which people acquire, wield, or influence the distribution of power and authority within social structures.
2. The *economic* order; establishments by which people organize labor, resources, and technical implements in order to produce and distribute goods and services.
3. The *military* order; institutions in which people organize legitimate violence and supervise its use.
4. The *kinship* order; institutions which regulate and facilitate legitimate sexual intercourse, procreation, and the early bearing of children.
5. The *religious* order; institutions in which men organize and supervise the collective worship of God or deities, usually at regular occasions and at fixed places.

Mills was especially critical of his own profession, for what he saw as excessive reliance on quantitative methodology and lack of interest in real-world problems.

Major Literature

Mills, Charles Wright. *The Puerto Rican Journey: New York's Newest Immigrants.* New York: Harper, Hamish Hamilton, 1950.

___. *White Collar: The American Middle Classes.* New York: Oxford University Press, 1951.

Gerth, Hans, and Charles Wright Mills. *Character and Social Structure: The Psychology of Social Institutions.* New York: Harcourt, Brace and Company, 1953.

Mills, Charles Wright, and Alan Wolfe. *The Power Elite.* New York: Oxford University Press, 1956, 2000.

Mills, Charles Wright. *The Causes of World War Three.* New York: Taylor and Francis Group, Routledge, 1958.

___. *Images of Man.* New York: George Braziller, 1960.

___. *Sociology and Pragmatism.* New York: Oxford University Press, 1964.

Moore, Barrington, Jr. (1913–2005)

POLITICAL SOCIOLOGY

Barrington Moore, Jr., was a classics major at Williams College, Williamstown, Massachusetts, where he was elected to Phi Beta Kappa. He gained a Ph.D. in sociology (1941) from Yale University, New Haven, Connecticut. Moore then worked as a policy analyst for the Office of Strategic Services (OSS) during World War II under Herbert Marcuse (see entry). After the war, he taught in the interdisciplinary Social Science Division at the University of Chicago from 1945 to 1947. He joined the Russian Research Center at Harvard University in Cambridge, Massachusetts, in 1947, where he remained an affiliate until his retirement.

Major Contributions

In 1958 Moore published a book of essays on methodology and theory entitled *Political Power and Social Theory*, in which he attacked the methodological outlook of 1950s social science. In *Social Origins of Dictatorship and Democracy: Lord and Peasant in the Making of the Modern World* (1968) he studied how social structures are created and how they change (sociogenesis). He looked particularly at the democratic, fascist and communist regimes, especially how industrialization and the pre-existing agrarian regimes interacted to produce those different political outcomes. He drew particular attention to the violence that preceded the development of democratic institutions.

In *Social Origins of Dictatorship and Democracy* (1966) — the cornerstone to what is now called comparative-historical analysis in the social sciences — Moore introduced the concept "no bourgeoisie, no democracy." In Britain, the effect of the "bourgeois impulse" was to change the attitudes of a portion of the landed elite toward commercial farming, leading to the destruction of the peasantry through the enclosure system and the English Civil War, which led to an aristocratic but moderate democracy. In France, the French Revolution did directly include the bourgeoisie, but it was the overwhelming influence of the peasantry that determined the outcome of the Revolution. Much the same happened in the United States when the victory of Northern industrialists over the Southern "planter elite" led to a liberal democracy. Moore also addressed the changes in China, Japan and Russia.

Major Literature

Moore, Barrington, Jr. *Terror and Progress — USSR*. Harvard University Press, Cambridge, 1954.

___. *Political Power and Social Theory: Six Studies*. Cambridge, Massachusetts: Harvard University Press, 1958.

___. *Reflections on the Causes of Human Misery and Upon Certain Proposals to Eliminate Them*. Beacon Press, 1972, 1997.

___. *Injustice: the Social Basis of Obedience and Revolt*. New York: Random House Inc., 1979.

___. *Privacy: Studies in Social and Cultural History*. New York: M.E. Sharpe, Inc., 1984.

___. *Moral Purity and Persecution in History*. New Jersey: Princeton University Press, 2000.

Mosca, Gaetano (1858–1941)

ELITES

Born in Palermo, Sicily, Gaetano Mosca was educated at the University of Palermo and earned his degree in law in 1881. From 1885 to 1888 he taught constitutional law at Palermo and from 1888 to 1896 at the University of Rome. He was chair of constitutional law at Turin (1896–1924), then public law at the University of Rome. A member of the Italian Chamber of Deputies from 1908, he served as undersecretary of state for the colonies from 1914 to 1916 and was made a senator for life by King Victor Emmanuel III in 1919. During the fascist dictatorship, Mosca retired to teach and research. His final speech in the Senate was an attack on the Italian fascist leader Benito Mussolini. Mosca also worked as a political journalist for the *Corriere della Sera* of Milan (after 1901) and the Rome *Tribuna* (1911–1921).

Major Contributions

Mosca is credited with developing the theory of elitism and the doctrine of the political class. With Vilfredo Pareto and Robert Michels (see entries), he is one of the three members constituting the Italian School of Elitists. In *The Ruling Class* (originally published in Italian, 1896; republished by Westport, Connecticut: Greenwood Press, 1980), Mosca asserts that societies are necessarily governed by minorities: by military, priestly, or hereditary oligarchies or by aristocracies of wealth or of merit. For him the will of God, the will of the people, the sovereign will of the state, and the dictatorship of the proletariat were all mythical, and that even in democracies the people do not rule. His theory seemed to have its greatest influence on supporters of fascism who used his theory to promote fascism.

Mosca opposed the racist elitism preached

by the Nazi Party in Germany, condemned Marxism, which in his view expressed the hatred within Karl Marx, and mistrusted democracy, seeing extension of universal suffrage as the greatest threat to liberal institutions. Mosca viewed the most enduring social organization as a mixed government of all classes, particularly those with superior organizational skills. Mosca's elites are not drawn from one social class, like the aristocracy; peoples from all classes of society can theoretically become "elite." He also adhered to Pareto's "the circulation of elites," where there is constant competition between elites, with one elite group replacing another repeatedly over time. Different elites rise up within different societies, often according to the needs of that society. In modern societies an important section of the ruling class is always the bureaucracy, the body of salaried officials professionally entrusted with the administration of the machinery of political, economic, and social life.

Related Literature

Nye, Robert A. *Anti-democratic Sources of Elite Theory: Pareto, Mosca, Michels.* London, England: Sage Publications, Ltd., 1977.

Albertoni, Ettore. *Mosca and the Theory of Elitism.* Lake Oswego, Oregon: Blackwell Publishers, 1987.

Finocchiaro, Maurice A. *Beyond Right and Left: Democratic Elitism in Mosca and Gramsci.* New Haven, Connecticut: Yale University Press, 1999.

Myrdal, Alva (1902–1986)

SOCIAL CHANGE

Alva Reimer was born in Uppsala, Sweden, and graduated from university in 1924 and married the Swedish economist Gunnar Myrdal (1898–1987) in the same year. She was a teacher and sociologist who, in the 1930s, with her husband initiated a national program establishing state responsibility for child care. She was also actively engaged in the discussion on housing and school problems, thus making a considerable contribution to social welfare in Sweden.

Myrdal focused primarily on issues of peace and war, population planning, the family, and women's rights. She believed in the importance of sociological analysis and understanding for progressive social change. She was a prominent member of the Social Democrat Party in Sweden, and in 1943 was appointed to that party's committee with the task of drafting a post-war program. Also in that year she was appointed to the Government Commission on International Post-War Aid and Reconstruction. She served as principal director of the United Nations Department of Social Welfare during 1949–1950 and became director of the UNESCO Department of Social Sciences in 1951.

From 1955 to 1961 she served as ambassador of the Swedish government to India, with related duties in neighboring Burma (Myanmar), Ceylon (Sri Lanka) and Nepal. After she served as a member of Sweden's Parliament (1962–1970), she led Sweden's delegation to the United Nations Disarmament Conference in Geneva (1962–1973) and was minister of disarmament and church affairs (1967–1973).

For her work in the nuclear disarmament movement, she won the 1982 Nobel Peace Prize, which she shared with Alfonso García Robles (1911–1991) of Mexico. She helped establish the Stockholm International Peace Research Institute. The aim of the institute is to conduct research on questions of conflict and cooperation of importance for international peace and security, and to contribute to an understanding of the conditions for peaceful solutions of international conflicts and for a stable peace. In addition to the Nobel Prize, Myrdal received the West German Peace Prize (1970; jointly with her husband), the Albert Einstein Peace Prize (1980), and the Jawaharlal Nehru Award for International Understanding (1981).

Major Literature

Myrdal, Alva. *Nation and Family: The Swedish Experience in Democratic Family and Population Policy.* Cambridge, Massachusetts: MIT Press, 1941, 2nd ed., 1965.

___, and V. Klein. *Women's Two Roles.* London, England: Routledge and Kegan Paul, rev. ed., 1968.

___. *The Game of Disarmament: How the United States and Russia Run the Arms Race.* 1976. New York: Pantheon, rev. ed., 1982.

Myrdal, Alva. *War, Weapons and Everyday Violence.* Manchester, New Hampshire: University of New Hampshire Press, 1977.

___. *Dynamics of European Nuclear Disarmament.* Nottingham, England: Spokesman Books, 1981.

Related Literature

Carlson, Allan C. *The Swedish Experiment in Family Politics: The Myrdals and the Interwar Population Crisis.* New Jersey: Transaction Publishers, 1990.

Oakley, Ann Rosamund (1944–)

MEDICAL SOCIOLOGY

Born in London, England, Ann Rosamund Oakley gained a B.A. in politics, philosophy and economics (sociology special option) at Somerville College, University of Oxford (1966), and was a postgraduate student (Social Science Research Council Studentship) (1969–1972). She gained a Ph.D. in sociology at Bedford College, University of London (1974), where she was research officer (1974–1979). At the Department of National Perinatal Epidemiology Unit, University of Oxford, Oakley was consultant (1979–1980); Wellcome Research Fellow (1980–1983); and senior research officer (1983–1984).

Oakley was visiting fellow, Department of Sociology, University of Warwick (1983–1987); deputy director, Thomas Coram Research Unit, University of London Institute of Education (1985–1990); director, Social Science Research Unit, University of London Institute of Education (1990–2005); professor of sociology and social policy, University of London (1991); and honorary professor in social sciences, Division of Public Health Medicine, Institute of Child Health, University College, London (1996).

Oakley was visiting professor at the University of Lund, Sweden (1986), University of Auckland, New Zealand (1989), and the University of Tulane, New Orleans (1990). She was also Torgny Segerstedt Distinguished Visiting Professor of Higher Education and Learning, Swedish Collegium for Advanced Study in the Social Sciences, University of Uppsala, Sweden (1997). She was awarded an honorary D.Litt. from the University of Salford, England (1995), and an honorary fellowship, Somerville College, University of Oxford (2001).

Major Contributions

Oakley was the only child of Kay Titmuss, a social worker, and Richard Titmuss (1907–1973), one of the 20th century's foremost social policy theorists and an architect of Britain's Welfare State. Her *Sex, Gender and Society* (1972) was later credited with introducing the term "gender" into academic and everyday discourse, and providing a critical tool for the new women's studies, which needed a way of distinguishing the social treatment of men and women from the biology of sex.

Oakley has maintained her interest in feminism throughout her academic career. In *Gender on Planet Earth* (2002), she links many of today's most pressing social problems with gender ideologies and arrangements. Issues such as rising crime and disaffected youth, and pollution and the "rape" of the environment are connected through an ethos about gender in which women remain cultural outsiders and men are alienated from the full range of human experiences.

Major Literature

Oakley, Ann. *Sex, Gender and Society: Towards a New Society.* London, England: Taylor and Francis Books, Ltd., Arena, 1985.

___. *The Captured Womb: History of the Medical Care of Pregnant Women.* Oxford, England: Blackwell Publishing, 1986.

___. *From Here to Maternity: Becoming a Mother.* London, England: Penguin Books, Ltd., 1986.

___. *The Men's Room.* London, England: Virago Press, Ltd., new edition, 1999.

___. *Experiments in Knowing: Gender and Method in the Social Sciences.* Cambridge, England: Polity Press, 2000.

___. *Gender on Planet Earth.* Cambridge, England: Polity Press, 2002.

___. *The Ann Oakley Reader: Gender, Women and Social Science.* Cambridge, England: Polity Press, 2005.

Odum, Howard Washington (1884–1954)

FOLK SOCIOLOGY

Born near Bethlehem, Georgia, Howard Washington Odum gained a B.A. in English and classics at Emory College, Atlanta, Georgia (1904); an M.A. in classics at the University of Mississippi, Oxford, Mississippi (1906); a Ph.D. in psychology at Clark University, Worcester, Massachusetts (1909); and a Ph.D. in sociology at Columbia University, New York (1910).

Odum was professor of educational sociology, University of Georgia, Athens (1912–1919); director of civilian relief for the southern division of the Red Cross (1918); and professor of ecology and dean of liberal arts at Emory (1919–1920). From 1919 to 1944, he worked for the Commission on Interracial Cooperation. From 1920 to 1954 at the University of North Carolina, Chapel Hill, he established and directed a new school of public welfare (later renamed the School of Social Work) (1920–1932), founded the Institute for Research in Social Science (1924),

and founded *Social Forces* (1922) (now *Social Forces: International Journal of Social Research*). He was president of the American Sociological Society (1930) and president of the newly formed Southern Regional Council (1944–1946).

Major Contributions

Odum's own work was based on the belief that sociology must provide social guidance. A specialist in the social problems of the southern United States and a pioneer of sociological education in the South, he worked to replace the Southern sectionalism with a sophisticated regional approach to social planning, race relations, and the arts, especially literature. Odum was ahead of his time in urging equal opportunity for African-Americans. His goal was unity through diversity; he stressed the role of folk culture in strengthening and vitalizing state civilization.

At Oxford, Odum began collecting songs and tales of blacks in nearby communities, which he fashioned into his first doctoral dissertation, "Religious Folk-Songs of the Southern Negroes." His second dissertation — published as *Social and Mental Traits of the Negro*, a compendium of detail concerning black society — challenged the status quo. He was criticized for his too ready acceptance of disfranchisement and segregation, and for his failure to make clear distinctions between cultural and racial traits.

In *Rainbow Round My Shoulder* (1928), *Wings on My Feet* (1929), and *Cold Blue Moon* (1931), Odum described the wanderings of Left-Wing Gordon, a semi-fictional black Ulysses whose ripe wisdom dramatized the richness of folk culture. At President Herbert Hoover's request, Odum and William Fielding Ogburn (see entry) edited the report *Recent Social Trends in the United States* (2 vols., 1933), for the President's Research Committee on Social Trends.

Major Literature

Odum, Howard. *The Negro and His Songs: Study of Typical Negro Songs in the South.* Westport, Connecticut: Greenwood Press, 1925.

___, and Guy Benton Johnson. *Negro Workaday Songs.* Westport, Connecticut: Greenwood Press, 1926.

Odum, Howard. *An Approach to Public Welfare and Social Work.* Chapel Hill: University of North Carolina Press, 1926.

___. *Man's Quest for Social Guidance.* New York: Henry Holt and Company, Inc., 1927.

___. *Southern Regions.* Chapel Hill: University of North Carolina Press, 1936.

___. *American Regionalism.* New York: Henry Holt and Company, Inc., 1938.

___. *Understanding Society: The Principles of Dynamic Sociology.* Basingstoke, Hampshire, England: Macmillan, Ltd., 1947.

Ogburn, William Fielding (1886–1959)

STATISTICAL SOCIOLOGY

Born in Butler, Georgia, William Fielding Ogburn gained a B.S. at Mercer University in Macon, Georgia (1905), and an M.A. (1909) and Ph.D. in sociology (1912) at Columbia University, New York. He was instructor in economics, politics and history, Princeton University, New Jersey (1911), professor of sociology and economics, Reed College, Portland, Oregon (1912–1917); professor of sociology, University of Washington, Seattle (1917–1918); examiner and head of the cost-of-living department of the National War Labor Board; special agent of the U.S. Bureau of Labor Statistics (1918–1919); professor of sociology, Columbia University, New York (1919–1927); and professor of sociology, University of Chicago, Illinois (1927–1951).

He was also director of the President's Research Committee on Social Trends established by President Herbert Hoover and running from 1930 to 1933; Sewell L. Avery distinguished service professor (1933); research consultant to the National Resources Committee (1935–1943); visiting professor, Nuffield College, Oxford, England (1952–1953); visiting professor of sociology at Florida State University, Tallahassee (1953–1959); and professor of American History and Institutions at the Indian School of International Studies, University of Delhi (1956–1957).

Ogburn was 19th president of the American Sociological Society (Association, 1959) (1929); president, American Statistical Association (1931); vice-president, American Association for the Advancement of Science (1932); chairman, Social Science Research Council and chairman of its Problems and Policy Committee (1937–1939); president, Society for the History of Technology (1959); and editor, *Journal of American Statistical Association* (1920–1926). He received the honorary degree of LL.D. from Columbia University and from the University of North Carolina, Chapel Hill.

Major Contributions

Ogburn believed passionately in research and argued that many sociologists run away from the long, hard, slow tasks of research for the quicker, easier prestige of counseling in public affairs. Such counselors Ogburn calls "committee bums." He believed that if he and others succeeded in building up a respect for the reliability of social science among statesmen, responsible educators, and capable congressmen, and among business and social leaders, universities and the students will follow. He maintained that social theory has no place in scientific sociology, if it is not built upon sufficient data. Although Ogburn may not be as noted as his teacher Franklin Henry Giddings (see entry) was for the creation of sociological terms and concepts, Ogburn's term "cultural lag," defined sociologically for the first time in his book *Social Change*, has become a classic (see also, Mirra Komarovsky).

Ogburn's articles appeared in many learned and technical journals, including fifty-three sociological journals, including *The American Journal of Sociology, Social Forces, Publications of the American Sociological Society, Annals of the American Academy of Political and Social Science*, and *Sociology and Social Research*.

Major Literature

Ogburn, William Fielding. *Social Change with Respect to Culture and Original Nature*. New York: B.W. Huebsch, 1922.

___. *A Handbook of Sociology*. London, England: Routledge and Kegan Paul, 1953, 1964.

___. *On Culture and Social Change: Selected Papers*. Chicago, Illinois: University of Chicago Press, 1964.

___. *American Society in Wartime: Franklin D. Roosevelt and the Era of the New Deal*. Cambridge, Massachusetts: Da Capo Press, 1972.

Oppenheimer, Franz (1846–1943)

POLITICAL SOCIOLOGY

Born in Berlin, Franz Oppenheimer studied medicine at Freiburg and Berlin, Germany (1881–1885), and practiced as a physician in Berlin (1886–1895). From 1890 onward, he followed parallel occupations of medicine with social-political problems and the science of social economics. Thereafter he was a journalist, serving as editor-in-chief of the *Welt am Montag* (*World on Monday*). He gained a Ph.D. at Kiel University (1909) and was then a private teacher in Berlin until 1917.

He was honorary professor, Berlin (1917–1919), and university professor of sociology and theoretical national economics, Johann Wolfgang Goethe University, Frankfurt am Main (Germany's first professorship of sociology) (1919–1929). From 1933 to 1938, he taught at the liberal rabbinical seminary in Berlin, and from 1934 to 1935, in Palestine. Oppenheimer was honorary member of the American Society of Sociology (1936). In 1938, he immigrated via Tokyo and Shanghai to Los Angeles. In 1942 he was co-founder and publisher of the *American Journal of Economics and Sociology*.

Major Contributions

In his influential book *The State*, Oppenheimer rejected the idea of the "social contract" and contributed to the "conquest theory." In essence, he said there are only two ways for men to acquire wealth:

1. By producing goods or services and voluntarily exchanging those goods for the product of somebody else. This is the method of exchange, the method of the free market; it's creative and expands production; it benefits both parties. Oppenheimer called this method the "economic means" for the acquisition of wealth.

2. The second method is seizing another person's property without his consent, i.e., by robbery, exploitation, looting, and one person benefits and the expense of the producer.

For Oppenheimer, "the State" is a social institution, forced by a victorious group of men on a defeated group, with the sole purpose of regulating the dominion of the victorious group over the vanquished, and securing itself against revolt from within and attacks from abroad. This dominion has no other purpose than the economic exploitation of the vanquished by the victors. *The State* sketches the two basic means by which men satisfy their material needs: through their own labor or through expropriating the labor of others. The former is the economic means; the latter is the political means.

Major Literature

Oppenheimer, Franz. "A First Program for Zionist Colonization" (1903). In: I.H. Bilski (Ed.), *Means and Ways Towards a Realm of Justice: A Collection of Articles Dedicated to the Memory of Professor Franz Oppenheimer (1864–1943)*. Mesharim, Tel Aviv: 1958, pp. 71–82.

___. *State: Its History and Development Viewed Sociologically*. Indianapolis, Indiana: Bob-Merrill Co., 1914. Manchester, New Hampshire: Ayer Co. Publishers, 1972. New Jersey: Transaction Publishers, 2nd edition, 1999.

___. *The State*. New York: B.W. Huebsch, 1922. New York: Fox and Wilkes, 1997.

___. "A Post-Mortem on Cambridge Economics." *The American Journal of Economics and Sociology*, Vol. 2, No. 3 (1942-1943) 369–376.

Pareto, Vilfredo (1848–1923)

CIRCULATION OF ELITES

Vilfredo Pareto was born in Paris, France, to an exiled noble family; his father was an Italian civil engineer, his mother was French. His family returned to Italy in 1858, where Pareto received a high standard of education. In 1867 he graduated in mathematical sciences and in 1870 gained a doctorate in engineering from what is now the Polytechnic University of Turin. His dissertation was entitled "The Fundamental Principles of Equilibrium in Solid Bodies." His later interest in equilibrium analysis in economics and sociology can be traced back to this paper. Pareto became an engineer and later a director of an Italian railway and was also employed by a large ironworks. Residing in Florence, he studied philosophy and politics and wrote many articles analyzing economic problems employing mathematical tools. In 1893 he was appointed to the chair of political economy at the University of Lausanne, Switzerland, where he remained for the rest of his life.

Pareto's first work, *Cours d'Économie Politique* (1896–1897), included his famous but much-criticized "law of income distribution," a complicated mathematical formulation in which he attempted to prove that the distribution of incomes and wealth in society exhibits a consistent pattern throughout history, in all parts of the world and in all societies. He introduced the concept "Pareto Optimum," which states that in the optimum allocation of resources of a society, improvement is not achieved if one person's situation is made better while others remain the same.

In 1906 he made the famous observation that in Italy, twenty percent of the population owned eighty percent of the property; this was later generalized into the "Pareto Principle" (also termed the 80–20 rule) and generalized further to the concept of a "Pareto Distribution." Believing that there were problems that economics could not solve, Pareto turned to sociology, writing what he considered his greatest work, *Mind and Society* (1916), in which he explored the nature and bases of individual and social action. Pareto saw societies as machines governed by various elites. In his theory of the elites, the lower classes constantly strive to better themselves, challenging the position of the upper-class elite. There is a constant moving in and out of power in an endless cycle that leaves little room for participation by the masses of people. This gave rise to the concept of the "circulation of elites." (See also, Gaetano Mosca and Robert Michels.)

Because of his theory of the superiority of the elite, Pareto sometimes has been associated with fascism. His concept of society as a social system influenced the development of sociology and theories of social action in the United States after World War II.

Major Literature

Pareto, Vilfredo. *Sociological Writings*. Lake Oswego, Oregon: Blackwell Publishers, 1976.

___. *The Other Pareto*. New York: Palgrave Macmillan, 1980.

___. *The Transformation of Democracy*. New Jersey: Transaction Publishers, 1984.
___. *The Rise and Fall of Elites: Application of Theoretical Sociology*. New Jersey: Transaction Publishers, 1991.
___. *Mind and Society* (4 volumes). Whitefish, Montana: R.A. Kessinger Publishing Co., 2003.

Park, Robert Ezra (1864–1944)

HUMAN ECOLOGY

Born in Harveyville, Pennsylvania, Robert Ezra Park grew up in Red Wing, Minnesota, then spent 11 years as a newspaper reporter in various large cities. He earned an A.B. at the University of Michigan, Ann Arbor (1887), and an A.M. in psychology and philosophy at Harvard University, Cambridge, Massachusetts (1899). He studied philosophy and sociology in Berlin (1899–1900) with Georg Simmel (see entry) and gained his Ph.D. in psychology and philosophy at the University of Heidelberg, Germany (1904). He taught at Harvard (1904–1905), the University of Chicago, Illinois (1914–1933), and Fisk University, Nashville, Tennessee (1936–43). At various times Park was president of the American Sociological Association and of the Chicago Urban League, and was a member of the Social Science Research Council.

Major Contributions

In 1892, Park established the world's first sociology department at the University of Chicago. Under him and his colleague, William Isaac Thomas (see entry), this department became the center of the later famous Chicago School of anthropology and sociology. Park's own contribution was mainly to studies of urban subcultures and ethnic minorities, as well as to methodological issues with relevance for these themes.

Park formulated the "melting pot" theory of multiethnic integration, based on his experience of the ethnic mix in Chicago.

In 1906 Park wrote two magazine articles about the oppression of the Congolese by Belgian colonial administrators. Turning to the study of the black population in America, he became secretary to Booker T. Washington and is said to have written most of Washington's *The Man Farthest Down* (1912). Park believed that a caste system produced by sharp ethnic differences, because of the division of labor among the castes, tends to change into a structure of economic classes. Park is noted for his work on ethnic minority groups, particularly African-Americans, and on human ecology (the branch of sociology that studies the characteristics of human populations), a term he is credited with coining.

Park was influential in developing the theory of assimilation (also known as "acculturation") as it pertains to immigrants in the United States. He argued that there are four steps to the Race Relations Cycle in the story of the immigrant: contact, competition, groups accommodate one another, and assimilation occurs when accommodation fails. Groups who do not surrender their own cultures entirely form the basis for "cultural pluralism." Assimilation is a two-way process; incomers lose something but also give something to the host society.

Major Literature

Park, Robert Ezra. *The Man Farthest Down: A Record of Observation and Study in Europe* (with Booker T Washington). New York: Doubleday, 1912.
___. *Introduction to the Science of Sociology* (with Ernest Burgess). Chicago: University of Chicago Press, 1921.
___. *The Immigrant Press and Its Control*. New York: Harper and Brothers, 1922.
___. "Human Migration and the Marginal Man." *American Journal of Sociology* 33 (1928): 881–893.
___. *The Crowd and the Public and Other Essays*.

Chicago, Illinois: University of Chicago Press, 1975.

Parsons, Talcott (1902–1979)
SOCIAL ACTION THEORY

Born at Colorado Springs, Colorado, Talcott Parsons gained a B.A. in biology, leisure and tourism, and philosophy (1924) at Amherst College, Massachusetts. After studying at the London School of Economics, he gained a Ph.D. in sociology and economics (1927) at the University of Heidelberg, Germany. From 1931 to 1973 he was on the faculty of Harvard University, Cambridge, Massachusetts, first as an instructor in economics and sociology, then full professor (1944). He was chairman of Harvard's department of social relations (1946–1956), created by Parsons to reflect his vision of an integrated social science. He retired in 1973. He was elected president of the American Sociological Association in 1949 and served as secretary from 1960 to 1965.

Major Contributions

Parsons' theory of social action had a profound influence on many different branches of sociology, although he was concerned more with creating his grand theory of society — an attempt to integrate all the social sciences into an overarching theoretical framework — than with empirical studies, known as "structural-functionalism." Parsons is credited with uniting clinical psychology and social anthropology with sociology. His work is generally thought to constitute an entire school of social thought. In his first major book, *The Structure of Social Action*, Parsons drew on elements from the works of several European sociologists — Max Weber, Vilfredo Pareto, Émile Durkheim (see entries) and the British economist Alfred Marshall (1842–1924); from their output he attempted to derive a single "action theory" based on the assumptions that human action is voluntary, intentional, and symbolic. This common systematic theory was based on the choices between alternative values, for which actions must be at least partially free.

Unlike Sigmund Freud and Max Weber, for whom socialization arose from the personality of people, Parsons saw socialization arising externally within the institutional structures developed by society. People are socialized into a system by internalizing key values and norms and behave in ways that support the system's needs in order to keep it alive and functioning. Later, Parsons became intrigued with, and involved in, medical sociology; he developed the concept of the sick role and studied in psychoanalysis, personally undergoing full training as a lay analyst; anthropology; small group dynamics, working extensively with the psychologist Robert Freed Bales (1916–2004); race relations; economics; and education.

Major Literature

Parsons, Talcott. *The Structure of Social Action.* New York: McGraw-Hill, Inc., 1937. New York: Free Press, 1967.

___, and Robert Freed Bales. *Family: Socialization and Interaction Process.* New York: Free Press, 1955. New York: Taylor and Francis Books, Ltd., Routledge, 1998.

Parsons, Talcott, and Neil J. Smelser. *Economy and Society: A Study in the Integration of Economic and Social Theory.* New York: Taylor and Francis Books, Ltd., Routledge, 1956, 1998.

Parsons, Talcott. *Sociological Theory and Modern Society.* New York: Free Press, 1968.

___. *The Social System.* New York: Free Press, 1951. New York: Taylor and Francis Books, Ltd., Routledge, 1970.

___. *Action Theory and the Human Condition.* New York: Free Press, 1978.

Patterson, Orlando (1940–)

SOCIOLOGY OF SLAVERY

Born in Savlamar, Jamaica, Orlando Patterson gained a B.Sc. at the University College of the West Indies, studied economics at London University (honors: external) (1962), and earned a Ph.D. in sociology (1965) at the London School of Economics, where he was assistant lecturer in sociology (1965–1967). He was lecturer in sociology, University of the West Indies (1967–1970). At Harvard University, Cambridge, Massachusetts, he was professor of sociology (1971); Cowles Professor of Sociology (1993); chair, Committee on Higher Degrees, Department of Sociology (1986–1992); and acting chairman, Department of Sociology (1989–1990). Patterson has been Phi Beta Kappa visiting professor, and visiting professor at Doshisha University in Japan, University of Stockholm in Sweden, and the University of Chicago. He was visiting scholar at Universitat Trier, Federal Republic of Germany; visiting fellow, Wolfson College, Cambridge University, England; and visiting member, Institute for Advanced Study, Princeton, New Jersey.

His awards and honors include Best Novel in English, Dakar Festival of Negro Arts (1965); Ralph Bunche Award for the Best Scholarly Work on Pluralism (co-winner) (1983); Distinguished Contribution to Scholarship (formerly Sorokin Prize), American Sociological Association (1983); chair, Political Economy of the World System, American Sociological Association (1990–1991); Walter Channing Cabot Faculty Prize, Harvard, University (1997); and Order of Distinction, Government of Jamaica (1999). Patterson was associate editor, *American Sociological Review* (1989–1992). He received honorary degrees from the universities of Harvard, Cambridge, Massachusetts; Trinity College, Connecticut; The New School,

New York; Northeastern University, Boston, Massachusetts; and the University of Chicago, Illinois. He was fellow, American Academy of Arts and Sciences; Ernest W. Burgess Fellow, American Academy of Political and Social Sciences; and member, American Sociological Association. He was a member of the Technical Advisory Council, Government of Jamaica (1972–1974), and founding member, Board of Cultural Survival, Inc., Cambridge, Massachusetts (1975).

Major Contributions

Patterson's major focus of research was and is slavery. His academic interests have moved in three main directions:

1. the comparative study of slavery aimed at an understanding of power at its limits on both the personal and systemic levels
2. the study of its antithesis, freedom
3. the study of socio-economic underdevelopment with special reference to Jamaica and the Caribbean Basin.

During his tenure as special advisor for social policy and development to Prime Minister Michael Manley of Jamaica (1972–1980), Patterson explored the problem of underdevelopment on the Caribbean in many papers and in many policy-oriented reports prepared for the government of Jamaica. His study of slavery and domination prompted interest in, and the study of, the nature and development of its shadow concept, freedom. He has published a number of anthologized short stories, numerous reviews and critical essays, and three novels, *The Children of Sisyphus* (Hutchinson, U.K., 1964), *An Absence of Ruins* (Hutchinson, U.K., 1967) and *Die the Long Day* (William Morrow, U.S., 1972).

Major Literature

Patterson, Orlando. *The Sociology of Slavery: Jamaica, 1655–1838*. London, England: MacGibbon and Kee, 1967. Cranbury, New Jersey, Associated University Presses, 1969.

____. *Slavery and Social Death: A Comparative Study*. Cambridge, Massachusetts: Harvard University Press, 1982, 2005.

____. *The Ordeal of Integration: Progress and Resentment in America's "Racial" Crisis*. Washington, D.C.: Counterpoint/Civitas, 1997.

____. *Rituals of Blood: Consequences of Slavery in Two American Centuries*. Washington, D.C.: Counterpoint/Civitas, 1999.

Piven, Frances Fox (1932–)

SOCIOLOGY OF REFORM

Frances Fox Piven was born in Calgary, Alberta, Canada, moved to the U.S. in 1933 and became an American citizen in 1953. At the University of Chicago, Illinois, she gained a B.A. in city planning (1953), an M.A. (1956), and a Ph.D. (1962). She is distinguished professor of the Political Science and Sociology Graduate School and University Center, City University of New York.

Her awards and honors: Guggenheim Fellowship (1973); Council of Learned Societies Fellowship (1982); the Eugene V. Debs Foundation Prize, for "published work which evidences social vision and commitment to social justice" (1986); Fulbright Distinguished Lectureship at the University of Bologna, Italy (1990); Lee/Founders Award of the Society for the Study of Social Problems, for "distinguished career-long contributions to the solution of social problems" (1991); President's Award of the American Public Health Association (1993); Annual Award of the National Association of Secretaries of State, for her work in the field of voter registration reform (1994); Tides Foundation Award for Excellence in Public Advocacy (1995); first recipient of the Lifetime Achievement Award of the Political Sociology Section of the American Sociological Association (1995); the Mary Lepper Award from the Women's Caucus of the American Political Science Association (1998); and Distinguished Career Award for the Practice of Sociology, American Sociological Association (2000).

Major Contributions

Piven is recognized as one of America's most thoughtful and provocative commentators on America's social welfare system. Her *Regulating the Poor*—winner of the C. Wright Mills Award in 1972, and co-authored with Richard Cloward — is a landmark historical and theoretical analysis of the role of welfare policy in the economic and political control of the poor and working class in the United States. In it, Piven and Cloward argue that any advances the poor have made throughout history were directly proportional to their ability to disrupt institutions that depend upon their cooperation. Inspired by the August 1965 riots in the black district of Watts in Los Angeles, Piven and Cloward published "The Weight of the Poor: A Strategy to End Poverty" in the May 2, 1966, issue of *The Nation*. From this, the "Cloward-Piven Strategy" was created.

Piven's work with the Human Service Employees Registration and Voter Education Campaign culminated in the 1994 passage of the National Voter Registration Act, or the "Motor-Voter" bill, designed to increase voter registration, especially among low-income groups.

Major Literature

Piven, Frances Fox. *Regulating the Poor*. London, England: Tavistock Publications, 1972. New York: Random House Inc., Vintage, 1993.

____. *The New Class War: Reagan's Attack on the Welfare State and Its Consequences*. New York: Pantheon Books, 1982, updated 1985.

____. *The Breaking of the American Social Compact*. London, England: The New Press, 1997.

___, and Richard A. Cloward. *Why Americans Still Don't Vote: And Why Politicians Want It That Way*. Boston, Massachusetts: Beacon Press, 2000.

Piven, Frances Fox. *The War at Home: The Domestic Costs of Bush's Militarism*. London, England: The New Press, new edition, 2006.

Porter, John Arthur (1921–1979)

SOCIAL STRATIFICATION

Born in Vancouver, Canada, John Arthur Porter completed his education at the London School of Economics (LSE) in England. While at the LSE, he became interested in studies of social class. On returning to Canada he joined the faculty of Carleton University, Ottawa, Ontario, Canada. He remained at Carleton as a professor and, later, as department chairman, dean and academic vice-president. Porter was also visiting professor at Harvard University, Cambridge, Massachusetts, and the University of Toronto. He was director of the Social Science Division at Carleton University from 1963 to 1966 and vice-president (academic) during 1977–1978. For many years he was a member and later chairman of the Subcommittee on Research and Planning of the Committee of Presidents of the Universities of Ontario; he helped to plan Ontario's postsecondary educational system.

Porter's work in the field of social stratification opened up new areas of inquiry for many sociologists in Canada. Regarded by many as Canada's leading sociologist, he published in 1965 his most important work, *The Vertical Mosaic: An Analysis of Social Class and Power in Canada*, a study of equality of opportunity and the exercise of power by bureaucratic, economic and political elites in Canada. Porter's chief concerns were to challenge the image that Canada was a classless society, which had no barriers to opportunity. Porter concluded that Canada, like other developed nations, relied heavily on its elite groups to make major decisions and to determine the shape and direction of its development. He saw this as inevitable; older models were no longer appropriate. However, accepting the situation — that power and decision-making must always rest with elite groups — adequate safeguards should be put in place to ensure open recruitment from all classes into the elite.

The Vertical Mosaic was influential in formulating multiculturalism policy in Canada and has led to the adoption of the term *cultural mosaic* by Canadian government agencies such as Statistics Canada. "Cultural mosaic" describes the "patchwork quilt" of ethnic groups, languages and cultures that co-exist within Canadian society. The idea of a cultural mosaic is intended to champion an ideal of multiculturalism to contrast with that of a melting pot, which is often used to describe the United States' supposed ideal of assimilation. The "vertical" implies that these ethnic and racial groups are arranged into a hierarchy. A similar term would be ethnic stratification.

Porter, along with Peter Pineo, developed the Pineo-Porter index of socioeconomic status (1971). Shortly before his death Porter put together what he regarded as his 10 most significant essays in a volume, entitled *The Measure of Canadian Society: Education, Equality, and Opportunity* (Canada: Carleton University Press, 1979). In honor of Porter and his importance in the development of sociology in Canada, the Canadian Sociology and Anthropology Association now has an annual award called the Porter Award.

Portes, Alejandro (1944–)

IMMIGRATION AND URBANIZATION

Born in Havana, Cuba, Alejandro Portes gained a B.A. in sociology at Creighton

University, Omaha, Nebraska (1965), and a PhD. In sociology at the University of Wisconsin, Madison (1970). He was assistant professor of sociology, University of Illinois, Urbana-Champaign (1970–1971); tenured associate professor and associate director of Latin American studies at the University of Texas, Austin (1971–1975); professor, Duke University, Durham, North Carolina (1975–1979); and professor of sociology, Johns Hopkins University, Baltimore (1981–1997).

He has been at Princeton University's Department of Sociology since 1997 and currently serves as chair, and he co-founded the Center for Migration and Development (1998). He was elected fellow, American Academy of Arts and Sciences (1998); was 90th president, American Sociological Association (1999); and fellow, National Academy of Sciences (2001). He received an honorary doctorate from the University of Wisconsin (1998).

Major Contributions

Professor Portes' main interests are immigration, economic sociology, comparative development, and Third World urbanization. His presidential address — "The Hidden Abode: Sociology as Analysis of the Unexpected" — was published in the *American Sociological Review* (65, No. 1 [2000]: 1–18). During his time at Duke, Portes spent a year in Brazil as a program adviser for the Ford Foundation conducting a study on housing policy and the urban slums of Rio de Janeiro, during the military dictatorship. For another year, he was a fellow at the Center for Advanced Study in the Behavioral Sciences in Stanford, California.

He has spent his career tracking the lives of different immigrant nationalities in the United States and has chronicled the causes and consequences of immigration to the United States, with an emphasis on informal economies, transnational communities, and ethnic enclaves. He examined the inte-

gration of Cuban refugees who landed in southern Florida from Mariel, Cuba, in the late 1980s. Portes and his colleague Rubén G. Rumbaut (see entry) of Michigan State University launched a project called the Children of Immigrants Longitudinal Study (CILS) in the school systems of Miami, Fort Lauderdale, and San Diego. The key concept that came out of CILS was that of "segmented assimilation," integration into different segments of American society rather than into one mainstream community. He has also researched Colombian, Dominican, and Salvadorian immigrant groups settling in different regions of the United States.

While pursuing his academic career, Portes has participated actively in the politics of reconciliation between the United States and Cuba, for example as a founding member of the Cuban Committee for Democracy. He has served on the editorial boards of several journals dealing with immigration.

Major Literature

Portes, Alejandro, and Harley L. Browning (Eds.). *Current Perspectives in Latin American Urban Research.* Austin, Texas: University of Texas Press, 1977.
Portes, Alejandro (Ed.). *The New Second Generation.* New York: Russell Sage Foundation, 1996.
____. *The Economic Sociology of Immigration: Essays on Networks, Ethnicity and Entrepreneurship.* New York: Russell Sage Foundation, 1998.
Portes, Alejandro, and Rubén G. Rumbaut. *Immigrant America: A Portrait.* Berkeley, California: University of California Press; 3rd edition, 2006.

Queen, Stuart Alfred (1890–1987)

SOCIAL WORK AND SOCIOLOGY

Born in Fredonia, Kansas, Stuart Alfred Queen gained an A.B. degree at Pomona

College, Claremont, California, where he majored in Greek, and earned an A.M. at the University of Chicago, Illinois. Queen was executive secretary of the California Board of Charities and Corrections (1913–1917) and director, Texas School of Civics and Philanthropy (1917–1918). He gained a Ph.D. at the University of Chicago (1919) and was director of educational service for the Potomac Division of the American Red Cross.

He was also associate professor of social technology at Goucher College, Baltimore, Maryland (1919–1920); head of the Simmons School of Social Work, Boston, Massachusetts (1920–1922); professor of sociology, University of Kansas, Lawrence (1922–1930); and executive, Community Fund, Detroit, Michigan (1930–1932). At Washington University, St. Louis, Missouri, Queen was professor of sociology (1932–1946) and dean of the College of Liberal Arts (1946–1949). He was 31st president of the American Sociological Society (Association, 1959) (1941).

Major Contributions

In his presidential address — "Can Sociologists Face Reality?" — Queen recounts the problems brought about by economic depression, armament races, bureaucracy and centralization, dictatorships, urbanism, family decline, and other issues. He noted that sociologists are called upon to furnish factual data and some interpretations for certain social phenomena. This means that sociological research is the means by which sociologists play roles in contemporary society, especially with reference to governments. He also pointed to the need for more information about cultural lags, the social processes involved in revolution, changing values (social security vs. individual thrift, production for use rather than for profits, home ownership, international peace, "the art of living" rather than "making a living," etc.). The sociologist must study origins, processes, and trends in a scientific manner.

For sixteen years Queen developed research projects that reached into both sociology and social work, and concluded that they have more points of contact than differences, and that sociology was fundamental to the practice of social work. Sociology, however, had to develop specific applications and academic course work that relates to the real world. He stressed that students should be helped to assemble reliable information about significant problems; to think clearly about them; analyze situations to see what they are, how they came to be, what are their implications; are there any alternative possibilities; if so, what they are, and at what cost might they be realized. Queen knew what it was like to work at the grass roots level as a social worker and could speak with authority on the role of the social worker and the contribution of sociology to social work.

Major Literature

___. *Social Work in the Light of History*. Philadelphia, Pennsylvania: J.B. Lippincott Company, 1922.
___. *Social Pathology*. New York: Thomas Y. Crowell, 1925.
___. *Social Organization and Disorganization*. New York: Thomas Y. Crowell, 1935.
___. *Research Memorandum on Social Work in the Depression*. New York: Social Science Research Council, 1937.
___. Lewis Francis Thomas. *The City*. New York: McGraw-Hill Book Company, 1939.
Queen, Stuart Alfred, and David Bailey Carpenter. *The American City*. New York: McGraw-Hill Book Company, 1953. London, England: Greenwood Press, 1972.

Quételet, Adolphe Jacques Lambert (1796–1874)

SOCIAL PHYSICS

Born in Ghent, Flanders, Belgium, Adolphe Quételet is considered the founder of modern statistics and demography. In 1819 he gained his doctorate in mathematics at the University of Ghent and was appointed to the chair of elementary mathematics at the Athenaeum. Shortly thereafter he was elected to membership in the Royal Academy of Sciences and Belles-lettres of Brussels. In 1823 he went to Paris to study astronomy, meteorology, and the management of an astronomical observatory. In 1828 he founded the Royal Observatory in Brussels and directed it until he died. He served as perpetual secretary of the Belgian Royal Academy (1834–1874) and organized the first International Statistical Congress (1853).

For the Dutch and Belgian governments, he collected and analyzed statistics on crime, mortality, and other subjects and devised improvements in census taking. He also developed methods for simultaneous observations of astronomical, meteorological, and geodetic phenomena from scattered points throughout Europe. He was influential in introducing statistical methods to the social sciences.

In *Sur l'homme et le développement de ses facultés, ou essai de physique sociale* (1835; *A Treatise on Man and the Development of His Faculties*), he presented his conception of the *homme moyen* ("average man") as the central value about which measurements of a human trait are grouped according to the "normal distribution." According to Quételet's "theory of oscillation," as social contacts increase and racial groups intermarry, differences between men will decrease in intensity through a process of social and cultural oscillation, resulting in an ever-increasing balance and, eventually, international equilibrium and world peace. This new science of "social physics" would discover the laws of society upon which human happiness depends.

His studies of the numerical constancy of such presumably voluntary acts as crimes stimulated extensive studies in "moral statistics" and wide discussion of free will versus social determinism. In trying to discover through statistics the causes of antisocial acts, Quételet conceived of the idea of relative propensity to crime of specific age groups. This idea, like his *homme moyen*, evoked great controversy among social scientists in the 19th century.

Although the science of probability and statistics was mainly used in astronomy at the time, Quételet was among the first who attempted to apply it to social science, planning what he called a "social physics." His goal was to understand the statistical laws underlying such phenomena as crime rates, marriage rates or suicide rates. Quételet was an influential figure in criminology. In criminology, using statistical analysis, Quételet gained insight into the relationships between crime and other social factors. Among his findings were strong relationships between age and crime, as well as gender and crime. Other influential factors he found included climate, poverty, education, and alcohol consumption. In public health Quételet established the Body Mass Index, which remains the only widely recognized raw material for obesity statistics and the policy discussions related to them.

Major Literature

Quételet, Adolphe Jacques Lambert. *Treatise of Man and the Development of His Faculties.* New York: Burt Franklin, 1968.

Reskin, Barbara F.
SOCIAL JUSTICE

Barbara F. Reskin was born in St. Paul, Minnesota. At the University of Washington, Seattle, she gained a B.A. (1968), M.A. (1970) and Ph.D. in sociology (1973). Reskin was acting assistant professor, University of California, Davis (1971); assistant, associate professor of sociology, Indiana

University, Bloomington (1973–1983); study director, Committee on Women's Employment and Related Social Issues, National Research Council/National Academy of Sciences, Washington, D.C. (1981–1982); professor of sociology and women's studies, University of Michigan, Ann Arbor (1983–1985); professor of sociology and director of graduate studies, University of Illinois, Urbana (1985–1991); and visiting scholar, Institute for Research on Women and Gender, Stanford University, California (1987).

At Ohio State University, Athens, she was professor of sociology (1991–1997) and chair, Department of Sociology (1993–1995). She was professor of sociology, Harvard University, Cambridge, Massachusetts (1997–2002); chair of the American Sociological Association Section on Occupations, Organizations, and Work (1997–1998); Simon Visiting Professor, Manchester University, Manchester, U.K. (1999); 93rd president, American Sociological Association (2002); and S. Frank Miyamoto Professor of Sociology, University of Washington, Seattle (2002).

Her awards and honors include the Distinguished Scholar Award, on Sex and Gender, American Sociological Association Section (1995); distinguished professorship, Ohio State University (1997); and fellow, National Academy of Science (2006).

Major Contributions

Reskin's presidential address, "Modeling Ascriptive Inequality — From Motives to Mechanisms," was published in *American Sociological Review* (68, No. 1 [February 2003]: 1–21). In it, she states that sociologists need to develop four levels of analysis in order to contribute meaningfully to social policies that will promote social equality: intrapsychic, interpersonal, societal, and organizational.

At a young age she was involved in the Congress on Racial Equality, for which she organized rent strikes, participated in sit-ins, and helped to organize a summer Freedom School. She experienced first-hand American racism against black people. With fellow student Lynn White, she started the Reproductive Counseling Center at the University of Washington, which gave undergraduates information about birth control.

Reskin's study of social stratification spotlighted discrimination in academia. She discovered great resistance in academic circles to studying the sociology of inequality from a feminist perspective. During her tenure at Indiana, Reskin spent a sabbatical year at the National Academy of Sciences, directing a study of sex segregation in the workplace. From her studies she concludes that no one will necessarily act on social science research that shows a situation or process to be unfair or discriminatory. Even writing about it is not enough; social scientists need to seek people out and tell them. This is what Reskin does.

Major Literature

Reskin, Barbara F., *Sex Differences in the Professional Life Changes of Chemists*. Manchester, New Hampshire: Ayer Co. Publishers, 1980.
___. *Sex Segregation in the Workplace: Trends, Explanations, Remedies*. Washington, D.C.: National Academy Press, 1985.
___, and Patricia A. Roos. *Job Queues, Gender Queues: Explaining Women's Inroads into Male Occupations*. Philadelphia, Pennsylvania: Temple University Press, 1991.
___, and Irene Padavic. *Women and Men at Work*. Thousand Oaks, California; Sage, 2002.

Reuter, Edward Byron (1880–1946)
SOCIOLOGY OF RACE

Born in Holden, Missouri, Edward Byron Reuter gained A.B. and B.S. degrees (1910) and an M.A. (1911) at the University of Missouri, St. Louis. He was then principal of a high school in Tuolumne, California (1911–1914). He gained a Ph.D., with honors, at the University of Chicago, Illinois (1919), and was then professor of sociology, Goucher College, Baltimore, Maryland (1919), and professor of sociology and director of the Red Cross School of Social Work, Tulane University, New Orleans (1920).

At State University of Iowa, Ames, Reuter was associate professor of sociology (1921–1924); professor of sociology; and chairman of the department of sociology (1924–1944). He was also professor of sociology and consultant in racial research, Fisk University, Nashville, Tennessee (1944–1946); fellow of the American Association for the Advancement of Science (1928); 22nd president, American Sociological Society (1933); visiting professor, University of Hawaii, Honolulu (1930–1931); University of Puerto Rico (1941–1942); secretary-treasurer of the Sociological Research Association (1936–1938); and president (1939). He was a summer lecturer at the universities of Colorado, Boulder (1928); Cornell, Ithaca, New York (1930); Michigan, East Lansing, Michigan (1939); and Stanford, California (1941). From 1928 to 1946 Reuter was consulting editor of the McGraw-Hill "Publications in Sociology" series and advisory editor of *The American Journal of Sociology*.

Major Contributions

In his 1928 presidential address, Reuter focused on the theme of "Race and Culture Contact." During the period 1917 to 1946 he published over thirty major articles in various professional journals and over 115 reviews of contemporary books in the field of sociology. Reuter's work falls into three definite areas of sociological interest: race and culture, population, and sociological theory. Five of his books, nearly two-thirds of his articles and more than one-half of his reviews deal with race problems or population theory, or consider the nature of the relationship between biological and social phenomena. Nearly all his other works are systematic presentations of general sociological theory or discussions of specific questions within the general realm of theory. He made several brief excursions into other areas, such as the family, the sociological theory of adolescent behavior, education, social work, and birth control.

Major Literature

Reuter, Edward Byron. *Population Problems*. New York: J.B. Lippincott, 1905, 1923, revised, 1937.
____. *The Mulatto in the United States*. London, England: Greenwood Press, 1918. Honolulu, Hawaii: University Press of the Pacific, 2004.
____. *The American Race Problem*. New York: Thomas Y. Crowell, 1927, revised, 1938.
____. *Race Mixtures*. London, England: Greenwood Press, 1931.
____(Ed.). *The Family*. Whitby, Ontario, Canada: McGraw-Hill, 1931.
____. *Introduction to Sociology*. Whitby, Ontario, Canada: McGraw-Hill, 1933.
____(Ed.). *Race and Culture Contacts*. New York: D.C. Heath and Company, 1934.
____, and Clyde W. Hart. *Handbook of Sociology*. New York: The Dryden Press, 1941, 1950.

Riesman, David (1909–2002)
SOCIAL SYSTEMS

Born in Philadelphia, Pennsylvania, David Riesman gained an A.B. (1931) and LL.B. (1934) from Harvard University Law School Cambridge, Massachusetts. Riesman served as clerk to U.S. Supreme Court Justice Louis D. Brandeis (1935–1936) and taught law at the University of Buffalo (now State University of New York at Buffalo) (1937–1941). He was a professor of social sciences at the University of Chicago, Illinois (1946–1958), and from 1958–1980 he was

Henry Ford II Professor of Social Sciences at Harvard until he retired. He then joined the new sociology department, focusing on his celebrated undergraduate course, "American Character and Social Structure."

Although Riesman had no formal training in sociology, he ranks as an influential American sociologist and author most noted for *The Lonely Crowd: A Study of the Changing American Character* (1950), a work dealing primarily with the social character of the urban middle class. "The lonely crowd" became a catchphrase denoting modern urban society in which the individual feels alienated.

Also entering common speech were the labels he applied to three character types he identified in the book: "tradition-directed," "inner-directed," and "other-directed." Tradition-directed relates to pre-industrial societies with personal values being determined by the traditions of a highly structured society or by power relations within its major divisions, such as classes, professions, castes, or clans. Inner-directed relates to societies when the population is growing but has not reached the stage of crowding (e.g., western Europe from the Renaissance to the early 20th century). Personal values — determined early by the immediate family — are not necessarily related to any wider social forces, and are also likely to remain unchanged. Other-directed societies are heavily industrialized societies, where the population is dense and perhaps beginning to decline. Life is in large part shaped by "peer groups" of persons of similar age, social class, or otherwise, and values are adjusted to conform to those of his group in a constant process of change.

Riesman argued that as conformity and the fear of losing the approval of others become increasingly important — especially in corporate settings — people grow increasingly anxious and "other-directed." This contrasts with being "inner-directed" and depending on a deeper and more stable sense of personal identity and integrity.

Major Literature

Riesman, David. *Faces in the Crowd: Individual Studies in Character and Politics*. New Haven, Connecticut: Yale University Press, 1952.
___. *Individualism Reconsidered and Other Essays*. New York: The Free Press, 1964.
___. *Academic Values and Mass Education*. Columbus, Ohio: McGraw-Hill Education, 1975.
___. *Abundance for What?* New Jersey: Transaction Publishers, 1993.
___. *On Higher Education: The Academic Enterprise in an Era of Rising Student Consumerism*. New Jersey: Transaction Publishers, 1998.
___, Nathan Glazer, and Reuel Denney. *The Lonely Crowd: A Study of the Changing American Character*. New Haven, Connecticut: Yale University Press, 2001.

Riley, Matilda White (1911–2004)

SOCIOLOGY OF AGING

Matilda White was born in Boston, Massachusetts, but was raised in Brunswick, Maine, by her grandmother, who adopted her following the death of her uncle and grandfather in the sinking of the *Titanic*. She earned both her bachelor's and master's degrees from Simmons College, Radcliffe College, Cambridge, Massachusetts. She married John (Jack) Riley (1908–2002) in 1931 and remained married until Jack died. They were frequent co-authors of professional papers, starting in the 1930s with the publication of a joint scientific paper on contraceptive behavior. Riley was a student of Talcott Parsons (see entry) at Harvard University, Cambridge, Massachusetts. She taught at Rutgers University, New Jersey, from 1950 to 1973.

Major Contributions

A pioneer in the field of social gerontology, Riley was the first woman to be named a full professor and chair of the Department of Sociology and Anthropology at Bowdoin College, Brunswick, Maine (1973 to 1981), and afterward remained an active part-time professor emeritus. The founding director of the National Institute on Aging (NIA), Dr. Robert Butler, recruited Riley to set up and direct the NIA's behavioral and social science program in 1979. She continued her work at the NIA and the National Institutes of Health for over twenty years. During that time she also served as president of the American Sociological Association (ASA) in 1985, co-president (with her husband) of the District of Columbia Sociological Society (1984–1985), and chair of the ASA Section on Aging (1989). In 2000, she returned to Bowdoin College as honorary research professor in sociology.

Riley challenged scientists, policy makers, and students alike to think of aging as a sociological and psychological as well as a biological process — this was unheard of at that time — and she argued that the realities of aging were far more positive than the prevailing stereotype would have us believe. One of her favorite sayings was, "people don't grow up and grow old in laboratories — they grow up and grow old in changing societies."

Matilda White Riley House, home of the Department of Sociology and Anthropology at Bowdoin College, was dedicated on May 8, 1996. In addition to Riley House, her name is found on an undergraduate prize, as well as the Matilda and John Riley Fund for Sociology and Anthropology, which, according to Bowdoin's Alumni website, promotes "the education of students in sociology and anthropology through engagement in the research of faculty, in their own independent research, and in the professional worlds of the two disciplines."

Major Literature

Riley, Matilda White. *Sociological Research*. New York: Harcourt, Brace and Company, 1963.

___(Ed.). *Aging and Society: An Inventory of Research Findings*. New York: Russell Sage Foundation, 1971.

Merton, Robert K., and Matilda White Riley. *Sociological Traditions from Generation to Generation*. Norwood, New Jersey: Ablex Publishing Corporation, U.S., 1981.

Riley, Matilda White (Ed.). *Aging from Birth to Death*. Boulder, Colorado: Westview Press, Inc., 1982.

___(Ed.). *Social Change and the Life Course: Social Structures and Human Lives* (3 volumes). London, England: Sage Publications, Ltd., 1988.

Ritzer, George (1940–)
SOCIOLOGY OF CONSUMPTION

Born in New York City, George Ritzer graduated from Bronx High School of Science and then gained a B.A. in psychology (1962) at City College of New York and an M.B.A. (1964) at the University of Michigan, Ann Arbor, then worked in personnel management for the Ford Motor Company. He gained a Ph.D. in organizational behavior at the School of Labor and Industrial Relations, Cornell University, Ithaca, New York (1968). He was assistant professor, Tulane University, New Orleans (1968–1970) and associate professor, University of Kansas (1970–1974). At the University of Maryland, College Park, he was professor (1974–2001) and distinguished university professor (2001). Ritzer was visiting professor at the universities of Surrey, England (1984, 1990); Shanghai and Peking, China (1988); Tampere, Finland (1996); Bremen, Germany (2001); and l'Associazione per l'Istituzione della Libera Università Nuorese, Sardinia, Italy (2002, 2004, 2005, 2006).

His honors and awards include the Fulbright-Hays Fellowship to the Netherlands (1975); fellow-in-residence, Netherlands Institute for Advanced Study (1980–1981); University of Maryland, Behavioral and

Social Sciences Teaching Excellence Award (1985–1986); Distinguished Scholar-Teacher (1984–1985); fellow-in-residence, Swedish Collegium for Advanced Study in the Social Sciences (1989); UNESCO chair in social theory, Russian Academy of Sciences (1992); Panhellenic Association Outstanding Teacher Award (1995); Distinguished Contributions to Teaching Award, American Sociological Association (2000); First Fulbright Chair at York University, Toronto, Ontario, Canada (2001); honorary doctorate from LaTrobe University, Victoria, Australia (2004); and honorary patron, University Philosophical Society, Trinity College, Dublin, Ireland (2006).

Major Contributions

A largely self-taught sociologist, Ritzer is most widely known for his contributions to the study of:

1. *Consumption*— often the source of the most unreasonable features of contemporary social life, particularly as experienced in the world's dominant postindustrial societies
2. *Globalization*—generally referring to the rapidly increasing world-wide integration and interdependence of societies and cultures
3. *Metatheory*— which analyzes the strengths and weaknesses of a variety of major and less common models of society and culture.

Ritzer is an academic celebrity as a result of *The McDonaldization of Society* (Thousand Oaks, California: Sage, 4th edition, 2004; first published in 1993), which is among the most popular monographs ever penned by a sociologist. Ritzer is prolific writer of articles, textbooks and encyclopedias (including the massive *Blackwell Encyclopedia of Sociology*, 2006). As popular as his books are, he has been criticized for pandering to the mass audiences by simplifying complex ideas and theories to increase book sales; for theories critics say lack substance; and by Marxists, for not recognizing capitalism as the principal cause of McDonaldization.

Major Literature

Ritzer, George. *Explorations in Social Theory: From Metatheorizing to Rationalization.* Thousand Oaks, California: Sage, 2001.
___. *Contemporary Sociological Theory and Its Classical Roots: The Basics.* Columbus, Ohio: McGraw-Hill, Education, 2002.
___. *Modern Sociological Theory.* Columbus, Ohio: McGraw-Hill, Education, 6th edition, 2003.
___. *The Globalization of Nothing.* Thousand Oaks, California: Sage, 2003.
___(Ed.). *The Blackwell Companion to Major Contemporary Social Theorists.* Ames, Iowa: Blackwell Publishing, 2003.
___(Ed.). *Encyclopedia of Social Theory.* Thousand Oaks, California: Sage, 2004.
___. *McDonaldization: The Reader.* Thousand Oaks, California: Sage; 2nd edition, 2006.

Rose, Arnold Marshall (1918–1968)

SOCIOLOGY AND LAW

Arnold Marshall Rose was born in Chicago, Illinois. At the University of Chicago, he earned an A.B. in sociology (1938), an A.B. in economics (1939), an M.A. in sociology (1940), and a Ph.D. in sociology (1946). He was professor of sociology, Bennington College, Bennington, Vermont (1946–1947), and associate professor of sociology, Washington University, St. Louis, Missouri (1947–1949). At the University of Minnesota, Minneapolis, he was associate professor of sociology, (1949–1952) and professor of sociology (1952–1968). He was elected to the Minnesota Legislature from the 41st District in 1962 and represented that district from 1963 to 1965. He declined a second term when he learned he had terminal cancer, from which he died.

Major Contributions

Rose was regarded as a president of the American Sociological Association even though he died a few months before he was to take office. His presidential address was read at the 1969 annual meeting by his widow. In 1967, Rose and his wife donated $200,000 to the American Sociological Association to establish the Arnold and Caroline Rose Fund as a legacy to scholarly publication.

Rose strove to educate all people involved in law-making and law-enforcement of the principles of sociology and about the nature of man and society. He saw this as being more important and worthwhile than constructing theories. Troubled because so much social theory was inadequate precisely because it failed to consider law as a factor in social change, he undertook to remove this "blind spot," as he called it.

He believed that legislation against discrimination was an important means of breaking tradition of prejudice but not sufficient by itself. He pointed to the sociological input in the United States Supreme Court decision that led to the desegregation of schools as evidence that sociology did have a vital input to social justice. He was honored by being named co-chairman, with the historian John Hope Franklin, of the 100th anniversary of the Emancipation Proclamation celebration at Wayne State University in Detroit, Michigan, in 1963. At the Emancipation Centennial he said: "The changes may seem slow to those who labor under discrimination ... but the changes are coming."

Rose believed passionately in the American Creed and lived his life by it. He was also a champion of trade unions and what they had achieved for liberty and equality.

Active in building bridges between law and social sciences on the national level, he helped to found the Law and Society Association and served on the editorial advisory board of the *Law and Society Review* published by the association.

Major Literature

Rose, Arnold Marshall. *America Divided*. New York: Knopf, 1950.

___. *The Roots of Prejudice*. Paris: UNESCO, 1951.

___. *Mental Health and Mental Disorder: A Sociological Approach*. London, England: Routledge and Kegan Paul, 1956.

___. *Libel and Academic Freedom: A Lawsuit Against Political Extremists*. Minneapolis, Minnesota: University of Minnesota Press, 1968.

Myrdal, Gunnar, Richard Sterner, Edvard Mauritz, and Arnold Marshall Rose. *An American Dilemma: The Negro Problem and Modern Democracy; 001*. New York: Random House, Inc., 1975.

Ross, Edward Alsworth (1866–1951)

SOCIAL CONTROL

Born at Virden, Illinois, Edward Alsworth Ross gained a B.A. at Coe College, Cedar Rapids, Iowa (1886), then taught at Ford Dodge Commercial Institute in Iowa (1886–1888) and did graduate study at the University of Berlin. He gained a Ph.D. in economics at the Johns Hopkins University, Baltimore, Maryland (1891). He was professor, Indiana University, Bloomington (1891–1892); secretary, American Economic Association (1892); professor, Cornell University, Ithaca, New York (1892); professor of administration and finance, Leland Stanford University, California (1893–1900); and was at University of Nebraska, Lincoln (1901–1905). At the University of Wisconsin, Madison, he was professor of sociology, then department chairman (1906–1937).

He was fifth president of the American Sociological Society (1914 and 1915); he sponsored sessions on freedom of expression and helped create the American Association of University Professors. He retired in 1937.

Major Contributions

Following his dismissal from Stanford in 1900 — because of his political views on populism — several other Stanford faculty members resigned in protest. A national debate ensued concerning the freedom of expression and control of universities by private interests. From this grew the organized movement to protect tenured academics.

Ross was a founder of sociology in the United States and one of the first sociologists to pursue a comprehensive sociological theory. He was an advocate of the application of sociology for the benefit of social reform. In addition to his work on social reform in the United States, he published many books on social conditions in Europe, Asia, and Africa. In 1917 he went to Russia to report on the Bolshevik Revolution and for many years advocated recognition of the Soviet Union by the U.S. government and an appreciation of the improvements the Soviets brought to the economic and social life of the Russian people.

In his early career Ross upheld the view of the superiority of the Anglo-Saxon peoples and advocated immigration restriction to prevent a large-scale influx of southern and eastern Europeans to the United States. In the 1920s he supported eugenics and the nationwide prohibition of liquor. By 1930 Ross shed these notions and spent the greater part of his efforts promoting the New Deal reform and the freedoms of the individual. He served as the national chairman of the American Civil Liberties Union (1940–1950). Ross believed that the primary purpose of the field of sociology was to identify and cure the ills of society.

Major Literature

Ross, Edward Alsworth. *Social Control: A Survey of the Foundations of Order.* The Macmillan Company, 1901. University Press of the Pacific, 2002.

___. *Principles of Sociology.* New York, The Century Co., 1905.

___. *The Russian Soviet Republic.* George Allen and Unwin, Ltd., 1905.

___. *Social Psychology.* The Macmillan Company, 1908. Manchester, New Hampshire: Ayer Co. Publishers, 1974.

___. *Changing America.* New York, The Century Co., 1912.

___. *Old World in the New: The Significance of Past and Present Immigration to the American People.* New York: The Century Co., 1914. Englewood, New Jersey: Jerome S. Ozer Publisher, 1971.

Rowntree, Benjamin Seebohm (1871–1954)
SOCIOLOGY OF POVERTY

Born in York, the third child of Quaker chocolate manufacturer Joseph Rowntree, Benjamin Seebohm Rowntree joined the family firm in 1889 and in 1897 he was appointed as a director. The Rowntrees' religion impacted their business practices; they implemented wage increases for the 4,000 workers their company employed. They believed the existence of companies that paid low wages was bad for the nation's economy and humanity.

Rowntree instituted several major Company reforms: an eight-hour working day (1896); a works doctor appointed (1904); a pension scheme (1906); a five-day working week and work councils (1919); a psychology department (1922); and a profit-sharing plan (1923). Rowntree assisted in the foundation of the Industrial Welfare Society (1918) and of the National Institute of Industrial Psychology (1921), remaining a member of its executive committee until

1949 and serving as chairman in 1940–1947. Rowntree is best known for his exhaustive, fact-based studies of poverty in his native city of York. He developed specific criteria for defining poverty, estimating precisely what was necessary to keep a person out of abject poverty.

In his first York study, *Poverty: A Study of Town Life* (1899), he surveyed poor families in York and drew a poverty line at a minimum weekly sum of money that covered fuel and light, rent, food, clothing, household items, and personal items, and was adjusted according to family size. To live below this poverty line was to live in *primary poverty*— unable to obtain the basic necessities of life. To live above the line was to live in *secondary poverty*— on the edge of poverty but able to obtain necessities.

His second York study, *Progress and Poverty* (1936), revealed that York had experienced a 50 percent reduction in poverty. In the 1890s poverty was caused by low wages, whereas in the 1930s it was unemployment.

The third York study, *Poverty and the Welfare State* (1951), showed that poverty appeared to be a minor problem, due largely an expanding economy and the Welfare State. The basic diet Rowntree and other experts drew up was criticized for not taking into account the customs of life of ordinary people.

In 1952, Rowntree was presented an honorary fellowship of the British Institute of Management in recognition of the debt the management movement owed to him.

Major Literature

Rowntree, Benjamin Seebohm. *Poverty: A Study of Town Life.* London, England: Macmillan, 1901. University of Bristol: Policy Press, 2001.
___. *The Human Needs of Labor.* London, England: Longmans Green and Co., 1905.
___. *The Land.* London, England: Thomas Nelson and Sons, 1913.
___. *How the Laborer Lives.* London, England: Thos. Nelson and Sons, 1913. New York: Arno Press, 1975.
___. *The Human Factor in Business.* London, England: Longmans Green and Co., 1921. Bristol, England, Thoemmes Press, 2003.
___. *Progress and Poverty.* London, England: Longmans Green and Co., 1941.
___. *Poverty and the Welfare State.* London, England: Longmans Green and Co., 1951.

Rumbaut, Rubén G. (1948–)
SOCIOLOGY OF IMMIGRATION

Born in Havana, Cuba, Rubén G. Rumbaut gained a B.A. in sociology, anthropology and biology at Washington University, St. Louis, Missouri (1969). At Brandeis University, Waltham, Massachusetts, he was National Institute of Mental Health predoctoral research fellow, and teaching fellow in the Department of Sociology (1971–1973); he gained an M.A. in sociology (1973) and a Ph.D. in sociology (1978).

He was research fellow, Department of Sociology, University of California, San Diego (1973–1974); research social scientist, City of San Diego Police Department (1973–1976); and research director, California Public Interest Research Group (1977–1978). At the University of California, San Diego, Rumbaut was assistant professor, Department of Sociology (1978–1985); research associate, Center for U.S.-Mexican Studies (1982–1985); associate professor, Department of Sociology (1985–1988); professor, Department of Sociology (1988–1993); and senior research fellow, Center for U.S.-Mexican Studies (1992–1993).

He was also visiting scholar, Center for Research on Social Organization, University of Michigan, Ann Arbor (1993–1994); visiting scholar, Russell Sage Foundation, New York (1997–1998); fellow, Center for Advanced Study in the Behavioral Sciences, Stanford University, California (2000–2001); professor, Department of Sociology, Michigan State University; senior faculty associate,

Julián Samora Research Institute, and Institute for Public Policy and Social Research, Michigan State University (1993–2002); professor, Department of Sociology, University of California, Irvine (UCI); and co-director, Center for Research on Immigration, Population, and Public Policy, UCI (2002).

His awards and honors include an Exceptional Performance Citation, City of San Diego Police Department (the first ever awarded to a civilian in San Diego Police Department history) (1975); elected to the "Honor Roll," National Conference of Christians and Jews (annual award for outstanding contributions to the community) (1981); Regents' Summer Faculty Fellowship, University of California, San Diego (1981); Meritorious Performance and Professional Promise Award, San Diego State University (1990); elected (founding) chair, International Migration Section, American Sociological Association (1994–1995); member, Sociological Research Association (1998); elected member, General Social Survey Board of Overseers (1998–2004); and W.I. Thomas and Florian Znaniecki Award of the ASA's International Migration Section (2002).

Major Contributions

Rumbaut's research has focused on intergenerational differences in adaptation, bilingualism and language loss, ethnic identity, citizenship, infant health and mortality, fertility, socioeconomic mobility and inequality, educational achievement and aspirations, depression and self-esteem, modes of acculturation, and difficulties of assimilation. Throughout the 1980s Rumbaut directed the Indochinese Health and Adaptation Research Project and the Southeast Asian Refugee Youth Study, concerning the migration and incorporation of refugees from Vietnam, Laos, and Cambodia who were resettled in the United States in the aftermath of the Indochina War. (See also, Alejandro Portes.)

Major Literature

Silvia Pedraza, and Rubén G. Rumbaut. *Origins and Destinies: Immigration, Race and Ethnicity in America*. Belmont, California: Wadsworth, 1995.

Portes, Alejandro, and Rubén G. Rumbaut. *Legacies: The Story of the Immigrant Second Generation*. Berkeley, California: University of California Press, 2001.

Foner, Nancy, Rubén G. Rumbaut, and Steven J. Gold (Eds.). *Immigration Research for a New Century: Multidisciplinary Perspectives*. New York: Russell Sage Foundation, 2003.

Portes, Alejandro, and Rubén G. Rumbaut. *Immigrant America: A Portrait*. Berkeley, California: University of California Press; 3rd edition, 2006.

Sampson, Robert J.
SOCIOLOGY OF CRIME

Robert J. Sampson gained a B.A. at State University of New York, Buffalo (1977); was senior staff associate, Columbia University, New York (1981–1983); gained an M.A. and Ph.D. at State University of New York, Albany (1983), and was post-doctoral fellow, School of Urban and Public Affairs, Carnegie-Mellon University, Pittsburgh, Pennsylvania (1983–1984). At the University of Illinois, Urbana, Champaign, he was associate professor, Department of Sociology (1988–1991) and assistant professor (1984–1988). He was scientific director of the "Project on Human Development in Chicago Neighborhoods" (1994). At the American Bar Foundation he was research fellow (1994–1999) and senior research fellow (1999–2002). At the University of Chicago, Illinois, he was professor of sociology (1991–1999); Lucy Flower Professor in Urban Sociology (1997–2001); and Fairfax M. Cone Distinguished Service Professor (2001–2002). He also was chair of the Crime, Law, and Deviance Section, American Sociological Association (2000–2001) and council member, Community and

Urban Section, American Sociological Association (2000–2003).

At Harvard University, Cambridge, Massachusetts, Sampson is Henry Ford II Professor of the Social Sciences (since 2003); chair, Department of Sociology (since 2005); and steering committee, Center for Geographic Analysis (since 2005). Since 2006 he has been on the Committee on Law and Justice, National Academy of Sciences. His awards, honors and fellowships: fellow, American Society of Criminology (1992); Distinguished Scholar Award, American Sociological Association, Crime, Law, and Deviance Section (1995); Robert Park Award, Community and Urban Sociology Section, American Sociological Association (2000, 2006); Edwin H. Sutherland Award, presented by the American Society of Criminology for outstanding contributions to theory and research by a North American criminologist (2001); fellow of the American Academy of Arts and Sciences (2005); and elected member of the National Academy Sciences (2006).

Major Contributions

Sampson's research interests center on crime, deviance, and stigma; the life course; neighborhood effects; and the social organization of cities. The Chicago Collective Civic Participation Study project aims to introduce change through cooperative efforts between various social movements by focusing on activities that are not initiated by the state or political professionals, but by groups of people who are motivated by a particular issue to act together in public (i.e., civic) space. His research shows that dense social ties, group memberships, and neighborly exchange do not predict a greater tendency for collective action at the community level in the city of Chicago; what does seem to matter is the density of community non-profit organizations.

Sampson engaged in a longitudinal study from birth to death of 1,000 disadvantaged men born in Boston during the Great Depression era. The resulting book, *Shared Beginnings,* received several book awards.

Major Literature

Sampson, Robert J., and John H. Laub. *Crime in the Making: Pathways and Turning Points Through Life.* Cambridge, Massachusetts: Harvard University Press, 1993.

Laub, John, and Robert J. Sampson. *Shared Beginnings, Divergent Lives: Delinquent Boys to Age 70.* Cambridge, Massachusetts: Harvard University Press, 2003.

Sampson, Robert J., and John H. Laub (special editors). "Developmental Criminology and Its Discontents: Trajectories of Crime from Childhood to Old Age." *Annals of the American Academy of Political and Social Science* 602 (2005).

Sanderson, Ezra Dwight (1878–1944)

RURAL SOCIOLOGY

Born at Olio, Michigan, Ezra Dwight Sanderson gained a B.S. in agriculture at Cornell University, Ithaca, New York (1898), then was assistant state entomologist, Maryland Agricultural College, College Park, Maryland (1898); entomologist, Delaware Agricultural Experiment Station (1899–1902); entomologist, State of Texas, and professor of entomology in the Texas Agricultural and Technical College, Waco, Texas (1902–1904). At New Hampshire College (now the University of New Hampshire), he was professor of zoology (1904–1907) and director of the Agricultural Experiment Station (1907–1910). From 1910 to 1915 he was dean of the College of Agriculture and director of the Agricultural Experiment Station, Morgantown, West Virginia; from 1916 to 1917 he was a fellow, Department of Sociology, University of Chicago, Illinois. At Cornell

University he was professor and head of department of Rural Sociology (1918–1944). He gained a Ph.D. at Chicago in 1921.

Major Contributions

Sanderson spent twenty successful years in entomology and he brought many skills into the study of sociology. He served as the 31st president of the American Sociological Society (1942). Sanderson's address, "Sociology a Means to Democracy," was published in the *American Sociological Review* (8, No. 1 [1943]: 1–9). He was also president of the Rural Sociological Society and of the American Country Life Association. He was a recognized entomologist as well as a sociologist, having been president of the American Association of Economic Entomologists in 1910.

Sanderson was a pioneer in the field of rural sociology, which later founded its own society and its own journal, *Rural Sociology*. In addition to his books and articles on entomology, his contributions to rural sociology included approximately twenty main articles and as many book reviews. His articles were published in *Social Forces, Rural Sociology, The American Journal of Sociology, American Sociological Review, The Survey,* and *The Family*. Sanderson sought in his writing to contribute to rural sociology as such rather than primarily to the study of rural problems. His main contribution was to describe the community in terms of structure and function in the realistic patterns of centers and hinterlands.

In his presidential address, Sanderson proposed:

- that democracy involves the principles of the supreme worth of the individual and his responsibility for participating in activities for the common good;
- that democracy is not merely a system, but a moral issue and a religious faith;
- that the task of sociology is to furnish knowledge of the structure and processes

of society, which is necessary if men are to assume responsibility for its intelligent control.

Major Literature

Sanderson, Dwight. *Rural Community Organization*. Wiley and Sons, Inc., 1905.

___. *Research Memorandum on Rural Life in the Depression*. New York: Social Science Research Council, 1924. New York: Arno Press, 1972.

___. "Scientific Research in Rural Sociology." *The American Journal of Sociology* 33, 2 (1927): 177–193.

___. *The Rural Community: The Natural History of a Sociological Group*. Boston, Massachusetts: Ginn and Co., 1932.

___. *Rural Sociology and Rural Social Organization*. New Jersey: John Wiley and Sons Inc., 1942.

Sassen, Saskia (1949–)

HUMAN MIGRATION

Born at The Hague, the Netherlands, Saskia Sassen grew up in Buenos Aires from 1950 and also spent some time in Italy. She studied philosophy and political science at the Université de Poitiers, France, the Università degli Studi di Roma, and the Universidad Nacional de Buenos Aires. Sassen gained an M.A. at the Université de Poitiers, France (1973); a Ph.D. in sociology and economics, University of Notre Dame, Indiana (1974); and a French master's degree in philosophy, de Poitiers (1974). She was at the Harvard University, Cambridge, Massachusetts, Center for International Affairs in 1974–1975.

Sassen has held various academic positions both in and outside the U.S. She is currently Ralph Lewis Professor of Sociology at the University of Chicago, Illinois, and Centennial Visiting Professor of Political Economy in the Department of Sociology at the London School of Economics.

Major Contributions

Sassen's work concentrates on Chicago as a global city, especially its connections to world financial markets and its location in international migration networks. During the 1980s and 1990s, she studied the impact of globalization processes, and the movements of labor and capital which they involve, on urban life. She also studied the influence of communication technology on government. In addition, she observed how nation states begin to lose power to control these developments, and she studied increasing general transnationalism (the increased connection that people all around the world have and the loosening of boundaries between countries, including human migration). She identified and described the phenomenon of the global city.

She has served as co-director of the Economy Section of the Global Chicago Project; is a member of the National Academy of Sciences Panel on Urban Data Sets; a member of the Council of Foreign Relations; and chair of the newly formed Information Technology, International Cooperation and Global Security Committee of the Social Science Research Council. Her books have been translated into thirteen languages. She has written for *The Guardian*, *The New York Times*, *Le Monde Diplomatique*, *International Herald Tribune*, *Vanguardia*, *Clarin*, *Financial Times*, and *The Nation*, among others. Her most recent award is an honorary doctorate from Delft University, the Netherlands.

Major Literature

Sassen, Saskia. *The Mobility of Labor and Capital*. Cambridge, England: Cambridge University Press, 1988.
___. *Losing Control? Sovereignty in an Age of Globalization*. New York: Columbia University Press, 1996.
___. *Globalization and Its Discontents: Selected Essays 1984–1998*. New York: New Press, 1998.
___. *The Global City: New York London Tokyo*. Princeton, New Jersey: Princeton University Press, 1991, new ed., 2001.
___. "Towards a Sociology of Information Technology." *Current Sociology, Special Issue: Sociology and Technology* 50, No. 3 (2002): 365–388.
___. *Global Networks/Linked Cities*. London, England: Taylor and Francis Books, Ltd., Routledge, 2002.
___. "The Global City: Introducing a Concept." *Brown Journal of World Affairs* 11 (2) (2005): 27–43.
___, with Robert Latham. *Digital Formations: Information Technologies and New Architectures in the Global Realm*. Princeton, New Jersey: Princeton University Press, 2005.
___. *Territory, Authority, Rights: From Medieval to Global Assemblages*. Princeton, New Jersey: Princeton University Press, 2006.

Schelsky, Helmut (1912–1984)
APPLIED SOCIOLOGY

Born in Chemnitz (Saxony/Germany), Helmut Schelsky was a most gifted German sociologist of the post-war period. Schelsky studied philosophy and history at the University of King Mountain (Albertina) and the University of Leipzig from 1931, from where he earned his doctorate (1935). In 1937 he became member of the National Socialist German Labor Party. From 1938 to 1940 he was an assistant to the philosopher Arnold Gehlen (1904–1976) in Leipzig, and from 1940–1941 to Hans Freyer at the University of Budapest. He was habilitated at the University of Königsberg (now Kaliningrad, Russia). He was called into the Germany army in 1941, and although called to his first chair of sociology at the University of Strasbourg (1944), he had to wait until after the fall of the Third Reich to take up his appointment.

In 1945, Schelsky joined the German Red Cross and formed its *Suchdienst* (service to trace down missing persons). From 1949 to 1953, he was professor at the Hamburg "Hochschule für Arbeit und Politik" (University for Work and Politics); from 1953 to 1960 he was professor of social economy at Hamburg University. In 1960 he was professor at the University of Münster, where he headed what was then the biggest West German center for social research. From 1970 to 1973 Schelsky was the first rector of the newly founded Bielefeld University, which led to the first German Faculty of Sociology and the Center of Interdisciplinary Research, the first sociological faculty in the Federal Republic.

On account of student unrest, Schelsky moved back to Münster until 1978. He was influential in helping many sociologists qualify as lecturers and helped spawn a dramatic increase in sociological chairs at German universities. In his writing he disagreed with the Utopian idealism approach fostered by the Frankfurt School. After the Second World War, no longer a National Socialist, Schelsky became one of the great men of applied sociology, due in part to his great gift of anticipating social and sociological developments. He published books in the fields of theory of institutions, stratification, sociology of family, sociology of sexuality, sociology of youth, industrial sociology, sociology of education, sociology of the university system, and sociology of law.

Major Literature

Schelsky, Helmut. *Die Arbeit Tun die Anderen: Klassenkampf und Priesterherrschaft der Intellektuellen* (*The Others Do the Work: Classes Battle and Priest Domination of the Intellectuals*). Berlin: Walter de Gruyter, Verlag, 1975.
___. *Der Selbständige Und Der Betreute Mensch: Politische Schriften Und Kommentare* (*The Independent and the Looked After Person: Political Writings and Commentaries*). Munich: Richard Seewald, 1976.
___. *Recht und Gesellschaft: Festschrift für Helmut Schelsky zum 65. Geburtstag.* (*Right and Company: Commemorative Volume for Helmut Schelsky to the 65th Birthday*). Berlin: Duncker and Humblot, 1978.
___. *Thomas Hobbes: Eine Politische Lehre.* (*Thomas Hobbes: A Political Apprenticeship*). Berlin: Duncker and Humblot, 1981.

Scott, W. Richard (1932–)
SOCIOLOGY OF ORGANIZATIONS

Born in Parsons, Kansas, W. Richard Scott gained an associate of arts degree (A.A.) at Parsons Junior College (1952), a B.A. with honors (1954) and an M.A. in sociology (1955) from University of Kansas, Lawrence, and a Ph.D. in sociology from the University of Chicago, Illinois (1961). Since 1960, Scott has held appointments at Stanford University, California, from assistant professor to professor emeritus, in the Departments of Sociology and Medicine; organization behavior, Graduate School of Business; and the School of Education. He was vicechair, Department of Sociology (1968–1972) and chair (1972–1975); and founding director of the Stanford Center for Organizations Research (1988–1996). After becoming professor emeritus in 1999, he was recalled by the dean to active service and continues to teach doctoral-level seminars in the department.

He was adjunct professor in public policy and administration, University of Tromsø in Tromsø, Norway (1991–1992); visiting professor, Copenhagen Business School (1992); visiting professor of organization behavior, Kellogg Graduate School of Management, Northwestern University, Evanston, Illinois (1997); and was visiting professor, School of Management, Hong Kong University of Science and Technology (2000).

Scott has received many awards, including honorary doctorates from Copenhagen School of Business (2000) and Helsinki School of Economics (2001); the Richard D. Irwin Award (1996) from the Academy of

Management for a career of distinguished scholarly contributions to management; and the Distinguished Scholar Award from the Management and Organization Theory Division of the Academy of Management (1988). He was faculty member, Stanford Overseas Studies Program, Stanford-in-Germany (1967 and 1971), Stanford-in-Britain (Reading) (1982), and Stanford-in-Britain (Oxford) (1988).

Major Contributions

Scott's initial research at Stanford was devoted to the psycho-sociological study of authority and control relations within organizations. His major field is organizational studies and among the many types of organizations studied are education, research, and healthcare. He has researched changes in the healthcare delivery systems in the San Francisco Bay area during the second half of the 20th century. He looked at specific changes in five populations of healthcare organizations related to the wider changes taking place in material resource and institutional environments.

He continues to focus on the general issues of institutional influences on organizational structures and functions, including changes in political regimes and policies. In 2000, the American Sociological Association, Section on Organizations, Occupations and Work created the W. Richard Scott Award to recognize annually the outstanding article contributing to the advancement of the field.

Major Literature

Blau, Peter, and W. Richard Scott. *Formal Organizations*. San Francisco, California: Chandler Press, 1961. Stanford University Press, 2004.

Scott, W. Richard, and Sanford Dornbusch. *Evaluation and the Exercise of Authority*. New Jersey: Jossey-Bass, 1975.

Scott, W. Richard, and Gerald Davis. *Organizations and Organizing: Rational, Natural and Open Systems*. Upper Saddle River, New Jersey: Prentice-Hall, 1981, 2006.

Scott, W. Richard, et al. *Institutional Change and Healthcare Organizations: From Professional Dominance to Managed Care*. Chicago, Illinois: University of Chicago Press, 2000.

Scott, W. Richard. *Institutions and Organizations*. Thousand Oaks, California: Sage, 2nd ed., 2001.

Sewell, William Hamilton (1909–2001)
SOCIOLOGY OF EDUCATION

Born in Perrinton, Michigan, William Hamilton Sewell gained B.A. and M.A. degrees in sociology from Michigan State University, East Lansing, Michigan, and a Ph.D. from the University of Minnesota, Minneapolis, then taught sociology at Oklahoma State University, Stillwater (1937–1944). From 1944 to 1946 he was a lieutenant in the U.S. Naval Reserve, then served in the postwar strategic bombing survey of Japan. At the University of Wisconsin, Madison, he was chair, Department of Rural Sociology (1949–1953); chair, Department of Sociology (1957–1962); Vilas Research Professor of Sociology (1964–1980); chancellor (1967–1968).

He was president of the Sociological Research Association (1953–1954); president, Rural Sociological Society (1955–1956); and 62nd president of the American Sociological Association (ASA) (1971). His honors and awards: Career of Distinguished Scholarship Award, ASA (1997), and chair of the National Commission on Research (1978–1980). He is a member of the National Academy of Sciences, American Philosophical Society, and American Academy of Arts and Sciences.

Major Contributions

Sewell's presidential address, "Inequality of Opportunity for Higher Education," was published in the *American Sociological Review* (36, No. 5 [1971]: 793–809). Sewell is widely credited with transforming the Madison sociology departments into a major international center for research and graduate training in sociology. His early recognition came with his pioneering research on measuring socioeconomic status in farm families and on childhood socialization practices. In one widely publicized and controversial study, Sewell tested some 360 hypotheses derived from Freudian ideas about infant training practices and children's personalities. Exactly 18 of these were statistically significant, that is, no more relationships appeared than would be expected by chance alone.

In the early 1960s, Sewell initiated and guided the Wisconsin Longitudinal Study of more than ten thousand Wisconsin high school graduates of 1957. He traced their post-secondary schooling, careers, and marriages to identify, measure, and explain the linkages between social background and social and economic achievements in adulthood. The results flew in the face of popular belief of the day that neighborhoods play a powerful role in creating social inequalities. Sewell and his colleagues also developed the "Wisconsin Model of Socioeconomic Attainment," which dominated American and international comparative studies of the life course for several decades.

In 2005 the Social Science Building at the University of Wisconsin-Madison was renamed the William H. Sewell Social Science Building.

Major Literature

Sewell, William H. *The Construction and Standardization of a Scale for the Measurement of the Socio-Economic Status of Oklahoma Farm Families.* Oklahoma Agricultural and Mechanical College, Agricultural Experiment Station, 1940.
___. "Infant Training and the Personality of the Child." *American Journal of Sociology*, 58.2 (1952): 150–59.
___, and Robert M. Hauser. *Education, Occupation and Earnings: Achievement in the Early Career.* New York: Academic Press Inc., 1975.
Sewell, William H., Robert M. Hauser, and David L. Featherman (Eds.). *Schooling and Achievement in American Society.* New York: Academic Press, Inc., 1976.
Sewell, William H., et. al "As We Age: The Wisconsin Longitudinal Study, 1957–2001." In *Research in Social Stratification and Mobility*, 20, ed. Kevin Leicht, 3–111. London, England: Reed Elsevier Group, 2004.

Shils, Edward (1911–1995)

GENERAL SOCIOLOGY

Edward Shils grew up in Philadelphia, Pennsylvania, and gained a B.A. at the University of Pennsylvania, Philadelphia (1931). At Chicago University, Illinois, he was research assistant (1934); instructor (1938); associate professor (1947); professor (1950); and distinguished service professor in the Committee on Social Thought and in Sociology (1971). During World War II he served with the British Army and the United States Office of Strategic Services and gained an M.A. at Cambridge University, England (1961).

For many years, Shils held joint appointments at Chicago and universities abroad: reader in sociology, London School of Economics (1946–1950); fellow, King's College, Cambridge (1961–1970); fellow, Peterhouse, Cambridge (1970–1978); honorary professor in social anthropology, University of London (1971–1977); professor, University of Leiden Netherlands 1976–1977); honorary fellow, London School of Economics (1972); and honorary fellow, Peterhouse (1979). Shils was a member of the American Academy of Arts and Sciences and the American Philosophical Society.

His awards and honors include selection by the National Council on the Humanities to give the Jefferson Lecture, the highest U.S.

award given in the humanities (1979), and the Balzan Prize, International Balzan Prize Foundation, an honor given in fields in which the Nobel Prize is not awarded (1983).

Major Contributions

The Times Higher Education Supplement (London, Feb. 2, 1995 Vol. 14, No. 11) wrote of Shils, "He is essentially an intellectual's intellectual and scarcely a single corner of the Western cultural tradition has not benefited from the illumination afforded by his penetrating and often pungent attention." Shils is known for his research on the role of intellectuals and their relations to power and public policy. He taught sociology, social philosophy, English literature, history of Chinese science and many other subjects to students who went on to become the leading scholars in their fields throughout the world. A specialist in the works of Max Weber, Shils also translated the works of Karl Mannheim into English (see entries).

Early in his career, Shils became the bridge between the research traditions of European and American sociology, connecting scholarship in America with work being done at European universities. At Chicago, he attracted leading European scholars to teach at the university. Shils was the founder and editor of *Minerva*, the world's leading journal of the social, administrative, political and economic problems of science and scholarship. He also was a co-founder of the *Bulletin of the Atomic Scientists*.

Major Literature

Parsons, Talcott, and Edward Shils. *Toward a General Theory of Action*. New York: Harper and Row, 1952. New Jersey: Transaction Publishers, abridged edition, 2001.

Shils, Edward. *The Intellectual Between Tradition and Modernity: The Indian Situation*. The Hague, Netherlands: Mouton and Co., 1961.

___. *The Calling of Sociology, and Other Essays on the Pursuit of Learning*. Chicago, Illinois: University of Chicago Press, 1980.

___. *Tradition*. Chicago, Illinois: University of Chicago Press, 1981, 2006.

___. *On the Constitution of Society*. Chicago, Illinois: University of Chicago Press, 1982.

___. *The Academic Ethic*. Chicago, Illinois: University of Chicago Press, 1984.

___, and Carmen Blacker (Eds.). *Cambridge Women: Twelve Portraits*. New York: Cambridge University Press, 1996.

Simmel, Georg (1858–1918)
SOCIAL STRUCTURE

Born in Berlin, Germany, Georg Simmel was one of the first generation of German sociologists, and is ranked by some authorities as second in importance only to Max Weber, Émile Durkheim, and Karl Marx (see entries). He was born to a Jewish family, but after the early death of his father, a Catholic guardian was appointed for him and from whom he inherited a large fortune. He received his doctorate in 1881 and was a *privatdozent* at the University of Berlin from 1885 to 1901. In 1901, the academic authorities consented to grant him the honorary title of Ausserordentlicher professor, although that failed to remove the stigma of the outsider.

In 1909 Simmel was co–founder of the German Society for Sociology with Ferdinand Tönnies and Max Weber (see entries). In 1914 Simmel received an ordinary professorship with chair, at what was then the German University of Strasbourg. During World War I, all academic activities and lectures were halted as lecture halls were converted to military hospitals. In 1915 he applied — without success — for a chair at the University of Heidelberg.

Major Contributions

Simmel argued that society is the outcome of interactions of individuals and groups, and so it is the interactions, rather than the individuals or social institutions themselves, that need to be studied. He drew attention to the phenomenon that when a dyad becomes a triad, the structure shifts as the possibility arises that two will combine against one, and control of the interaction becomes unpredictable. Simmel also argued that urban life in the early 20th century was incompatible with a positive community culture. The main reason for this was that specialization, started in the 19th century, and gaining momentum in the 20th, led to one person (or group) being incomparable to another, yet each of them being indispensable to one another. He speaks of a "metropolitan type individual" who with others forms an "organ" to protect themselves from the threatening nature of the city. The "organ" leads individuals to become insensitive and remote.

Simmel is also known for his classic analysis of the development and social significance of money, in which he relates the breakdown of "trust," reciprocity and primitive relations to the emergence of monetary exchange. Shortly before the end of the war he died from liver cancer, a man of great eminence, whose fame had spread to other European countries as well as to the United States, yet barely honored in his own country.

Major Literature (Modern editions)

Simmel, G. "The Sociology of Sociability" (translator, Everett C. Hughes). *American Journal of Sociology*, 55.3 (November 1949): 254–261.
___. *On Individuality and Social Forms*. Chicago, Illinois: University of Chicago Press, 1973.
___. *On Women, Sexuality and Love*. New Haven, Connecticut: Yale University Press, 1987.
___. *Simmel on Culture: Selected Writings*. London, England: Sage Publications, Ltd., 1997.
___. *A Chapter in the Philosophy of Value*. Whitefish, Montana: R.A. Kessinger Publishing Co., 2004.
___. *Philosophy of Money*. London, England: Taylor and Francis Books Ltd., Routledge, 2004.

Skocpol, Theda (1947–)
POLITICAL SOCIOLOGY

Born in Detroit, Michigan, Theda Skocpol gained a B.A. at Michigan State University, East Lansing, Michigan (1969). At Harvard University, Cambridge, Massachusetts, she gained an M.A. (1972) and Ph.D. (1975) and was assistant and associate professor of sociology (1975–1981); professor of sociology (1986–1994); professor of government and of sociology (1995–1997); Victor S. Thomas Professor of Government and Sociology (1998); director, Center for American Political Studies (1999–2006); dean, Graduate School of Arts and Sciences (since 2005); and senior advisor in the social sciences, Radcliffe Institute for Advanced Study (since 2006). At the University of Chicago, Illinois, she was associate professor of sociology and political science, and of social science in the College (1981–1984); director, Center for the Study of Industrial Societies (1982–1985); professor of sociology and political science, and of social science in the College (1984–1986).

She was visiting distinguished professor, Amsterdam School for Social Science Research, Netherlands (1997). Her awards and honors: honorary member, Radcliffe Chapter of Phi Beta Kappa (1991); president, Politics and History Section, American Political Science Association (1991–1992); Graduate Society Medal of the Radcliffe Alumnae Association (1994); fellow of the American Academy of Arts and Sciences (1994); president, Social Science History Association (1996); and president, American Political Science Association (2002). Skocpol received honorary degrees from Northwestern University, Evanston, Illinois, and Amherst College, Massachusetts.

Major Contributions

In the early 1980s, Skocpol successfully challenged Harvard University in denying her tenure because she was a woman, and in 1985 she became first ever tenured female sociologist at Harvard. Skocpol is one of the most cited and widely influential scholars in the modern social sciences; her work has contributed to the study of comparative politics, American politics, comparative and historical sociology, U.S. history, and the study of public policy. Her works and opinions have been associated with the structuralist school. Active in civic as well as academic life, Skocpol contributed to policy discussions with President Bill Clinton at the White House and Camp David. She writes for scholarly outlets and for publications appealing to the educated public; her books have won a number of awards.

Major Literature

Skocpol, Theda. *States and Social Revolutions: A Comparative Analysis of France, Russia and China*. New York: Cambridge University Press, 1979.

Rueschemeyer, Dietrich, and Theda Skocpol (Eds.). *States, Social Knowledge and the Origins of Modern Social Policies*. Princeton, New Jersey: Princeton University Press, 1995.

Skocpol, Theda. *Boomerang: Health Care Reform and the Turn Against Government*. New York: W.W. Norton and Co., Ltd., 1997.

___. *Diminished Democracy: From Membership to Management in American Civic Life*. Norman, Oklahoma: University of Oklahoma Press, 2003.

Jacobs, Lawrence R., and Theda Skocpol (Eds.). *Inequality and American Democracy: What We Know and What We Need to Learn*. New York: Russell Sage Foundation Publications, 2005.

Skocpol, Theda, Ariane Liazos and Marshall Ganz. *What a Mighty Power We Can Be: African American Fraternal Groups and the Struggle for Racial Equality*. Princeton, New Jersey: Princeton University Press, 2006.

Small, Albion Woodbury (1854–1926)

BASIC SOCIOLOGY

Born in Buckfield, Maine, Albion Woodbury Small graduated, from Colby College, Waterville, Maine (1876), and from Andover Newton Theological School, Massachusetts (1879), but was never ordained. He studied history, social economics and politics at the German universities of Berlin (1879–1880) and Leipzig (1880–1881). He then taught history and political economy at Colby (1881–1888) and studied history at Johns Hopkins University, Baltimore, Maryland (1888–1889), where he gained a Ph.D. (1889). Small was professor of sociology and president of Colby (1889–1892).

He was the first professor of sociology at the University of Chicago, Illinois, the earliest position of its kind in the United States (1892), and he founded and chaired the department for over 30 years. He founded and edited the *American Journal of Sociology,* the first such journal in the United States (1895); was dean of the Graduate School of Arts and Literature at the University of Chicago (1905–1925); helped found the American Sociological Society and was its fourth president (1912 and 1913).

Major Contributions

Small did much to establish sociology as a valid field for academic study, and he occupied a leading place as a historian of sociological thought. *General Sociology* is the chief of his several works. The title of his Ph.D. dissertation, which today can be found in the special collections at Johns Hopkins University, was "The Beginnings of American Nationality: The Constitutional Relations between the Continental Congress and the Colonies and States from 1774 to 1789." At Colby College, Small replaced the traditional moral philosophy course with one on sociology; it was one of the first three sociology courses in the United States. Under his leadership as department head at Chicago, the university became the major center for sociology during the first thirty years of the twentieth century. Small was particularly interested in the discipline of sociology itself, as well as the interrelations between the various social sciences.

He wrote *An Introduction to the Study of Society* with George E. Vincent (see entry) in 1894, the world's first sociological textbook. In his first major work, *General Sociology*, he explained the focus of sociology as the process by which groups come into conflict and subsequently resolve the divergence through adjustment and social innovation. His treatise "Fifty Years of American Sociology," published in the *American Journal of Sociology* in 1916, is still regarded as the standard reference.

Major Literature

Small, Albion Woodbury. *Introduction to a Science of Society*. American Book Company, 1890.
___. *The Beginnings of American Nationality*, 1899. New York: Johnson Reprint Corporation, 1973.
___. *General Sociology*. Chicago, Illinois: University of Chicago Press, 1905.
___. *Adam Smith and Modern Sociology*, 1907. Whitefish, Montana: R.A. Kessinger Publishing Co., 2004.
___. *The Meaning of Social Science*. Chicago: 1910.
___. *Between Eras: From Capitalism to Democracy*. Texas: Inter-Collegiate Press, 1913.

Sombart, Werner (1863–1941)

HISTORICAL SOCIOLOGY

Born in Ermsleben, Saxony, Prussia, Werner Sombart gained his Ph.D. (1888) from the University of Berlin. Until 1890 he was head lawyer for the Bremen Chamber of Commerce. From 1890 to 1906 he taught political science at the universities of Breslau and Berlin. Heidelberg and Freiburg universities offered him professorships, but because of his left-wing politics, the respective governments vetoed his appointments. In 1906, Sombart was appointed a full professor of sociology at the Berlin School of Commerce, and in 1917, professor for economic political sciences, Berlin University where he remained until 1931. He continued teaching until 1940. He was one of the leading sociologists, much more prominent than his friend Max Weber (see entry), who later of course eclipsed him.

Initially a supporter of Marxism, Sombart grew increasingly conservative and anti–Marxist. *The Jew and Modern Capitalism* refutes Max Weber's theory of the Protestant ethic, arguing that Jews introduced the spirit of capitalism into Northern Europe after being dispersed by the Spanish Inquisition. At the time, Sombart regarded Jews as a positive economic force, but his later writings reflect the anti–Semitism of the Nazi regime.

In one of his last publications, *A New Social Philosophy*, Sombart analyzed social problems from the perspective of the national socialist (Nazi) Party. Sombart was the head of the Historical School of Economics Youngest branch, and one of the leading Continental European social scientists during the first quarter of the 20th century. Between 1902 and 1927, his magnum opus, *Der moderne Kapitalismus*, appeared in six volumes. It is a systematic history of economics and economic development through the centuries and very much a work of the Historical School. The book has been translated into many languages, except English.

Sombart insisted that sociology was a part of the humanities, necessarily so because it deals with human beings and therefore requires inside, empathic understanding rather than outside objectivity. This view was not well received at a time when the world was looking toward all things scientific and provable. Sombart's place in sociology has been harmed by his earlier socialist affinities and his later sympathies with Nazi ideology; however, his studies of urban societies are significant. His theories also influenced the economist and political scientist Joseph Alois Schumpeter (1883–1950).

Sombart has always been very popular in Japan; one reason for his lack of recognition in the United States is that most of his works were for a long time not translated into English.

Major Literature

Sombart, Werner. *Why Is There No Socialism in the United States?* 1906. New York: Macmillan, 1976.

___. *The Jews and Modern Capitalism.* 1911. New Jersey: Transaction Publishers, new edition, 1982.

___. *A New Social Philosophy.* Westport, Connecticut: Greenwood Press, 1937.

___. *Socialism and the Social Movement.* 1896. New York: Kelley Publishers, 1970.

___. *Economic Life in the Modern Age.* New Jersey: Transaction Publishers, 2001.

Sorokin, Pitirim Alexandrovich (1889–1968)

SOCIAL CYCLE THEORY

Born in Turya, a remote village in Northern Russia, Pitirim Alexandrovich Sorokin had a hard life. At the age of eleven, he and his older brother were left to fend for themselves as itinerant artisans. Sorokin won a series of competitive scholarships that eventually took him to the University of St. Petersburg. He was one of the founders of Kovalevsky Russian Sociological Society (1916). By 1922 Sorokin had finished his magistrant of criminal law and Ph.D. degrees. He had also been jailed six times for political defiance and was a prisoner of both the Czar and the Bolsheviks (he preferred the monarch's jails; they were cleaner, books

were provided and treatment was more humane). Because he was a highly vocal and persuasive anti-communist, during his last incarceration, Lenin ordered him shot. Only pleas from former political allies persuaded Lenin to exile him instead.

He and his wife left Russia in 1923 and in 1924 arrived in the United States, where he went to work in the department of sociology, University of Minnesota, Minneapolis, and stayed for six years. He moved to Harvard University, Cambridge, Massachusetts, to chair the University's first Department of Sociology, where he remained for thirty years. His magnum opus, the monumental *Social and Cultural Dynamics* (1957), spanned 2,500 years. (In 1962 the Bedminister Press reissued *Social and Cultural Dynamics* in a four volume set.)

Sorokin speculated that the world was moving toward a difficult and bloody period of transition. For the next twenty years he wrote prolifically on war, integralism and altruism. As a humanistic scholar he wanted to understand the conditions that led to war and the methods by which they could be treated and reduced. Similar values informed his later works on revolution and institutional violence. Sorokin further argued that sociologists spend too much time studying destructive social behaviors. If they wished to improve the human condition, they should learn how to make people more humane, compassionate and giving.

This concern led Sorokin to a decade-long study of altruism and the study of friendship. With support from the Lilly Endowment, he established the Harvard Center for Creative Altruism; he believed politics was unlikely to bring about peace in the future without the people, groups, institutions, and cultures becoming more altruistic. Sorokin's work was controversial and the center did not survive.

He was 55th President of the American Sociological Association in 1965, an honor that brought him into the sociological limelight three years before his death.

Major Literature

Sorokin, P.A. *Social and Cultural Mobility.* New York: Free Press, 1959.

___. *A Long Journey* (Autobiography). Lanham, Maryland: Rowman and Littlefield Publishers, Inc., 1963.

___. *The Sociology of Revolution.* New York: Howard Fertig, 1967.

___. *Social and Cultural Dynamics.* Boston, Massachusetts: Porter Sargent Publishers, 1970. New Jersey: Transaction Publishers, 1991.

___. *On the Practice of Sociology,* edited by Barry V. Johnson. Chicago: University of Chicago Press, 1998.

___*The Ways and Power of Love: Types, Factors, and Techniques of Moral Transformation.* Conshohocken, Pennsylvania: Templeton Foundation Press, 2002.

Spencer, Herbert
(1820–1903)

SURVIVAL OF THE FITTEST

Born in Derby, Derbyshire, England, Herbert Spencer was a philosopher and one of the early sociologists. He supported the theory of evolution, advocated that the individual was more important than society, and believed that science was more important than religion. His magnum opus was *A System of Synthetic Philosophy,* a comprehensive work completed in 1896 and containing volumes on the principles of biology, psychology, morality, and sociology. He thought of social life as a social system and societies as organisms that progressed through a process of evolution, similar to living species, which gave rise to his being termed the father of social Darwinism, a term that Spencer never used. Spencer coined the phrase "survival of the fittest" in his *Principles of Biology* (1864).

In *Social Statics*—which predates Charles Darwin's *The Origin of Species* (1959)—Spencer began developing his view of civilization as a natural and organic product of social evolution. He stressed the importance of looking at the long-term effects of social policy with respect to the nature of man. Spencer spelled out the "law of equal liberty," a basic tenet of libertarianism that says that each individual should be allowed to do as he or she wills as long as it doesn't infringe on the rights of another person. In *Principles of Psychology,* Spencer explored a theory of the mind as a biological counterpart of the body rather than as an estranged opposite. It was published at his own expense, as publishers were suspicious of his evolutionary approach. He continued to write throughout his life, often by dictation in his later years, until he succumbed to his poor health at the age of 83.

Although Spencer never had a wide following among his colleagues, his ambitious attempt to systematize all knowledge within the framework of modern science, and especially in terms of evolution, earned him an enduring place among the foremost thinkers of the late 19th century. Spencer's works were widely read during his lifetime and by 1869 he was able to support himself solely on the profit of book sales. Translations of his various works were made in German, Italian, Spanish, French, Russian, Japanese and Chinese, and he was offered honors and awards from all over Europe and North America. In 1902, shortly before his death, he was nominated for the Nobel Prize for literature.

Major Literature

Spencer, Herbert. *Social Statics.* London: Chapman, 1851. Abridged and revised with *The Man Versus the State.* Honolulu, Hawaii: University Press of the Pacific, 2003.

___. *The Principles of Psychology.* London: Longmans, 1855. Cuckfield, West Sussex, England: Gregg Publishing, 1971.

___. *The Principles of Sociology.* London: Williams and Norgate, 1861. 4 volumes. Honolulu, Hawaii: University Press of the Pacific, 2004.

___. *First Principles.* London: Williams and

Norgate, 1862. Honolulu, Hawaii: University Press of the Pacific, 2002.

___. *The Study of Sociology.* New York: D. Appleton, 1880. Honolulu, Hawaii: University Press of the Pacific, 2002.

Straus, Murray A. (1926–)

FAMILY SOCIOLOGY

From 1944 to 1946, Murray A. Straus served with the U.S. Army's Unit Information and Education as an interpreter. At the University of Wisconsin, Madison, he gained a B.A. in international relations (1948) and an M.S. in sociology (1949). He was instructor in the Department of Economics and Sociology (1949) and gained a Ph.D. in sociology and anthropology (1956).

Straus was lecturer in sociology, University of Ceylon, Colombo (Sri Lanka) (1949–1952); assistant professor, Department of Sociology and Rural Sociology, Washington State University, Pullman, Washington (1954–1957); assistant professor, Department of Sociology and Rural Sociology, University of Wisconsin, Madison (1957–1959); associate professor of family sociology, Department of Child Development and Family Relationships, Cornell University, Ithaca, New York (1959–1961); visiting professor, University of Bombay, Mumbai, India (1964–1965); professor of sociology and chairperson, University of Minnesota, College of Liberal Arts, Division of Family Social Science, Bloomington, Minnesota (1967–1968); and visiting professor, University of Kentucky, Lexington (1967).

At the University of New Hampshire, Durham, Straus was professor of sociology (1968); founder and director, Family Violence Research Program (1970); director, State and Regional Indicators Archives (1979–1988); and founder and co-director, Family Research Laboratory (1979). He was visiting professor, University of York, England (1974); visiting professor, University of Massachusetts in Boston, (1975); and visiting scholar, Columbia University, New York (1982).

His awards and honors include being named a fellow, American Association for the Advancement of Science (1971); the Ernest W. Burgess Award, National Council on Family Relations (1977); Contributions to Teaching, American Sociological Association (1979); Distinguished Contribution, New Hampshire Psychological Association (1992); Outstanding Contributions, North Hampshire Psychological Association (1993); Career Contributions to Child Abuse Research, American Professional Society on Child Abuse (1994); Citizen of the Year, National Association of Social Workers (1994); and Charles Holmes Pettee Medal, University of New Hampshire Alumni Association (2001).

Major Contributions

Straus has been called the world's most distinguished family researcher on violence and has also influenced research on child abuse. In sociological circles, Straus and his colleagues and students are known as the "New Hampshire School." They believe that conflict is universal, and there is no single cause of violence in the home; that the various forms of family problems are interrelated, both within the home and in society; and that much of the conflict and violence in society at large can be traced to roots in the family.

Straus started on his life-long crusade against family violence, including spanking, in 1979 when he discovered that one quarter of his students had been hit by their parents during their senior year in high school, and another quarter had been threatened with being hit.

Major Literature

Straus, Murray A. *Beating the Devil Out of Them: Corporal Punishment in American Children.* New Jersey: Transaction Publishers, 2nd edition, 2001.

___. *Primordian Violence.* Lanham, Maryland: Rowman and Littlefield Publishers, Inc., 2004.

___, Richard J. Gelles, and Suzanne K. Steinmetz. *Corporal Punishment of Children in Theoretical Perspective.* New Haven, Connecticut: Yale University Press, 2005.

Straus, Murray A. *Behind Closed Doors: Violence in the American Family.* New Jersey: Transaction Publishers, new edition, 2006.

Sumner, William Graham (1840–1910)

SOCIAL CHANGE

William Graham Sumner was an economist and sociologist, and heir apparent to the ideas of Herbert Spencer in the United States. He was born in Paterson, New Jersey, and grew up in Hartford, Connecticut, the son of a working-class English immigrant. He graduated from Yale University, New Haven, Connecticut, in 1863, studied for the ministry and eventually became a priest in the Protestant Episcopal Church. He left the ministry and was professor of political and social science in at Yale from 1872 until his death.

Sumner believed in individual liberty, and that inequalities among men was inevitable. Like Spencer, Sumner was a believer in laissez-faire economics, strongly opposing any government measures that he thought interfered with the natural economics of trade. He heavily criticized socialism and communism and opposed all government efforts to regulate business or to combat social inequality. For Sumner, competition for property and social status was something desirable, the result of which was the elimination of those less able—an echo of Spencer's "survival of the fittest." That some people had the ability to accumulate substantial wealth by frugal living and hard work was for him what made society great. The Protestant ethic of hard work, thrift, and sobriety was conducive to wholesome family life and sound public morality.

As a sociologist he did valuable work in charting the evolution of human customs, which he called mores and folkways. Sumner's work with folkways led him to conclude that attempts at government-mandated reform were useless. Foreseeing the drift toward the welfare state, but considering poverty the natural result of inherent inferiorities, he opposed all reform proposals that smacked of paternalism because they would impose excessive economic burdens on the middle class, his "forgotten man."

Sumner opposed the 1898 Spanish American War and the subsequent U.S. effort to quell the insurgency in the Philippines. He was a vice president of the Anti-imperialist League, which had been formed after the war in June 1898 to oppose the annexation of territories. According to Sumner, imperialism would enthrone a new group of "plutocrats," or businesspeople who depended on government subsidies and contracts. Sumner also originated the concept of ethnocentrism—a term now commonly used—to designate attitudes of superiority about one's own group in comparison with others. Sumner was elected president of the American Sociological Society for a two year term in 1908.

Major Literature

Sumner, William Graham. *Collected Essays in Political and Social Science.* New York: Henry Holt and Company, 1885.

___. *Folkways: A Study of the Sociological Importance of Usages, Manners, Customs, Mores, and Morals.* Boston, Massachusetts: Ginn and Co., 1906. Mineola, New York: Dover Publications, Inc., 2002.

___. *War, and Other Essays,* ed. with introduction, Albert G. Keller. New Haven, Connecticut:

Yale University Press, 1911. New York: Ams Press, Inc., 1970.

___. *The Science of Society*, with Albert G. Keller. 4 volumes. New Haven, Connecticut: Yale University Press, 1927.

___. *On Liberty, Society and Politics*. Robert C. Bannister (Ed.). Indianapolis, Indiana: Liberty Fund Inc., 1992.

Sutherland, Edwin H. (1883–1950)

CRIMINOLOGY

Born in Gibbon, Nebraska, Edwin H. Sutherland gained an A.B. degree at Grand Island College, Maine (1904), and a PhD. with a double major in sociology and political economy at the University of Chicago, Illinois (1913).

He was professor of sociology at William Jewell College, Liberty, Missouri (1913–1919); visiting professor of sociology, University of Kansas, Lawrence (1918); assistant professor of sociology, University of Illinois, Urbana, Champaign (1919–1935); visiting professor of sociology, Northwestern University, Evanston, Illinois (1922); associate professor of sociology, University of Illinois (1925–1926); professor of sociology, University of Minnesota, Minneapolis (1926–1929); professor of sociology, University of Chicago (1930–1935); head of the Department of Sociology, Indiana University, Bloomington (1935–1949); visiting professor of sociology, University of Washington, Seattle (1942); and 29th president, American Sociological Society (1939). He was also president of the Indiana University Institute of Criminal Law and Criminology, the American Prison Association, the Chicago Academy of Criminology, and the Sociological Research Association.

Major Contributions

Sutherland, like many of the leading sociologists, came to sociology from another field — teaching Latin and Greek in a small college. He had plans to take graduate work in history, but found that a course in sociology was a prerequisite for graduate work in history, and consequently he took a correspondence course in sociology to meet this requirement. From this he decided to select sociology as a minor while keeping history as a major. Sutherland's interest in criminal behavior was not in the control of crime, but through intense study of that behavior to throw light on society.

His presidential address in 1939 — "White-Collar Criminality" — received front-page publicity in the daily newspapers. In this address, he argued that many business and professional men commit crimes that should be brought within the scope of the theories of criminal behavior. In opposition to the dominant biological and psychological explanations, Sutherland maintained that criminal behavior is learned through delinquent peer groups, in which such behavior is considered normal. Delinquent groups develop motivations and rationalizations for engaging in criminal activity.

Sutherland also acknowledged the existence of a criminal life cycle, which he defined in terms of the ways in which these attitudes vary in content and intensity throughout the criminal's life. As a criminologist, Sutherland is best known for his development of the "differential association" theory of crime. In recognition of his influence, the most important annual award of the American Society of Criminology is given in his name.

Major Literature

Sutherland, Edwin H. *Criminology*. 1924. New York: Lippincott, Williams and Wilkin, 1978.

___. *Twenty Thousand Homeless Men*. Philadelphia:

J.B. Lippincott, 1936. New York: Arno Press, 1971.

___. *The Professional Thief.* Chicago, Illinois: University of Chicago Press 1937, 1988.

___. *Principles of Criminology.* Philadelphia: J.B. Lippincott, 1939. Dix Hills, New York: General Hall, Inc., 2002.

___. *White Collar Crime.* New York: Dryden Press, 1949. New York: Irvington Publishers, 1993.

___. *On Analyzing Crime.* Chicago, Illinois: University of Chicago Press, new edition, 1974.

___. *Prisons of Tomorrow.* Manchester, New Hampshire: Ayer Co., Publishers, 1974.

Taft, Jessie (1882–1961)

SOCIOLOGY AND SOCIAL WORK

Jessie Taft, psychologist, feminist, and scholar with limited academic ties to sociology, was a noted social work educator and a brilliant symbolic interactionist. She studied women, their view of the world, and the application of their values in various situations. Born in rural Iowa, she gained a B.A. (1904) from Drake University, Des Moines, Iowa, and a B.A. in philosophy (1905) from the University of Chicago, Illinois, then taught Latin and algebra at West High School in Des Moines. After returning to the University of Chicago in 1908, she was offered a fellowship in 1909 and completed her Ph.D. (1913) under George H. Mead (see entry).

At Chicago, Taft met Virginia Robinson; later they were to develop the "functional school" of social casework. Together, Taft and Robinson were hired, in 1912, to conduct interviews on the relation between crime and "feeble-mindedness," at Bedford Hills Reformatory for Women, New York. Academic barriers to women to become professors of sociology were insurmountable; she became assistant superintendent Bedford Hills. Her own experience of finding suitable employment in sociology was typical of many women in that era. From 1919 to 1929 Taft was a part-time psychology instructor in extension courses at the University of Pennsylvania, Philadelphia; only in 1929 was she finally allowed to teach advanced personality courses to vocational students.

Major Contributions

Although untrained, Taft became a leader in social work, first in Philadelphia, working in child and family services, and then nationally. From 1934 until she retired in 1950, she was the director of the School of Social Work, University of Pennsylvania. She met the psychoanalyst Otto Rank in 1924, underwent analysis by him in 1926, arranged for his immigration to the United States and his employment at the University of Pennsylvania, and translated his writings.

A prominent early national authority on child placement, Taft advocated raising the standard of adoption agencies to professional level. She carried some of the features of Rankian therapy into her own work but was one of the first to develop the nondirective approach to therapy more usually associated with Carl Rogers. Taft recognized the necessity for therapists to accept the limitation on the help it is possible to give others, but all the while acknowledging the tremendous pressure upon the therapist, who can see so clearly that something needs to be done.

Major Literature

Taft, Jessie. *The Woman Movement from the Point of View of Social Consciousness* (also doctoral dissertation). Chicago, Illinois: University of Chicago Press, 1916.

___. "Relation of Personality Study to Child Placing." Paper presented at the National Conference of Social Work (1919): 63–67.

___. "The Re-Education of a Psychoneurotic Girl." Paper presented at the American Psychiatric Association, Atlantic City, June 1924. *American Journal of Psychiatry* 4 (1925): 477–487.

___. "Early Conditioning of Personality in the

Pre–School Child." *School and Society* 21 (546) (1925): 695–701.

___. *The Dynamics of Therapy in a Controlled Relationship*. New York: Macmillan, 1933.

___. *Family Casework and Counselling*. Pennsylvania, Philadelphia: University of Pennsylvania Press, 1948.

Tarde, Gabriel (1843–1904)

CRIMINOLOGY

Philosopher and sociologist Gabriel Tarde made important contributions to general social theory and to the study of collective behavior, public opinion, and personal influence. Born in Sarlat, he read law in Toulouse and then Paris. From 1869 to 1894 he held several legal posts near Sarlat, and director of criminal statistics at the Ministry of Justice in Paris. After 1894 he lectured in numerous peripheral institutions outside the university, and from 1900 until his death he held the chair of modern philosophy at the Collège de France, Paris. During his years of public service as a magistrate, he became interested in the psychosocial bases of crime. In *Penal Philosophy* (1890, tr. 1912) and other early works he criticized the theory of criminality developed by the Italian psychologist Cesare Lombroso (1835–1909). Among the concepts that Tarde initiated were the "group mind" which relates to so-called herd behavior or crowd psychology, and economic psychology, where he anticipated a number of modern developments. In opposition to Gustave Le Bon, who analyzed modern society in terms of crowds, Tarde emphasized the importance of the public. Crowds depend on physical proximity; publics derive from shared experiences of their members, who may not be in immediate physical proximity. Trade unions, political parties, and churches all support different publics, and Tarde saw these overlapping but distinct publics as major sources of flexibility in modern industrial societies. For Tarde, society was based on small psychological interactions among individuals (much as if it were chemistry), the fundamental forces being imitation and innovation. His theory brought him into conflict with Émile Durkheim (see entry), who viewed society as a collective unity. Durkheim's sociology was a rational and impersonal discipline; Tarde's approach was more flexible and individualistic. Tarde saw "invention" as the ultimate source of all human innovation and progress, found in the minds of gifted individuals. The inventions most easily imitated are similar to those already institutionalized, and imitation tends to descend from social superior to social inferior. However, opposition takes place when conflicting inventions encounter one another. These oppositions may be associated with social groups — nations, states, regions, social classes — or they may remain largely inside the minds of individuals. Tarde held that an elite was necessary to govern society and to maintain creative innovation, basic cultural patterns, and a social and political stability. Crime, mental illness, and social deviance in general were seen by Tarde as frequent results of the disintegration of traditional elites. Migration, social mobility, and contact with deviant subcultures also further the tendencies toward deviance.

Major Literature (English translations)

Tarde, Gabriel. *Laws of Imitation*. Magnolia, Massachusetts: Peter Smith, Inc., 1940.

___. *On Communication and Social Influence*. Chicago, Illinois: University of Chicago Press, 1969.

___. *Underground Man*. New York: Hyperion Books, 1974.

___. *Penal Philosophy*. New Jersey: Transaction Publishers, 2000.

Thomas, Dorothy Swain (1899–1977)

DEMOGRAPHY

Dorothy Swain was born in Baltimore, Maryland, and gained her B.A. (1922) at Barnard College, New York, and Ph.D. (1924) at University of London School of Economics. She married William I. Thomas (see entry) in 1936. Between 1924 and 1948, she held research or academic appointments at: Federal Reserve Bank of New York; Social Science Research Council, Columbia University Teachers College, Yale University; Social Science Institute at the University of Stockholm; and University of California at Berkeley.

In 1948 Thomas became the first woman professor in the Wharton School of the University of Pennsylvania, where she was research professor of sociology. While at Pennsylvania she initiated an interdisciplinary doctoral training program in demography and helped found and direct the Population Studies Center. Following her retirement from Pennsylvania in 1970, she continued teaching at Georgetown University, Washington, D.C., for four years. She served on numerous occasions as technical consultant to the United Nations and United States government agencies.

She was the first woman elected president of the American Sociological Association (1952). She was president of the Population Association of America (1958–1959), and received an honorary doctorate from the University of Pennsylvania in 1970 for her influential work in demography. As chair of the Social Science Research Council's Committee on Migration Differentials, she authored a study (1938) that set the research agenda of the field for the next several decades. In her 1941 study, "Social and Economic Aspects of Swedish Population Movements," she focused on the long-term effects of demography on the economy.

Thomas' most famous work, not often cited by demographers, is her co-authored two volume study of the forced evacuation, detention, and resettlement of West Coast Japanese Americans during World War II (1946 and 1952). The Supreme Court accepted her study as unbiased evidence of crimes against fellow Americans. She co-directed with economist Simon Kuznets the University of Pennsylvania project (1957) on population redistribution and economic growth, which produced definitive estimates of internal migration in the United States by sex, age, race, nativity, and state of origin and destination. As chair of the Committee on Internal Migration of the International Union for the Scientific Study of Population, she collaborated in producing *United Nations Manual VI, Methods of Measuring Internal Migration* (1970).

At a time that professional careers in academia were virtually closed to women, she made a lasting contribution, and can justifiably be considered one of the founders of American demography.

Major Literature

Thomas, Dorothy S. *Social Aspects of the Business Cycle*. London: Routledge and Kegan Paul, 1925. (New York: Knopf, 1928.) Reprinted, New York: Gordon and Breach, 1968.
___. *Research Memorandum on Migration Differentials*. New York: Social Science Research Council, 1938.
Dorothy Swain Thomas Papers, 1929–1977, are available at http://www.archives.upenn.edu/faids/upt/upt50/thomasdot.html.

Thomas, William Isaac (1863–1947)

SOCIOLOGY OF MIGRATION

Born in Russell County, Virginia, William Isaac Thomas gained a B.A. in literature and classics at the University of Tennessee,

Knoxville (1884), and was adjunct professor of English and modern languages there (1884–1888). In 1888–1889 he studied classic and modern languages at the German universities of Berlin and Göttingen and sociology under Wilhelm Wundt. At Oberlin College in Oberlin, Ohio, Thomas was professor of English (1889) and professor of sociology (1894).

At the Department of Sociology, University of Chicago, Illinois, he was instructor, graduate studies in sociology and anthropology (1895); among the first to receive a doctorate in sociology with his Ph.D. in 1896; and was assistant professor (1896), associate professor (1900), full professor (1910), and dismissed (1918). He was lecturer, New School for Social Research, New York (1923–1928); visiting lecturer, Harvard University, Cambridge, Massachusetts, at the invitation of Pitirim A. Sorokin (see entry) (1936–1937); president, American Sociological Association (1927); co-editor, *American Journal of Sociology* (1895–1917).

Major Contributions

Thomas developed the biographic approach in sociology, which would later establish his lasting reputation in sociology, using this approach in his study of Polish immigrants. He used newspaper reports, archives of organizations, personal letters and diaries, and letters sent from Poland. His lifestyle did not conform with the image of a respectable professor and made him a controversial figure, including among colleagues. Disaster struck in 1918 when the FBI arrested Thomas under the Mann Act. Although Thomas was acquitted of the charge in court, his career was irreversibly damaged. The university immediately dismissed him without awaiting the outcome of his case, and without any relevant protest from his colleagues. After 1937, Thomas gradually withdrew into retirement in New York, New Haven, and finally Berkeley, California, where he died.

Sex and Society is considered the first fully secular work on the subject by an American sociologist. In it he called for an end to the subjection of women in society, although by today's standards, some of his views would be considered sexist, i.e., women didn't have the same intellectual capacity as men. *Source-Book for Social Origins* and *Primitive Behavior* reflect his interest in ethnology. *The Unadjusted Girl* is a psychological study of personality. His major work, *The Polish Peasant in Europe and America*, applies the comparative method to the study of nationalities and analyzes social problems by means of personal history.

Major Literature

Thomas, William I. The Relation of the Medicine-Man to the Origin of the Professional Occupations. Chicago, Illinois: University of Chicago Press, 1903.

____. *Sex and Society: Studies in the Social Psychology of Sex*. Chicago, Illinois: University of Chicago Press, 1907.

____(Ed.). *Source Book for Social Origins. Ethnological Materials, Psychological Standpoint, Classified and Annotated Bibliographies for the Interpretation of Savage Society*. Chicago, Illinois: University of Chicago Press, 1909.

____, and Florian W. Znaniecki. *The Polish Peasant in Europe and America: Monograph of an Immigrant Group*. Volumes 1 and 2. Chicago, Illinois: University of Chicago Press, 1918. Volumes 3–5, Boston, Massachusetts: Badger, 1919–1921.

Thorne, Barrie (1942–)
SOCIOLOGY OF GENDER

Born in Logan, Utah, Barrie Thorne gained a B.A. with great distinction and with honors in anthropology and honors in social thought and institutions at Stanford University, California (1964), then did graduate study in social anthropology at the London School of Economics, England

(1964–1965). She gained an M.A. (1967) and Ph.D. in sociology (1971) at Brandeis University, Waltham, Massachusetts. At Michigan State University, East Lansing, Michigan, Thorne was associate professor and assistant professor (1971–1983) and professor of sociology (1984–1987). At the University of Southern California, Los Angeles, she was Streisand Professor of Intimacy and Sexuality, Program for the Study of Women and Men in Society, and professor of sociology (1987–1995); and chair, Program for the Study of Women and Men in Society (1992–1995).

She was visiting associate professor of sociology and feminist studies, Stanford University (1981–1982). At University of California, Santa Cruz, she was visiting assistant professor of sociology (1976–1977) and visiting associate professor of sociology (1980–1981). At the University of California, Berkeley, she was professor of sociology and women's studies (1995); Berkeley Center for Working Families co-director (1998–2001); director (2001–2002); and chair, Women's Studies Department (2003). Thorne was U.S. editor of *Childhood: A Global Journal of Child Research* and the former chair of the American Sociological Association Section on the Sociology of Children and Youth.

Her awards and honors include the Phi Kappa Phi Award for Faculty Excellence, University of Southern California, Los Angeles (1988); University of Southern California Raubenheimer Award for Outstanding Teaching, Research, and Service to the University (1992); Sociologists for Women in Society Outstanding Mentorship Award (1993); Mentor of the Year Award, Society for the Study of Symbolic Interaction (1998); and the Jessie Bernard Award, American Sociological Association, in recognition of scholarly work encompassing fully the role of women in society (2002).

Major Contributions

Thorne's work focuses on the sociology of gender across institutional spheres of influence and in the constitution of conversation, identities, and everyday life; feminist theory; the sociology of age relations, childhood, families, and the social construction of childhoods; theorizing age relations; feminist theory; and study of group methods. She has helped to build an intellectual feminist community focused on the themes of "cultures of care" and the changing face of family life in the context of global economic change. In her study of playground behavior, related to gender identity, Thorne argues that because girls and boys interact in many social contexts — at home, in classrooms, in play groups — behavioral differences must somehow be transmitted to them by the adult culture and are not entirely related to comparison among peers.

Major Literature

Thorne, Barrie, and Nancy Henley. *Language and Sex: Difference and Dominance*. London, England: Thomson Learning, Newbury House, 1975.

Henley, Nancy, and Barrie Thorne. *She Said–He Said*. Pittsburgh, Pennsylvania: Know, Inc., 1976.

Thorne, Barrie (Ed.). *Language, Gender and Society*. Upper Saddle River, New Jersey: Pearson Education, Longman Group, 1991.

___. *Gender Play: Girls and Boys in School*. Piscataway, New Jersey: Rutgers University Press, 1993.

Laslett, Barbara, and Barrie Thorne (Eds.). *Feminist Sociology: Life Histories of a Movement*. New Jersey: Rutgers University Press, 1997.

Tocqueville, Alexis De (1805–1859)

HISTORICAL SOCIOLOGY

Alexis-Charles-Henri Clérel de Tocqueville was born in Verneuil-sur-Seine,

France. After finishing at the College Royal at age 18, Tocqueville moved to Paris, where he studied law. After obtaining his law degree, he was named auditor-magistrate at the court of Versailles. He held various legal posts and was active in French politics, first under the July Monarchy (1830–1848) and then during the Second Republic (1849–1851), which succeeded to the February 1848 Revolution.

In 1841 and 1846, he traveled to Algeria; his first travel inspired his *Travail sur l'Algérie*, in which he criticized the French model of colonization, based on an assimilationist view; he preferred the British model of indirect rule, which didn't mix different populations together, but advocated racial segregation between the European colonists and the Arabs.

After the fall of the July Monarchy (1830–1848) during the February 1848 Revolution, Tocqueville was elected a member of the Constituent Assembly of 1848, where he integrated the commission charged with the drafting of the new Constitution of the Second Republic (1848–1851). He quit political life after Louis Napoleon Bonaparte's December 2, 1851, coup and retreated to his castle (*château de Tocqueville*). There, he began the draft of *L'Ancien Régime et la Révolution*, publishing the first tome in 1856, and leaving unachieved the second one.

Gustave de Beaumont (1802–1865), a prosecutor substitute, and Tocqueville were sent to the United States to compare the democratic system with what was emerging in France. The success of *Democracy in America* (in two volumes, 1835 and 1840) became an early model for the science that would become known as sociology. In both *Democracy in America* and *The Old Regime and the Revolution*, Tocqueville explored the effects of the rising equality of social conditions on both the individual and the state in Western societies. He studied the positive and negative consequences of different forms of democracy on various aspects of social life,

from economics and law to religion and art. He argued that a purely democratic system could easily lead to what he called the "tyranny of the majority." He compared France and England and sought to explain why revolution occurred in the former but not the latter.

He was named *chevalier de la Légion d'honneur* (Knight of the Legion of Honor) (1837), and was elected the next year to the *Académie des sciences morales et politiques*. He was elected a member of the *Académie française* in 1841.

Major Literature

Tocqueville, Alexis de., J.P. Mayer, and A.P. Kerr (Eds.). *The Old Regime and the French Revolution*. New York: Vintage and Anchor Books, 1955.

____. *Recollections: French Revolution of 1848*. G. Lawrence (Translator). New Jersey: Transaction Publishers, 1987.

____. *Writings on Empire and Slavery*. Baltimore: Johns Hopkins University Press, 2003.

____. *Democracy in America*. New York: Barnes and Noble, Collector's Library, new edition, 2005.

____. *Memoir on Pauperism: Does Public Charity Produce an Idle and Dependent Class of Society?* New York: Cosimo Classics, 2006.

Tönnies, Ferdinand (1855–1936)

GEMEINSCHAFT AND GESELLSCHAFT

Ferdinand Tönnies was a German sociologist, born in Nordfriesland in Schleswig-Holstein, Germany, then under Danish rule. He studied at the universities of Jena, Bonn, Leipzig, Berlin, and Tubingen, where he received a doctorate in 1877. From 1881 to 1884 he was a private lecturer at the University of Kiel. He was denied professorship until 1913 because the Prussian government considered him to be a social democrat, having sympathized with the Hamburg

Dockers' strike of 1896. He was professor emeritus in 1921 and taught until 1933, when he was ousted by the Nazis due to his earlier publications criticizing them.

Major Contributions

Tönnies was a major contributor to sociological theory and field studies, and his work had a profound influence on the Chicago School of sociology. He is best known for his distinction between two types of social groups: *Gemeinschaft* (community) and *Gesellschaft* (society). Tönnies' conception of will was central to his sociological theory. He identified *Wesenwille* (natural will), which involves a judgment of the intrinsic value of an act rather than its practicality and which varies in degree of rationality, and *Kürwille* (rational or arbitrary will), which is a conscious choice of means to a specific end. In his view, *Wesenwille* is manifested in *Gemeinschaft*. *Gesellschaft* must be held together by deliberately formulated prescriptions and may be explained in terms of the social-contract theory.

Although Tönnies did not support totalitarianism (including Nazism in his own country) and found some degree of voluntarism in all social relationships, he believed that every social organization has a collective will, presenting aspects of both *Wesenwille* and *Kürwille*, because man's conduct is neither wholly instinctive nor wholly reasoned.

Tönnies was a prolific writer and a cofounder of the German Society for Sociology. He was well known in Great Britain for his English-language editions of writings by the 17th-century philosopher Thomas Hobbes (1588–1679). In 1889, Tönnies, who in part owed his notion of *Kürwille* to Hobbes, produced English editions of Hobbes's *Behemoth* and *Elements of Law, Natural and Politic;* both were reissued in 1928. He also wrote *Thomas Hobbes Leben und Lehre* (1896; *Thomas Hobbes's Life and Doctrine*). Many

of his writings on sociological theories — including *Gemeinschaft und Gesellschaft* (1887) — furthered pure sociology.

Tönnies coined the term "voluntarism." He also contributed to the study of social change, particularly on public opinion, customs and technology, crime, and suicide. He also had a vivid interest in methodology, especially statistics, and sociological research.

Major Literature (English translations)

Tönnies, Ferdinand, and Werner J. Cahnmann (Ed.). *On Sociology: Pure, Applied and Empirical.* Chicago, Illinois: University of Chicago Press, 1971.
___. *On Social Ideas and Ideologies.* New York: Harper and Row, 1974.

Touraine, Alain (1925–)
SOCIOLOGICAL INTERVENTION

Born in Hermanville-sur-Mer, France, Alain Touraine received his history "agrégation" from the Ecole Normale Supèrieure of Paris in 1950. He was a Rockefeller Fellow in 1952 and 1953 at the universities of Harvard (Cambridge, Massachusetts), Columbia (New York) and Chicago (Illinois), and was a researcher at the CNRS (French National Research Council) until 1958. In 1956, Touraine founded the Research Center for the Sociology of Labor at the University of Chile, and in 1958 founded the Industrial Sociology Workshop of Paris, which became the Center for the Study of Social Movements in 1970.

In 1960 he became senior researcher at the now School of the High Études in Social Sciences and, after receiving his D.Litt., taught at the Department of Literature of the University of Paris–Nanterre from 1966 to 1969. In 1981, he founded the Center for Sociological Analysis and Intervention Cadiz, the direction of which he handed over to Michel Wieviorka in 1993.

Touraine received honorary degrees from seven European and American universities. He is a member of several French and international academies and committees dealing with issues such as bioethics, immigration, teaching and research, and of the World Bank Commission on sustainable development. He is an officer of the *Légion d'Honneur* and of the *Ordre National du Mérite*.

Major Contributions

Touraine is best known as the originator of the term "post-industrial society." He believes that society shapes its future through structural mechanisms and its own social struggles. His key interest for most of his career has been with social movements. He has studied and written extensively on workers' movements across the world, particularly in Latin America and in Poland, where he observed and aided the birth of the Trade Union Solidarity. While in Poland, he developed the research method of "sociological intervention."

Touraine has gained immense popularity in Latin America as well as in continental Europe, yet he has failed to gain anywhere near the same recognition in the English-speaking world. The body of Alain Touraine's work constitutes a "sociology of action" and can be divided into three periods:

1. The sociology of labor and workers' consciousness, mainly based on field studies in Latin America.
2. Social movements, starting with studies of the events of May 1968 military coups in Latin America and the birth of Solidarnosc in Poland.
3. Present period, mainly concerned with the subject as the fundamental agent of social movements, an area in which Touraine intends to continue working in the coming years.

Major Literature

Touraine, Alain. *Workers' Movement*. Cambridge, England: Cambridge University Press, 1987.
___. *The Return of the Actor*. Minneapolis, Minnesota: University of Minnesota Press, 1988.
___. *Facing the Future: Young People and Unemployment Around the World*. London, England: Sangam Books, 1991.
___. *Critique of Modernity*. Oxford, England: Blackwell Publishing, 1996.
___, and David Macey. *What is Democracy?* Westview Press, Inc., 1997.
Touraine, Alain. *Can We Live Together?* Cambridge, England: Polity Press, 2000.

Turner, Bryan Stanley (1945–)

MEDICAL SOCIOLOGY

Born in Birmingham, England, Bryan Stanley Turner gained a B.A. in sociology first class (1966), a Ph.D. (1970), and an M.A. (2002) at the University of Leeds, England. His dissertation was "The Decline of Methodism: An Analysis of Religious Commitment and Organization." At the University of Aberdeen, Scotland, Turner was lecturer in sociology (1969–1974); senior lecturer in sociology (1979–1980); and reader in sociology (1980–1982). He was then lecturer in sociology, University of Lancaster, Lancashire, England (1974–1978).

At Flinders University, Adelaide, South Australia, he was professor of sociology and head of the Department of Sociology (1982–1988), and foundation director, Center for Multicultural Studies (1986–1987). He was professor of general social sciences, with special reference to questions of social change and continuity, and department chairman, University of Utrecht, the Netherlands (1988–1990); professor of sociology, University of Essex, Colchester, Essex, England (1990–1993); and dean of arts and professor of sociology, Deakin University, Victoria, Australia (1993–1998). At the University of

Cambridge, England, he was professor of sociology (1998–2005); department head, Faculty of Social and Political Sciences (1999–2001); professorial fellow, Fitzwilliam College (2002–2005); professor of sociology and research leader, Asian Research Institute, National University, Singapore (since 2005).

Flinders University awarded Turner a doctor of literature degree (1986). He was Morris Ginsberg Fellow, London School of Economics, University of London (1981); fellow, Academy of Social Sciences, Australia (1987); Alexander von Humboldt Professorial Fellow, University of Bielefeld, Germany (1987–1978); distinguished visiting fellow, La Trobe University, Victoria, Australia (1992); and distinguished visiting professor, University of Helsinki, Finland (1995). He is or has been on the editorial boards of the *British Journal of Sociology*, *Ethnicities*, *Journal of Social Archaeology*, *Journal of Human Rights*, and *Social Theory and Health*.

Major Contributions

The focus of Turner's contemporary research projects is on:

1. *Religion, Globalization and Politics*. The growth and diversity of religion as a consequence of the globalization of labor markets and population flows; the emergence of citizenship and how it is regulated in Asia; emerging religious conflicts related to fundamentalism, the evolution of citizenship and human rights.
2. *Popular Religion*. The spread of popular religion through modern media — an important dimension of modern society — and how religion is treated as a commodity.
3. *Religion and Global Technology*. The impact of information technology and travel on the growth of modern religion, especially fundamentalism.
4. *Religion Globalization and the Body*.

Religion will continue to play a large part in debates over such issues as stem cell research and assisted reproduction, and the moral questions relating to cloning, genetics, new reproductive technologies, medical technology, human rights, aging and the diseased body.

Major Literature

Turner, Bryan S. *Regulating Bodies: Essays in Medical Sociology*. London, England: Taylor and Francis Books, Ltd., Routledge, 1992.
___. *Orientalism, Postmodernism and Globalism*. London, England: Taylor and Francis Books, Ltd., Routledge, 1994.
___. *The Body and Society*. London, England: Sage Publications, Ltd., 2nd edition, 1996.
___. *Classical Sociology*. London, England: Sage Publications, Ltd., 1999.
___(Ed.). *The Cambridge Dictionary of Sociology*. Cambridge, England: Cambridge University Press, 2006.
___. *Vulnerability and Human Rights*. University Park, Pennsylvania: Pennsylvania State University Press, 2006.

Urry, John Richard (1946–)
SOCIOLOGY OF MOBILITY

Born in London, England, John Richard Urry gained a B.A. and M.A. in economics, ('double first') (1967) and a Ph.D. in sociology (1972) Christ's College, Cambridge, England. At Lancaster University, Lancashire, England, he was lecturer in sociology (1970–1981); senior lecturer, sociology (1981–1985); head of the Department of Sociology (1983–1989); professor of sociology (1985–); founding dean of the faculty of social sciences (1989–1994); university dean of research (1994–1998); director of the Centre for Mobilities Research (2003); coordinator of Lancaster Complexity Network (2003); and director of the M.A. in tourism and leisure degree course.

In his recent professional activities, he has served as chair, Professors and Heads of Department of Sociology National Committee (1989–1992); chair, Sociology Panel, Research Assessment Exercises (1996, 2001); member and chair, advisory board, Central European University, Warsaw, Poland; and president, Global Studies Association (2003–2004).

His awards and honors include an honorary doctorate from Roskilde University, Roskilde, Denmark (2004); fellow, Royal Society of Arts; and founding academician, Academy of the Social Sciences, U.K. He has been editor, International Library of Sociology, Routledge (since 1988) and co-editor, *Mobilities*, launched by Taylor and Francis in 2006. He has or is serving on several editorial and advisory boards: *Annals of Tourism Research, Journeys, European Journal of Social Theory, Space and Culture, Theory, Culture and Society, British Journal of Sociology*, and *Tourist Studies*.

Recent international research collaborations include those at the Institute of Philosophy and Sociology, Warsaw, program of workshops and joint publications; Danish Tourism Centre, Roskilde University; visiting Professor; L'institut pour la ville en mouvement, Paris, funded by Peugeot-Citroen; Reflexive Modernisation Centre, Munich; and the Cosmobilities Network; EST Zurich, Social Networks and Future Mobilities project.

Major Contributions

Urry's original research interests were in the sociology of power and revolution, and this resulted in the publication of *Reference Groups and the Theory of Revolution* (Routledge and Kegan Paul, 1973) and *Power in Britain* (Heinemann Education, co-edited with John Wakeford, 1973). Early work at Lancaster was in the area of social theory and the philosophy of the social sciences. Recent research has focused on five main areas:

1. urban and regional research, mainly associated with the Lancaster Regionalism Group
2. general dimensions of economic and social change in Western capitalist societies
3. consumer services and especially tourist-related services, industries that are of particular significance in contemporary Western societies
4. the changing nature of mobility
5. exploring some implications of complexity theory for the social sciences.

Major Literature

Abercrombie, Nicholas, and John Urry. *Capital, Labour and the Middle Classes.* London, England: Harper Collins Publishers, Ltd., 1983.

Urry, John. *Consuming Places.* London, England: Taylor and Francis Books, Ltd., Routledge, 1995.

_____. *Touring Cultures: Transformations of Travel and Theory.* Taylor and Francis Books, Ltd., Routledge, 1997.

_____. *Sociology Beyond Societies: Mobilities for the Twenty-First Century.* London, England: Taylor and Francis Books, Ltd., Routledge, 1999.

_____. *The Tourist Gaze.* London, England: Sage Publications, Ltd., 2nd edition, 2002.

Featherstone, Mike, Nigel Thrift, and John Urry (Eds.). *Automobilities.* London, England: Sage Publications, Ltd., 2005.

Larsen, Jonas, John Urry, and Kay Axhausen. *Mobilities, Networks, Geographies.* London, England: Ashgate Publishing, 2006.

Veblen, Thorstein (1857–1929)

THE LEISURE CLASS

Born in Cato, Wisconsin, of Norwegian immigrant parents, Thorstein Veblen gained his B.A. in economics at Carleton College, Northfield, Minnesota (1880). He did his graduate work at Johns Hopkins University, Baltimore, Maryland, and gained a Ph.D. in moral philosophy (1884) at Yale University,

New Haven, Connecticut, under William Graham Sumner (see entry). His doctoral thesis was on the German philosopher Immanuel Kant (1724–1804). From 1891 to 1892, after six years of unemployment, Veblen continued studying as a graduate student, in economics, at Cornell University, Ithaca, New York. Between 1892 and 1919, when he helped found the New School for Social Research, New York (known today as The New School), Veblen was a professor at the newly opened University of Chicago, Illinois, served as managing editor of the *Journal of Political Economy*, and lectured in economics at the universities of Stanford, California, and Missouri-Columbia.

Major Contributions

As a sociologist Veblen concentrated on criticism of capitalism as an exploitative and greedy system; the dominant social classes, whom he called the leisure class and who benefit most from capitalism; and the influence of economic values on social life. Veblen was particularly critical, for example, of what he saw as the corruption of education by the obsessive pursuit of economic success. Veblen became well known through his book *The Theory of the Leisure Class* (1899), a satiric look at American society. He coined the widely used phrases "conspicuous consumption" and "pecuniary emulation," a description of the display of wealth made by the upper class.

His reputation was highest in the 1930s, when the Great Depression was seen as a vindication of his criticism of the business system. An important analytical contribution became associated with Veblen — the "ceremonial-instrumental dichotomy." The clash between the "ceremonial" related to the past, supporting the tribal legends, and the "instrumental" related to the technological aspects of group life.

Major Literature (Modern editions)

Veblen, Thorstein. *The Theory of the Leisure Class* (1899). Delhi, India: Aakar Books, 2005.
___. *The Theory of Business Enterprise* (1904). New Jersey: Transaction Publishers, 1978.
___. *The Instinct of Workmanship and the State of the Industrial Arts* (1914). New York: Cosimo Classics, 2006.
___. *Imperial Germany and the Industrial Revolution* (1915). New York: Cosimo Classics, 2006.
___. *The Higher Learning in America: A Memorandum on the Conduct of Universities by Businessmen* (1918). New York: Cosimo Classics, 2005.
___. *The Place of Science in Modern Civilization and Other Essays* (1919). New Jersey: Transaction Publishers, 1990.
___. *The Vested Interests and the Common Man* (1919). New York: Cosimo Classics, 2005.

Vincent, George Edgar (1864–1941)
SOCIOLOGY OF EDUCATION

George Edgar Vincent was born in Rockford, Illinois, the son of Bishop John Heyl Vincent, founder of the Chautauqua movement, a popular system of education and home study for children and adults. George Vincent spent the early years of his career working for the Chautauqua Schools, eventually succeeding his father in 1898. In 1886 he became the literary editor of the Chautauqua Press, then served as vice-president of the school from 1888 to 1889.

Vincent entered the University of Chicago, Illinois, in 1892, the same year the university was established, and became the first graduate student in the world's first sociology department. Along with Albion Small (see entry), chair of the new department, Vincent helped write *Introduction to the Study of Sociology*, the first sociology textbook ever published in the United States. He received his Ph.D. from the University of Chicago in 1896, with his dissertation entitled "Social

Mind and Education." After spending some time as a teaching fellow in sociology at the University of Chicago, he became a full professor of sociology in 1904. From 1900 to 1907 he was dean of the Junior College, and from 1907 to 1911 he served as the dean of arts, literature and sciences at Chicago.

In 1911, Vincent became the president of the University of Minnesota, Minneapolis, and built the university's reputation as one of the country's leading research universities. Influenced heavily by his experiences with Chautauqua, Vincent established the General Extension Division to provide access for adults to University of Minnesota classes. He also established a connection between the Graduate School and the Mayo Foundation and created the All-University Student Council. In 1917 he become the president of the Rockefeller Foundation.

He was a trustee of the Peiping Union Medical College from 1917 to 1929 and the China Medical Board, Inc., from 1930 to 1938. He was also a member of a variety of other groups, including the General Education Board from 1914 to 1929 and the United States Delegation to the Pan American Conference in Santiago, Chile, in 1923. Vincent retired in 1929 but kept active in many more outside activities and roles: lecturer at the Scandinavian University in 1933; member of the American Scandinavian Foundation; member of the Commission for Relief in Belgium and the Educational Foundation. He was one of the founding members of the American Sociological Society in 1895, and its sixth president in 1916. He was associate editor of the *American Journal of Sociology* from 1895 to 1915 and advisory editor from 1915 to 1933.

He was a pioneer of rural sociology, and his contribution to the development of the then new science of sociology was enormous. Possibly his greatest contribution was his popularization of the sociological point of view both in the classroom and in public address. He received many public honors, among which were LL.D. degrees from the universities of Chicago, Yale, Michigan, and Minnesota.

Wallerstein, Immanuel Maurice (1930–)

WORLD SYSTEM THEORY

Born in New York City, Immanuel Maurice Wallerstein gained a B.A. (1951), M.A. (1954), and PhD. (1959) and was lecturer (1958–1971) at Columbia University, New York. He was at Oxford University, England (1955–1956), and was professor of sociology, McGill University, Montreal, Canada (1971–1976). At State University of New York, Binghamton, he was distinguished professor of sociology (1976–1999) and director of the Fernand Braudel Center for the Study of Economics, Historical Systems, and Civilizations (1999–2005). He was chair of the international Gulbenkian Commission on the Restructuring of the Social Sciences (1993–1995); president of the International Sociological Association (1994–1998); and senior research scholar, Yale University, New Haven, Connecticut (2000).

Wallerstein held several positions as visiting professor at universities worldwide; he was awarded multiple honorary titles and intermittently served as director at the School for Advanced Studies in the Social Sciences in Paris.

Major Contributions

Until the early 1970s Wallerstein devoted himself to post-colonial African affairs, until he began to distinguish himself as a historian and theorist of the global capitalist economy, which developed into world system theory. His early criticism of global capitalism and championship of "anti-systemic movements" have made him a powerful adviser with the anti-globalization movement within and without the academic community, along with Noam Chomsky, Professor of Linguistics (1928–), and Pierre Bourdieu (see entry).

Wallerstein rejected the notion of a "Third World," claiming there was only one world, connected by a complex network of economic exchange relationships; i.e., a "world-economy" or "world-system" in which friction is caused by the separation of capital and labor, and the obsession with accumulating capital by people and nations competing with one another. In the world system, more and more economies that have remained on the periphery are sucked into the core. The task of the periphery economies is to supply raw materials, agricultural products and cheap labor for the ever-expanding core, which has a high level of technological development and manufactures complex products. The periphery is forced to sell its products at low prices, but has to buy the core's products at comparatively high prices, thus creating an unequal relationship.

Wallerstein writes in three domains of world-systems analysis: the historical development of the modern world-system; the contemporary crisis of the capitalist world-economy; and the structures of knowledge.

Major Literature

Wallerstein, Immanuel M. *The Modern World-System, Vol. I: Capitalist Agriculture and the Origins of the European World-Economy in the Sixteenth Century.* New York: Academic Press, 1974.

___. *The Modern World-System, Vol. II: Mercantilism and the Consolidation of the European World-Economy, 1600–1750.* New York: Academic Press, 1980.

___. *The Modern World-System, Vol. III: The Second Great Expansion of the Capitalist World-Economy, 1730–1840s.* San Diego: Academic Press, 1989.

___. *The End of the World As We Know It: Social Science for the Twenty-first Century.* Minneapolis: University of Minnesota Press, 1999.

___. *World-Systems Analysis: An Introduction.* Durham, North Carolina: Duke University Press, 2004.

___. *European Universalism: The Rhetoric of Power.* New York: New Press, 2006.

Ward, Lester Frank (1841–1913)

PIONEER SOCIOLOGIST

Lester Frank Ward was an American sociologist who was instrumental in establishing sociology as an academic discipline in the United States. Born in Joliet, Illinois, he fought for the Union in the American Civil War, then went on to gain degrees in botany and law. For most of his life he worked for the federal government, mainly in the fields of geology, paleontology, and botany, and made some significant contributions to botanical theory.

By 1876 Ward had shifted the focus of the work, which was begun in 1869, to sociology, and when he was 65 years old, he was appointed professor of sociology at Brown University, Providence, Rhode Island. Ward followed Auguste Comte (see entry) in thinking of sociology as the fundamental social science, the primary responsibility of which is to teach methods of improving society. Ward's emphasis on social function and planning, rather than social structure, had considerable effect on Thorstein Veblen (see entry) and on economic thought generally.

Although Herbert Spencer and Karl Marx disagreed about many things, they were similar in that their systems were static: they both taught that mankind was essentially helpless before the force of evolution. Ward disagreed with that static view. On the other hand, Ward was optimistic. For example, he believed that poverty, one of society's curses, could be minimized or eliminated by the systematic intervention. Humankind wasn't helpless before the impersonal force of nature and evolution; through the power of Mind, people could take control of the situation and direct the evolution of human society.

Ward was also scathing in his denunciation of the doctrine of laissez-faire. He also believed that the social sciences had already given mankind the information basic to happiness, and to further this state, he advocated a planned society in which nationally organized education would be the dynamic factor. In his "sociocracy" — similar to the utopian plan of Auguste Comte — social scientists would assemble into a legislative advisory academy in Washington, D.C. Ward was a strong advocate for equal rights for women and even theorized that women were naturally superior to men, much to the scorn of mainstream sociologists. Ward is now considered a feminist writer.

He served as the first president of the American Sociological Association (1906 and 1907).

Major Literature

Ward, Lester Frank. *Dynamic Sociology* (2 vols). New York: Appleton, 1883.
____. *Pure Sociology.* New York: Macmillan, 1903.
____. *A Textbook of Sociology* (with James Quayle Dealey). New York: Macmillan, 1905.
____. "Sociocracy." Chapter 38 in *Psychic Factors of Civilization.* Boston, Massachusetts: Ginn and Company, 1906.
____. *Applied Sociology.* Boston: Ginn and Company, 1906.
____. *Glimpses of the Cosmos.* New York: Putnam, 1913.

Waters, Mary C. (1957–)

SOCIOLOGY OF IMMIGRATION

Born in the Bronx, New York, Mary C. Waters gained a B.A. in philosophy at Johns Hopkins University, Baltimore, Maryland (1978). At the University of California, Berkeley, she earned an M.A. in sociology (1981), an M.A. in demography (1983), and a Ph.D. in sociology (1986), and was acting instructor, Department of Sociology (1983–1985). At Harvard University, Cambridge, Massachusetts, she was assistant to associate professor, Department of Sociology (1986–1990); John L. Loeb Associate Professor of the Social Sciences (1991–1993); Harvard College professor (1999–2004); chair, Department of Sociology (2001–2005); professor of sociology (1993); and M.E. Zukerman Professor of Sociology (since 2006).

Her awards and honors: Outstanding Teaching Award, University of California (1984); Hoopes Award for Excellence in Teaching (1990, 1996); George R. Kharl Award for Excellence in Teaching (1991); elected to the Sociological Research Association (1993); elected to the American Philosophical Society (2005); fellow, Radcliffe Institute for Advanced Study (2005–2006); and fellow, American Academy of Arts and Sciences (2006).

Major Contributions

Waters is the author of numerous important books and articles, including most recently *Black Identities,* which won numerous honors: the Mirra Komorovsky Award of the Eastern Sociological Society for the best book published in 1999–2000; the 2001 Otis Dudley Duncan Award of the Population Section of the American Sociological Association (ASA); the 2001 Thomas and Znaniecki Award of the International Migration Section of the ASA; the 1999 Best Book Award of the Section on Race, Ethnicity and Politics of the American Political Science Association, and the 1999–2000 Distinguished Book Award of the Center for the Study of Inequality at Cornell University, Ithaca, New York.

Waters carried out a large survey of the lives of young adult children of immigrant parents in New York City, based on analysis of in-depth life history interviews and ethnographic observations. The study examined the socioeconomic, cultural, and social adjustments of the new second generation. Waters also directed a cross-site qualitative study of the transition to adulthood in communities across the United States. This study ascertained how young people are leaving home, finishing education, finding work, choosing life partners, and becoming parents.

Major Literature

Lieberson, Stanley, and Mary C. Waters. *From Many Strands: Ethnic and Racial Groups in Contemporary America.* New York: Russell Sage Foundation, 1988, 1990.

Waters, Mary C. *Black Identities: West Indian Immigrant Dreams and American Realities.* Cambridge, Massachusetts: Harvard University Press, 1999.

Waters, Mary C., and Joel Perlmann (Eds.). *The New Race Question: How the Census Counts Multiracial Individuals.* New York: Russell Sage Foundation Press, 2002.

Waters, Mary C., and Peggy Levitt (Eds.). *The Changing Face of Home: The Transnational Lives of the Second Generation.* New York: Russell Sage Foundation Press, 2002.

Waters, Mary C., and Fiona Devine (Eds.). *Social Inequalities in Comparative Perspective.* Oxford, England: Blackwell Publishing, 2003.

Waters, Mary C., Philip Kasinitz, and John H. Mollenkopf (Eds.). *Becoming New Yorkers: Ethnographies of the New Second Generation.* New York: Russell Sage Foundation Press, 2004.

Waters, Mary C., and Tomas Jimenez. "Assessing Immigrant Assimilation: New Empirical and Theoretical Challenges." *Annual Review of Sociology,* 31 (2005) 105–25.

Weatherly, Ulysses Grant (1865–1940)

RACE RELATIONS

Born in West Newton, Indiana, of illiterate farming parents, Ulysses Grant Weatherly gained an A.B. at Colgate University, Hamilton, New York (1890), then did graduate work in history and political science at Cornell University, Ithaca, New York (1891–1892), and gained a Ph.D. (1894) having traveled in England, Germany, Austria and studying in Heidelberg and Leipzig Universities (1893–1894). He taught at Central High School in Philadelphia, Pennsylvania (1894–1895). At Indiana University, Bloomington, he was assistant professor of European history (1895); associate professor of history (1896–1899); professor of economics and sociology; and head of the Department of Economics and Social Science (1899–1935).

He was a founding member (1905) of the American Sociological Society (Association, 1959), member, executive committee (1907–1910), vice president (1920–1923), and president (1923). He was also president of the Indiana Conference of Charities and Corrections; chairman of the Indiana Child Labor Commission; and member of the Indiana Commission of Industrial Education. He was visiting professor during summer sessions at Columbia University, New York (1912); University of Illinois, Urbana, Champaign (1914); Cornell University (1923); University of Oregon, Eugene (1929); and University of Southern California, Los Angeles (1932).

Major Contributions

Weatherly's presidential address, entitled "Racial Pessimism," was delivered at the American Sociological Society's annual meeting in Pittsburgh on December 27, 1923, and was published in the Proceedings of the 1923 Annual Meeting. In his early years, Weatherly taught courses in general sociology, anthropology, criminology, charities, and race relations. During those years, he formed contacts with the social agencies of Indiana and took an active part in the state conferences of social work. He spent several months one year touring the West Indies with Robert E. Park (see entry), studying race relations, and wrote two journal articles on race relations in Haiti.

In 1906, he produced a small book, *Outlines in Sociology*, explaining his ideas of sociology; it was the forerunner of many sociology texts. In 1906 Weatherly wrote to the president and board of trustees of Indiana University, drawing attention to the urgent need for further developing the work in sociology. He contrasted the fragmentary nature of the sociology courses offered with those in the economics faculty. His concern was that students were being deprived of a proper foundation in sociology. He was not interested in abstract theoretical sociology but practical courses. Weatherly died in Cortland, New York.

Major Literature

Weatherly, U.G. *Outlines in Sociology*. Indianapolis, Indiana: Hollenbeck Press, 1906.
___. "How Does the Access of Women to Industrial Occupations React on the Family?" *American Journal of Sociology*, Vol. 14, No. 6 (1909): 740–65.
___. "Race and Marriage." *American Journal of Sociology*, Vol. 15, No. 4 (1910): 433–453.
___ "The West Indies as a Sociological Laboratory." *American Journal of Sociology*, 29, No. 3 (1923): 290–304.
___. "Haiti: An Experiment in Pragmatism." *American Journal of Sociology*, 32, No. 3 (1926): 353–366.
___. *Social Progress: Studies in the Dynamics of Social Change*. Philadelphia, Pennsylvania: Lippincott, 1927.

Weber, Max (1864–1920)

POLITICAL PSYCHOLOGY

Sociologist and political economist Max Weber is best known for his thesis of the Protestant ethic and for his ideas on bureaucracy. With Karl Marx and Émile Durkheim (see entries), he is considered to a key figure in the history of sociology. Born in Erfurt, Germany, Weber enrolled at the University of Heidelberg in 1882, served his two years of military service at Strasbourg, then completed his studies at the University of Berlin. In 1890, Weber wrote a comprehensive analysis of the agrarian problems of the German East for one of Germany's most important academic societies, the Union for Social Policy. In 1893 he received a temporary position in jurisprudence at the University of Berlin, and in 1895 he was appointed full professor in political economy at Freiburg University, then in 1896, at Heidelberg University.

In his inaugural address at Freiburg, Weber blasted the ruling Junker aristocracy as historically obsolete. In his view the only way Germany could achieve political power was if the whole nation were educated to political maturity by a conscious policy of overseas imperial expansion. Weber's Freiburg address thus advanced an ideology of "liberal imperialism." Between 1898 and 1903, following the death of his father, Weber had several periods of being institutionalized, suffering from depression, something that plagued him for the rest of his life and which interfered with his academic career.

Weber's definition of modern society as an iron cage — which would increasingly hold people's lives in its grip with little hope for escape or relief from its suffocating effects on the human spirit, determined by Western rationalism — hints that his strict Calvinistic upbringing placed a great amount of role conformity upon him. He argued that before Calvinism, capitalist enterprise was always fettered by the passive or active hostility of the prevalent religious order.

Weber's political sociology is concerned with the distinction between charismatic, traditional, and legal forms of authority. Charisma refers to the gift of spiritual inspiration underlying the power of religious prophecy and political leadership. Around

1916, Weber was engaged in efforts to gain respect for sociology as a discipline by defining a value-free methodology for it. Following World War I, he argued powerfully against Germany's annexationist war goals and in favor of a strengthened parliament. He assisted in drafting the new constitution and in the founding of the German Democratic Party. All of Weber's most important work appeared in the 17 years between the worst part of his illness and his death.

Major Literature (Modern editions)

Weber, Max. *Economy and Society.* Berkeley, California: University of California Press, 1978.
___. *Basic Concepts of Sociology.* New York: Citadel Press, Inc., 1994.
___. *The Protestant Ethic and the Spirit.* Mineola, New York: Dover Publications, Inc., 2003.
___. *From Max Weber: Essays in Sociology.* New York: Taylor and Francis Group, Routledge, 2004.
___. *Protestantism and the Rise of Capitalism.* Whitefish, Montana: R.A. Kessinger Publishing Co., 2004.

Wells-Barnett, Ida B. (1862–1931)

BLACK FEMINISM SOCIOLOGY

Ida B. Wells-Barnett was a fearless anti-lynching crusader, suffragist, women's rights advocate, journalist, and speaker. She stands as one of America's most uncompromising leaders and most ardent defenders of democracy. She delivered forceful blows against mainstream white male ideologies of the time, and helped to organize the National Association for the Advancement of Colored People (NAACP) along with W.E.B. Du Bois (see entry). Her parents were slaves in Holy Springs, Mississippi, and although emancipated after the Civil War (1861–1865), they remained on the plantation as employees of the master.

Until 1876 Wells-Barnett was at the (now) Rust College, Holly Springs, when both her parents died of yellow fever. Determined to keep her family together, she migrated to Memphis, Tennessee, and took a job as a schoolteacher. Because she needed qualifications in order to teach, she enrolled in Fisk University, Nashville, Tennessee, and gained her qualification in less than a year. In 1884 she caused a stir when she was forcibly moved from the ladies' compartment on a train into a smoking compartment to make room for a white person. She sued the railroad company and won the case, but the decision was reversed by the Supreme Court of Tennessee. Her teaching career ended in 1891 for protesting about the conditions in black schools.

In 1892, she founded and was part owner of the weekly newspaper *Memphis Free Speech and Headlights*, distributed throughout the black community; she was the editor and wrote a column under the pen name Lola. The printing press was destroyed and she was run out of town by a white mob. She settled in Chicago and became associated with the *Chicago Conservator*. It was here she met and married Ferdinand Lee Barnett in 1895.

Wells-Barnett's social theory is considered to be a radical non–Marxian conflict theory with a focus on pathological differences and power in U.S. society, characterized by repression, domination, subjugation and tyranny. Her social theory was also considered "black feminism sociology," which had four themes that found action in moral resistance: a method of social analysis appropriate to the project; her model of the social world; her theory of domination; and her alternative to domination. Wells-Barnett's significant contribution to the field ranks with top social thinkers of the day, including the African-American educator and social activist Anna Julia Cooper (1858–1964). Her theories also centered on legal issue pertaining to African American suffrage of the time, particularly Washington's policies for not protecting black people against lynching (See entry, Troy Duster).

Major Literature (Modern editions)

Wells-Barnett, Ida, and Jacqueline Jones Royster (Ed.). *Southern Horrors and Other Writings: The Anti-Lynching Campaign of Ida B. Wells, 1892–1900.* Basingstoke, Hampshire, England: Palgrave Macmillan, Ltd., St. Martins Press, 1997.

Wells-Barnett, Ida. *On Lynchings.* Loughton, Essex, England: Prometheus Books, 2002.

___. *The Red Record.* New York: Arno Press, 1969. Indypublish.com, 2005.

___. *Mob Rule in New Orleans.* New York: Arno Press, 1969. Indypublish.com, 2005.

Whyte, Martin King (1942–)
SOCIOLOGY OF CHINA

Born in Oklahoma City, Oklahoma, Martin King Whyte gained a B.A. in physics with a minor in Russian at Cornell University, Ithaca, New York (1964) with cum laude, Phi Eta Sigma and Phi Beta Kappa honors. In 1963 he went on a University of Michigan study tour of the USSR. At Harvard University, Cambridge, Massachusetts, he gained an M.A. in Russian area studies (1966) and was research assistant, Harvard Project on the Social and Cultural Aspects of Modernization (1967–1968); did thesis fieldwork involving interviewing refugees from China residing in Hong Kong, (1968–1969); and gained a Ph.D. in sociology (1971) with a thesis titled "Small Groups and Political Rituals in Communist China."

At the University of Michigan, Whyte was research associate, Center for Chinese Studies, (1969–1970); associate chairman, Department of Sociology (1972–1973, 1979–1981); assistant professor of sociology (1970–1976); associate professor of sociology (1976–1981); professor of sociology (1981–1994);

deputy director, Center for Chinese Studies, (1978–1979, 1989–1990); and director, Center for Research on Social Organization (1984–1988, 1990–1991). He was director, Universities Service Centre, Kowloon, Hong Kong (1973–1974); program director, Sociology Program, National Science Foundation (1993–1994); professor of sociology and international affairs, George Washington University, Washington, D.C. (1994–2000); professor of sociology, Harvard University, (since 2000); visiting professor, University of Aveiro, Portugal (2002).

His awards and honors include a faculty fellowship, Center of Asian and Pacific Studies, University of Hawaii, Honolulu (1982); fellow, Center for Advanced Study in the Behavioral Sciences, Palo Alto, California (1991–1992); visiting fellow, Contemporary China Centre, Australian National University, Canberra, Australia (1995); Eastern Sociological Society, Robin Williams Distinguished Lectureship (1997–1998); and member, Academic Advisory Committee, Institute of Sociology, Academia, Sinica, Taiwan (2004).

Major Contributions

Whyte's teaching and research interests include the comparative institutional development of China and the former Soviet Union; the American family; inequality and stratification; bureaucracy; and the sociology of post-communist transitions. *China's Revolutions* draws on a survey project that focused on relations between aging parents and their grown children in urban Chinese families. A national survey focusing on inequality and distributive justice issues was completed in the summer of 2004.

At Harvard, Whyte regularly teaches a course on social life in contemporary China and a course on the American family. He also offers seminars on contemporary Chinese society focused on issues of inequality and stratification, on the sociology of families and kinship, and on the sociology of economic development. He also teaches "Foreign Cultures 63: China's Two Social Revolutions," a general overview of the patterns of social life in China and how these have changed since the revolution in 1949.

Major Literature

Whyte, Martin King. *Small Groups and Political Rituals in China*. Berkeley: University of California Press, 1974.
___. *The Status of Women in Preindustrial Societies*. Princeton, New Jersey: Princeton University Press, 1978.
___, and William Parish. *Village and Family in Contemporary China*. Chicago, Illinois: University of Chicago Press, 1978.
Whyte, Martin King. *Marriage in America: A Communitarian Perspective*. Lanham, Maryland: Rowman and Littlefield, 2000.
___. *China's Revolutions and Inter-Generational Relations*. Ann Arbor, Michigan: University of Michigan Center for Chinese Studies, 2003.

Whyte, William Foote (1914–2000)

INDUSTRIAL SOCIOLOGY

Born in Springfield, Massachusetts, William Foote Whyte gained an A.B. in economics (1936) at Swarthmore College, Swarthmore, Pennsylvania. He was junior fellow, Harvard University, Cambridge, Massachusetts (1936–1940); taught at Swarthmore (1944–1948); and gained a Ph.D. in sociology at the University of Chicago, Illinois (1943), having taught at the University of Oklahoma, Norman (1942–1943). He was at School of Industrial and Labor Relations, Cornell University, Ithaca, New York, from 1948 until he retired in 1979. He was 72nd president of the American Sociological Association (1981).

Major Contributions

While at Harvard, Whyte lived on the streets of Boston in an Italian community, researching social relations of street gangs in Boston's North End. His experience — published as *Street Corner Society*— has been the model for urban ethnography ever since. He was among the first to demonstrate that a poor community need not be socially disorganized. Whyte contracted polio in 1943 but recovered some use of his legs, thanks in part to an experimental treatment offered in a Boston hospital; he conducted all of his field research with the aid of braces, crutches and canes.

He studied industrial and agricultural workers and workers' cooperatives in Venezuela, Peru, Guatemala, the Mondragon cooperative complex in Spain, and the oil fields of Oklahoma, working all the time for social reform and social change. His presidential address, "Social Inventions for Solving Human Problems," was published in the *American Sociological Review* (47, No. 1 [1982]: 1–13). As an emeritus professor at Cornell, Whyte was a co-founder and later research director of Programs for Employment and Workplace Systems.

After his death, a tribute was paid to Whyte by members of the Ohio Employee Ownership Center, of which Whyte was an early supporter "and a great friend of employee ownership the world over. He wrote the foreword for BUYOUT!, a collection and analysis of case studies of Ohio buyout committee experiences." Upon his death, friends and colleagues remembered Whyte in an article entitled "Colleagues Salute William Foote Whyte," which was published on page 6 of the September–October 2000 issue of *Footnotes*.

Whyte addressed questions that lie at the heart of sociology — how individuals, groups, and societies shape each other, how social processes operate at every scale of human activity — and illuminated them with his participant observation. It was his career-long, and still-controversial, assertion that social scientists can maintain objectivity while immersed in the societies they study. Whyte's work influenced methodologies in a range of disciplines from anthropology, social psychology and industrial relations to organizational behavior, agricultural development and sociology.

Major Literature

Whyte, William Foote. *Street Corner Society: The Social Structure of an Italian Slum.* Chicago, Illinois: University of Chicago Press, 1943, 4th edition, 1993.

___. *Human Relations in the Restaurant Industry.* McGraw-Hill Companies, Inc. 1948.

___. *Participatory Action Research.* Thousand Oaks, California: Sage, 1991.

___. *Social Theory for Action.* Thousand Oaks, California: Sage, 1991.

___. *Participant Observer: An Autobiography.* New York: Cornell University Press, 1994.

___. *Creative Problem Solving in the Field: Reflections on a Career.* Lanham, Maryland: Rowman and Littlefield Publishers, Inc., 1997.

Williams, Robin Murphy, Jr. (1914–2006)

RACE RELATIONS

Born in Hillsborough, North Carolina, Robin Murphy Williams, Jr., gained a B.S. (1933) and M.S. (1935) at North Carolina State University, Raleigh, and an M.A. (1939) and Ph.D. (1943) at Harvard University, Cambridge, Massachusetts. From 1942 to 1946 he worked for the Special Services Division of the U.S. War Department in Washington, D.C., and the European Theater of Operations. At Cornell University, Ithaca, New York, he was in the Sociology Department (1946); chair of the department (1956–1961); was Henry Scarborough Professor of Social Science (1967); and was emeritus professor (1985–2003). From 1990 to 2006 he was affiliated with the University of California, Irvine.

Williams was 48th president of the American Sociological Society (Association, 1959) (ASA) (1958). He was a member of the National Academy of Sciences; American Philosophical Society; National Research Council; Pacific Sociological Association; American Association for the Advancement of Science; and was president, Eastern Sociological Association. His awards and honors include the Commonwealth Award for Distinguished Service; Career of Distinguished Scholarship Award, ASA; and the Robin M. Williams, Jr., Distinguished Lectureship Award established in his honor by the Eastern Sociological Association.

Major Contributions

Williams' presidential address, "Continuity and Change in Sociological Study," was published in the December 1958 issue of the *American Sociological Review* (23, No. 6 [1958]: 619–633). He devoted much of his career and writing to studies of inter-group tensions, race relations, war and peace, ethnic conflict, and altruism and cooperation. As an Army researcher on the frontlines, he was a contributor to the classic work *The American Soldier.* In his retirement, Williams took on the chair of the National Research Council's Committee on the Status of Black Americans, publishing with Gerald David Jaynes in 1989 a major report on its findings: *A Common Destiny.*

In 1989 came the first publication of a paper based on data he collected in the 1950s in Elmira on women's roles. Williams was passionate about promoting understanding of ethnic conflicts within and across national borders. The result was, *The Wars Within: Peoples and States in Conflict.* In 1986 he founded *Sociological Forum*, the journal of the Eastern Sociological Society.

Major Literature

Williams, Robin M. *The Reduction of Intergroup Tensions*. New York: Social Science Research Council, 1947.

Stouffer, S.A., A.A. Lumsdaine, M.H. Lumsdaine, R.M. Williams, Jr., and M.B. Smith, et al. *The American Soldier: Combat and Its Aftermath*, Vol. 2. Princeton, New Jersey: Princeton University Press, 1949.

Williams, Robin M. *Schools in Transition: Community Experiences in Desegregation*. Chapel Hill, North Carolina: University of North Carolina Press, 1954.

___. *Strangers Next Door: Ethnic Relations in American Communities*. New Jersey: Prentice-Hall, 1964.

___. *American Society: A Sociological Interpretation*. New York: Knopf, 3rd edition, 1970.

___. *Mutual Accommodation: Ethnic Conflict and Cooperation*. Minnesota, Minneapolis: Minnesota University Press, 1977.

Jaynes, Gerald David, and Robin M. Williams. *A Common Destiny: Blacks and American Society*. Washington, D.C: National Academy Press, 1989.

Williams, Robin M. *The Wars Within: Peoples and States in Conflict*. New York: Cornell University Press, 2003.

Wilson, Bryan Ronald (1928–2004)

SOCIOLOGY OF RELIGION

Born in Leeds, Yorkshire, England, Bryan Ronald Wilson gained a B.Sc. in economics with first class honors at the University of London (1952) and a Ph.D. at the London School of Economics (1955), and was lecturer in sociology, University of Leeds (1955–1962). His M.A. was from the University of Oxford (1962). He was reader in sociology at All Souls College, Oxford, and was a fellow (1963), sub-warden (1988–1990), domestic bursar (1989–1993), and emeritus fellow (1993). He was Commonwealth Fund fellow (Harkness Foundation), University of California, Berkeley (1957–1958); visiting professor, University of Ghana

(1964); fellow of the American Counsel of Learned Societies, Berkeley (1966–1967); research consultant for the Sociology of Religion, University of Padua, Italy (1968–1972); president of what is now the International Society for the Sociology of Religion (1971–1975); visiting fellow, the Japan Society (1975); visiting professor, the Catholic University, Louvain, Belgium (1976, 1982, 1986, 1993); council member of the Society for the Scientific Study of Religion (U.S.A.) (1977–1979); and Snider Visiting Professor, University of Toronto, Canada (1978).

He was visiting professor in the sociology of religion and consultant for religious studies, Mahidol University, Bangkok, Thailand (1980–1981). He was also Scott Visiting Fellow, Ormond College, University of Melbourne, Australia (1981); visiting professor, University of Queensland, Australia (1986); and distinguished visiting professor, University of California, Santa Barbara (1987). His awards and honors include an honorary D.Litt., University of Oxford (1984); *doctor honoris causa*, Catholic University of Leuven, Louvain, Belgium, in recognition of his outstanding contribution to the sociology of religion (1992); honorary doctorate, Soka University, Japan (1994); fellow of the British Academy (1994).

Major Contributions

Wilson has made extensive contributions to the sociology of religion in the areas of sectarian religion and secularization, and set the research agenda for sociology of religion throughout the world. He was also a pioneer of studies of millennialism. He conducted research into minority religious movements in the United Kingdom, the United States, Ghana, Kenya, Belgium and Japan. He defended new religious movements and other minorities against the various waves of international anti-cult campaigns, for no other personal reason than his passionate love for freedom and justice; he defined himself as an agnostic. He argued that Scientology was precisely the kind of religion one might expect to find reflecting the preoccupations of a secularized society. He has been called as an expert witness on sects in courts in various parts of the world, and has given expert written evidence on religious movements for the Parliamentary Home Affairs Committee of the House of Commons.

Major Literature

Wilson, Bryan. *Sects and Society: The Sociology of Three Religious Groups in Britain*. London, England: Heinemann, 1961. Reprinted, Westport, Connecticut: Greenwood Press, 1978.

___(Ed.). *Patterns of Sectarianism* London, England: Heinemann, 1967.

___. *Magic and the Millennium*. London, England: Heinemann, 1973.

___. *Religion in Sociological Perspective*. Oxford, England: Clarendon Press, 1982.

___, and K.A. Dobbelaere. *Time to Chant: The Soka Gakkai Buddhists in Britain*. Oxford, England: Clarendon Press, 1994.

Wilson, William Julius (1935–)

URBAN POVERTY

Born in Derry township, Pennsylvania, William Julius Wilson gained a B.A. in sociology and history, Wilberforce University, Wilberforce, Ohio (1958), an M.A. sociology, Bowling Green State University, Ohio (1961), and a Ph.D. in sociology and anthropology, Washington State University, Pullman, Washington (1966). At the University of Massachusetts, Amherst, Department of Sociology, he was assistant (1965–1969) and associate professor of sociology (1969–1971). At the University of Chicago, Illinois, he was associate professor of sociology (1972–1975); chairman, Department of Sociology (1978–1981); acting director, Center for the Study of Industrial Societies (1984–1987); Lucy

Flower Professor of Urban Sociology (1980–1984); distinguished service professor, Department of Sociology and School of Public Policy (1984–1990); and university professor (1990–1996). At Harvard University, Cambridge, Massachusetts, he was director, Joblessness and Urban Poverty Research Program, Malcolm Wiener Center for Social Policy (1996–); Malcolm Wiener Professor of Social Policy (1996–1998); and Lewis P. and Linda L. Geyser University Professor (1998–). He won the National Medal of Science (1998).

Major Contributions

Wilson maintains that a large black underclass is created more by class divisions and global economic changes than by racism, and that chronic joblessness deprives those in the inner city of skills necessary to obtain and keep jobs. He also disagrees with the view that African-American poverty is due to cultural deficiencies and welfare dependency. He believes that sweeping changes in the global economy pull low-skilled manufacturing jobs out of the inner city, resulting in the flight from the ghetto of its most successful residents. Universal health care and government-financed jobs will relieve the problems of the underclass.

Wilson was one of the first to develop at length the "spatial mismatch" theory for the development of a ghetto underclass. In *Truly Disadvantaged* Wilson also argued effectively against the theory that welfare causes poverty. However, it has been observed that some minorities do much better than African-Americans, which might suggest that second and third generation northern African-Americans are hampered by overly high salary expectations, and the inability to find an economic niche.

Past president of the American Sociological Association, Wilson has received many honorary degrees and numerous awards and honors. In June 1996 he was selected by

Time magazine as one of America's 25 Most Influential People and in 2003 was awarded the Talcott Parsons (see entry) Prize in the Social Sciences by the American Academy of Arts and Sciences.

Major Literature

Wilson, William Julius. *The Declining Significance of Race: Blacks and Changing American Institutions.* Chicago, Illinois: University of Chicago Press, 1978.
___. *The Truly Disadvantaged: The Inner City, the Underclass, and Public Policy.* Chicago, Illinois: University of Chicago Press, 1987.
___. *When Work Disappears: The World of the New Urban Poor.* New York: Knopf, 1996.
___, and Richard P. Taub. *There Goes the Neighborhood: Racial, Ethnic, and Class Tensions in Four Chicago Neighborhoods and Their Meaning for America.* New York: Knopf, 2006.

Winship, Christopher (1950–)

STATISTICAL SOCIOLOGY

Born in Topeka, Kansas, Christopher Winship grew up in New Britain, Connecticut, and gained a B.A. in sociology (highest honors) and mathematics (highest honors) at Dartmouth College, Hanover, North Hampshire (1972). At Harvard University, Cambridge, Massachusetts, he gained a Ph.D. in sociology (1977) and was director of graduate studies, Department of Sociology (1995–1998); chair, Department of Sociology (1998–2001); director of graduate studies, Department of Sociology (2005); senior fellow, Hauser Center for Non-profit Organizations, Kennedy School of Government (1999); and Diker-Tishman Professor of Sociology (since 2005).

Winship was research associate, Institute for Research on Poverty, University of Wisconsin (1977–1978), and at the National Opinion Research Center, University of Chicago, he was research associate (1981–1993); senior study director (1978–1980); and acting director, (1983–1985). At Northwestern University, Evanston, Illinois, he was research associate, Center for Urban Affairs and Policy Research (1981–1993); director, Program in Mathematical Methods in the Social Sciences (1984–1987); chair, Department of Sociology (1988–1992); and founding member of the Department of Statistics. Since 1999 he has been research associate, Institute for Quantitative Social Science (formerly the Center for Basic Research in the Social Sciences) at Harvard.

Winship is a member of the American Sociological Association, American Economic Association, Population Association of America, American Statistical Association, the Society for the Advancement of Socio-Economics International Society for Social Justice Research, Academy of Management, and a fellow, Center for Advanced Study in the Behavioral Sciences, Palo Alto, California. His community activities are board of trustees, Hebrew College, Newton Center, Massachusetts; officer and board, Jewish Community Relations Council; board, Wilstein Institute, Newton Center, Massachusetts; chair, Evaluation Committee, Boston Freedom Summer, Ten-Point Church Coalition; co-chair, Demographic Survey Committee, Combined Jewish Philanthropies; and chair, Social Justice Committee, Jewish Community Relations Council.

Major Contributions

The Ten Point Coalition is a group of black ministers who are working with the Boston police to reduce youth violence. Winship challenges the bell curve hypothesis of psychologists Richard J. Herrnstein and Charles Murray, who claim a youth's intelligence (IQ) is a more important determinant of social and economic success in adulthood than is the socioeconomic status of his or her parents. Winship's challenge is that estimates based on a variety of methods, including analyses of siblings, suggest that parental family background is at least as important, and maybe more important, as IQ in determining socioeconomic success in adulthood.

Winship concludes that mental ability appears to be like some kinds of music and athletic ability — there are large innate differences, training is critical to performance, and being "in shape" has a substantial effect on performance. Another area of research is assessing changes in the racial differences in imprisonment rates over the past sixty years.

Major Literature

Winship, Christopher, and Jenny Berrien. "An Umbrella of Legitimacy: Boston's Police Department–Ten Point Coalition Collaboration." In *Securing Our Children's Future: New Approaches to Juvenile Justice and Youth Violence.* Gary Katzman (Ed.). Washington, D.C.: Brookings Institution Press, 2002.

Winship, Christopher, and Amy Reynolds. "Faith, Practice, and Transformation: A Theory-Based Evaluation of Faith-Based Teen Programs." In *Taking Faith Seriously,* Mary Jo Bane, Brent Coffin, and Richard Higgins (Eds.). Chicago, Illinois: Harvard University Press, 2005.

Wirth, Louis (1897–1952)

URBAN SOCIOLOGY

Born in Gemünden, Germany, Louis Wirth came to the United States at the age of fourteen. He earned a Ph.B. (1919), M.A. (1925), and Ph.D. (1926) at the University of Chicago, Illinois. From 1919 to 1922 he was a social worker, then studied at Tulane University, New Orleans (1928–1929). At the department of sociology, University of Chicago, he was assistant professor (1931), associate professor (1932), and full professor (1940). Wirth was secretary (1932) and president (1947) of the American Sociological Society. He was regional chairman of the National Resources Planning Board; director of planning, Illinois Post War Planning Commission; consultant and adviser for the Social Science Research Council of the National Resources Planning Board and the Federal Public Housing Authority; president of the American Council on Race Relations; editor, "Sociology Series" of the Macmillan Company; associate editor, *American Journal of Sociology*; and first president of the International Association of Sociologists, a position he held at the time of his death.

Major Contributions

Wirth was a leading figure in the Chicago School of social sciences and was a strong supporter of applied sociology, which takes the knowledge offered by sociology and uses it to solve real social problems. In the variety of fields Wirth studied, social scientists, scholars, government officials, foundations, research agencies, and action groups often sought his advice and guidance. His research was concerned with how Jewish immigrants adjusted to life in urban America, as well as the distinct social processes of city life. According to Wirth, the city is harmful to culture: primary contacts are replaced by secondary ones; bonds of kinship, family and neighborhood are weakened, resulting a loss of solidarity. He also postulated that city life would lead to a drop in reproduction, resulting in smaller families; that marriage would decline and the proportion of single people would increase.

His work with minority groups is applicable not only to immigrant groups but to ethnic minorities, disabled people, homosexuals, women, and the elderly, all of whom have also suffered or continue to suffer prejudice, discrimination and disenfranchisement from the more numerically dominant members of a host society. It is in this respect that Wirth's path-breaking and insightful work still amply rewards detailed study even today, some seventy years after his original investigations.

Major Literature

Wirth, Louis. *Our Cities: Their Role in the National Economy*. A Report to President Roosevelt, 1937.

___. "Urbanism as a Way of Life." *American Journal of Sociology* 44 (1938): 1–24; and in Vol. 74, No. 5 (March 1969): 492–499.

___. *The Ghetto*. Chicago, Illinois: University of Chicago Press, 1938. New Jersey: Transaction Publishers, 1998.

___. "The Problem of Minority Groups." In Ralph Linton, *The Science of Man in the World Crisis*. New York: Columbia University Press, 1945. New York: Irvington Publishers, 1993.

___. *Community Life and Social Policy*. With E. Wirth Marvick and Albert J. Reiss, Jr. Chicago, Illinois: University of Chicago Press, 1956.

___. *On Cities and Social Life*. Albert J. Reiss, Jr. (Ed.). Chicago, Illinois: University of Chicago Press, 1964.

Wright, Erik Olin (1947–)

SOCIAL CLASS

Born in Berkeley, California, Erik Olin Wright gained a B.A. in social studies (with honors) at Harvard College, Cambridge, Massachusetts, in 1968, was awarded a Social Science Research Council pre-doctoral research training fellowship in 1969 and gained a B.A. in history (first class honors) at Balliol College, Oxford, England (1970). He was awarded a University of California Chancellor's Science Fellowship (1971) and gained a Ph.D. in sociology at the University of California, Berkeley (1976).

At University of Wisconsin, Madison, Department of Sociology he was assistant professor, (1976–1980); associate professor (1980–1983); professor (1983); C. Wright Mills Distinguished Professor (1990); and Vilas Distinguished Research Professor of Sociology (1998). He was visiting professor at the University of California, Berkeley, Department of Sociology (1987–1988) and won a University of Wisconsin Distinguished Teaching Award (1998).

Major Contributions

Wright's work is concerned mainly with the study of social classes, and in particular with the task of providing an update to the Marxist concept of class. His research has focused especially on the changing character of class relations in developed capitalist societies. Wright has analyzed the suitability of various theories of class structure within the United States labor force and developed a theory of contradictory class locations and later a theory based on exploitation.

When defining "class," he focuses on the importance of the control of the means of production, at the same time trying to account for the situation of skilled employees. According to Wright, employees with sought-after skills are in a "contradictory class location," because, while they are not capitalists, they are more precious to the owner of the means of production than less skilled workers. The owner of the means of production therefore tries to "buy" their loyalty by giving them stakes in his enterprises and endowing them with authority over their fellow workers. Thus skilled workers tend to be closer to the interests of the "bosses" than other workers. Wright identifies three changes in class structure during the twentieth century: change in forms control of the labor process; differentiation of the functions of capital; and development of complex hierarchies.

Since 1992 Wright has directed the Real Utopias Project. It embraces the tension between dreams and practice. It is founded on the belief that what is practically possible is not fixed independently of our imaginations, but is itself shaped by our visions.

Major Literature

Wright, Erik Olin. *The Politics of Punishment: A Critical Analysis of Prisons in America.* New York: Harper and Row, Colophon Books, 1973.

___, Elliott Sober, and Andrew Levine. *Reconstructing Marxism: Essays on Explanation and the Theory of History.* London, England: Verso Books, 1992.

Wright, Erik Olin. *Class Counts: Comparative Studies in Class Analysis.* New York: Cambridge University Press, 1997. Student edition, 2000.

___, and Archon Fung. *Deepening Democracy: Institutional Innovations in Empowered Participatory Governance.* London, England: Verso Books, 2003.

Fung, Archon, and Erik Olin Wright. *The Real Utopias Project: Deepening Democracy, Institutional Innovations in Empowered Participatory Governance.* Vol. 4. London, England: Verso Books, 2003.

Wright, Erik Olin. *Approaches to Class Analysis.* New York: Cambridge University Press, 2005.

Young, Kimball (1893–1972)
URBAN SOCIOLOGY

The grandson of Brigham Young, Kimball Young was born in Provo, Utah, gained an A.B. at Brigham Young University, Salt Lake City, Utah (1915), then taught high school English and history in Arizona (1916). During World War I he was a Mormon missionary in Germany, then gained an M.A. in sociology under Robert Park (see entry), University of Chicago, Illinois (1918), and a Ph.D. in psychology under Lewis Terman (1877–1956), Stanford University, California (1921). Young was assistant professor, University of Oregon, Eugene, then from 1920 to 1927 was assistant professor, Clark University, Worcester, Massachusetts and associate professor of sociology, Oregon.

He was president of the Alpha Kappa Delta (1928–1930) and professor of social psychology at the University of Wisconsin, Madison (1930–1940), and chairman of the Department of Sociology, Queens College, New York (1940–1947). In 1945 he was at the American University (U.S. Army) installation in Shrivenham, Oxfordshire, England, then was head of the Department of Sociology, Northwestern University, Evanston, Illinois (1947–1962). He was 35th president, American Sociological Society (Association, 1959) (1945) and was member of the Social Science Research Council and American Psychological Association.

Major Contributions

Young's presidential address, "Society and the State: Some Neglected Areas of Research and Theory," was published in the *American Sociological Review* (11, No. 2 [1946]: 137–146). He carried out one of the first ecological field studies in Chicago, working the area north of the river along Clark Street to Chicago Avenue. In his own estimation, what he brought to sociology was his knowledge of social psychology and that basic to all cultural learning is social learning which is older than culture. Social learning is not restricted to humans; it is found in mammals, especially the primates. He considered himself to have done a tolerable job in bringing together cultural anthropology, sociology, and social psychology.

With Robert Seashore (psychology) and the Melville J. Herskovits (anthropology), Young established an integrated sociology-psychology-anthropology freshman course in 1948 at Northwestern. His intellectual curiosity led him to be psychoanalyzed, in the belief that his insights could contribute to social science. In addition to a large number of articles in the social science journals, Young was general editor of the "American Sociology Series" for the American Book Company and member of the board of editors of the *Journal of Social Psychology* and *The American Journal of Sociology*.

Soon after retiring from Northwestern, he suffered the detachment of both retinas, yet despite his resulting blindness, he continued to work and teach a seminar or two a year for several years at Arizona State University, Tempe, Arizona.

Major Literature

Young, Kimball. *Mental Differences in Certain Immigrant Groups*. University of Oregon Press, Eugene, Oregon, 1922.
___. *Source Book for Social Psychology*. New York: Knopf, 1927. Woodstock, Georgia: American Book Company, 1935.
___(Ed.). *Social Attitudes*. New York: Henry Holt, 1931.
___. *An Introductory Sociology*. Woodstock, Georgia: American Book Company 1934, 1942, 1949.
___. *Personality and Problems of Adjustment*. New Jersey: Appleton-Century-Crofts, Inc., 1941.
___. *Handbook of Social Psychology*. New York: Taylor and Francis Group, Routledge, 1957, 1998.

Znaniecki, Florian Witold (1882–1958)

POLISH PEASANT CULTURE

Born in, Swietniki, Poland, Florian Witold Znaniecki turned from philosophy to sociology and he helped make sociology a distinct academic discipline. A pioneer in the field of empirical investigation, he was a noted authority on Polish peasant culture. After being expelled from the University of Warsaw for his active support of Polish nationalism, he studied at various universities in France and Switzerland and received his Ph.D. in philosophy from the Jagiellonian University, Kraków, in 1909. He joined William Isaac Thomas (see entry) at the University of Chicago (1914), where they began their joint work — *The Polish Peasant in Europe and America*.

Znaniecki returned to Poland in 1920 and became professor of sociology at Poznan, where in 1922 he founded a sociological institute and began publishing *The Polish Sociological Review*. He lectured at Columbia University, New York, between 1931 and 1933 and during the summer of 1939. The outbreak of World War II prevented his return to Poland, so he joined the faculty at the University of Illinois, Champaign-Urbana, where he taught until his retirement and was a member of the Chicago School. He was the 44th president of the American Sociological Association (1954); his presidential address was "Basic Problems of Contemporary Sociology."

Major Contributions

Znaniecki was interested in understanding the relationship between sociology and other disciplines and argued that although the best sociological practice adhered to scientific principles and methods, its focus on social rather than natural phenomena made it a unique discipline. He was also interested in the general problem of how social systems are constructed through social interaction among individuals In 1934 Znaniecki formulated the principle of "analytic induction," designed to identify universal propositions and causal laws, which he contrasted with enumerative research dealing with statistical relationships. He perceived the world as being caught between the social beliefs of idealism on the one hand and realism on the other. He proposed a third way, which he labeled culturalism — a theory that suggests society uses technology to serve its needs.

Znaniecki identified four types of social relations: social actions, social relations, social group, and social persons. He also named four types of character and personality: the humorous man, the working man, the well-behaved man, and the deviant man.

Major Literature

Znaniecki, Florian. *Cultural Reality*. Chicago, Illinois: University of Chicago Press, 1919. Houston, Texas: Cap and Gown Press, 1983.

___. *The Laws of Social Psychology*. Chicago, Illinois: University of Chicago Press 1925.

___. *The Method of Sociology*. New York: Farrar and Rinehart, 1934.

___. *Social Actions*. New York: Farrar and Rinehart, 1936.

___. *The Social Role of the Man of Knowledge*. New York: Columbia University Press, 1940.

New Jersey: Transaction Publishers, 1986.

___. *Cultural Sciences*. Urbana, Illinois: University of Illinois Press, 1952. New Jersey: Transaction Publishers, 1980.

___. *Modern Nationalities: A Sociological Study*. Urbana, Illinois: University of Illinois Press, 1952.

Timeline

Dates	Name	Area of Interest
1332–1406	Ibn Khaldun	*Historical Sociology*
1723–1816	Ferguson, Adam	*Early Sociology*
1796–1874	Quételet, Adolphe Jacques Lambert	*Social Physics*
1798–1857	Comte, Auguste	*Pioneer of Sociology*
1802–1876	Martineau, Harriet	*Early Sociologist*
1805–1859	Tocqueville, Alexis de	*Historical Sociology*
1818–1883	Marx, Karl Heinrich	*Class Conflicts*
1820–1895	Engels, Friedrich	*Dialectic Materialism*
1820–1903	Spencer, Herbert	*Survival of the Fittest*
1833–1911	Dilthey, Wilhelm	*Historical Consciousness*
1838–1909	Gumplowicz, Ludwig	*Sociology of Conflict*
1840–1910	Sumner, William Graham	*Social Change*
1841–1913	Ward, Lester Frank	*Pioneer Sociologist*
1843–1904	Tarde, Gabriel	*Criminology*
1846–1943	Oppenheimer, Franz	*Political Sociology*
1848–1923	Pareto, Vilfredo	*Circulation of Elites*
1854–1931	Blackmar, Frank Wilson	*Sociology Pioneer*
1854–1926	Small, Albion Woodbury	*Basic Sociology*
1855–1931	Giddings, Franklin Henry	*Consciousness of Kind*
1855–1936	Tönnies, Ferdinand	*Gemeinschaft and* Gesellschaft
1857–1929	Veblen, Thorstein	*The Leisure Class*
1858–1917	Durkheim, Émile	*Suicide*
1858–1916	Kidd, Benjamin	*Social Evolution*
1858–1941	Mosca, Gaetano	*Elites*
1858–1918	Simmel, Georg	*Social Structure*
1860–1935	Addams, Jane	*Social Reform*
1862–1931	Wells-Barnett Ida B.	*Black Feminism Sociology*
1863–1931	Mead, George Herbert	*Symbolic Interactionism*
1863–1941	Sombart, Werner	*Historical Sociology*
1863–1947	Thomas, William Isaac	*Sociology of Migration*
1864–1929	Cooley, Charles Horton	*Socio-psychology*
1864–1929	Hobhouse, Leonard Trelawny	*Political Sociology*
1864–1944	Park, Robert Ezra	*Human Ecology*
1864–1941	Vincent, George Edgar	*Sociology of Education*
1864–1920	Weber, Max	*Political Psychology*
1865–1940	Weatherly, Ulysses Grant	*Race Relations*
1866–1949	Gillette, John Morris	*Rural Sociology*
1866–1951	Ross, Edward Alsworth	*Social Control*

1867–1861	Balch, Emily Greene *Gender Inequality*
1868–1963	Du Bois, William Edwards Burghardt *Racial Oppression*
1868–1928	Hayes, Edward Cary *Social Process*
1871–1958	Gillin, John Lewis *Criminology and Penology*
1871–1954	Rowntree, Benjamin Seebohm *Sociology of Poverty*
1872–1950	Mauss, Marcel *Comparative Religion*
1872–1952	Kollontai, Alexandra *Rights of Women*
1873–1946	Ellwood, Charles Abram *Psychological Sociology*
1876–1936	Michels, Robert *Iron Law of Oligarchy*
1877–1970	Hankins, Frank Hamilton *Scientific Sociology*
1878–1944	Sanderson, Ezra Dwight *Rural Sociology*
1880–1956	Fairchild, Henry Pratt *Eugenics*
1880–1946	Reuter, Edward Byron *Sociology of Race*
1881–1951	Bernard, Luther Lee *Social Attitudes*
1882–1973	Bogardus, Emory Stephen *Social Distance Scale*
1882–1970	MacIver, Robert Morrison *The Nature of Authority*
1882–1961	Taft, Jessie *Sociology and Social Work*
1882–1958	Znaniecki, Florian Witold *Polish Peasant Culture*
1883–1950	Sutherland, Edwin H. *Criminology*
1884–1965	Gini, Corrado *Demography*
1884–1954	Odum, Howard Washington *Folk Sociology*
1886–1966	Burgess, Ernest Watson *Urban Sociology*
1886–1966	Carr-Saunders, Sir Alexander Morris *Demography*
1886–1959	Ogburn, William Fielding *Statistical Sociology*
1888–1974	Chapin, Francis Stuart *Social Change*
1889–1970	Ginsberg, Morris *Cultural Sociology*
1889–1968	Sorokin, Pitirim Alexandrovich *Social Cycle Theory*
1890–1987	Queen, Stuart Alfred *Social Work and Sociology*
1891–1952	Geiger, Theodor *Social Mobility*
1891–1937	Gramsci, Antonio *Cultural Hegemony*
1893–1947	Mannheim, Karl *Sociology of Knowledge*
1893–1981	Marshall, Thomas Humphrey *Social Policy*
1893–1972	Young, Kimball *Urban Sociology*
1894–1962	Frazier, Edward Franklin *Sociology of Race*
1895–1973	Horkheimer, Max *Critical Theory*
1897–1990	Elias, Norbert *Process Sociology*
1897–1983	Hughes, Everett Cherrington *Race Relations*
1897–1952	Wirth, Louis *Urban Sociology*
1898–1979	Marcuse, Herbert *Political Theory*
1899–1985	Cottrell, Leonard Slater, Jr. *Empathy in Sociology*
1899–1977	Thomas, Dorothy Swain *Demography*
1900–1993	Lowenthal, Leo *Sociology of Literature*
1901–1976	Lazarsfeld, Paul Felix *Communication Theory*
1902–1978	Lasswell, Harold Dwight *Political Sociology*
1902-1986	Myrdal, Alva *Social Change*
1902–1979	Parsons, Talcott *Social Action Theory*
1903–1969	Adorno, Theodor *Authoritarian Personality*
1903–1996	Bernard, Jessie, Shirley *Marriage and Family*
1905–1983	Aron, Raymond *Ideology*
1905–1995	Loomis, Charles Price *Rural Sociology*
1906–1999	Komarovsky, Mirra *Sociology of the Family*
1906–1992	Lee, Alfred McClung *Humanist Sociology*
1908–1997	Davis, Kingsley *Demography*

1909–1994	Hauser, Philip Morris *Urban Studies*
1909–2002	Riesman, David *Social Systems*
1909–2001	Sewell, William Hamilton *Sociology of Education*
1910–2003	Clark, Samuel Delbert *Political Sociology*
1910–1989	Homans, George Casper *Exchange Theory*
1911–1978	Glass, David Victor *Demography*
1911–2004	Riley, Matilda White *Sociology of Aging*
1911–1995	Shils, Edward *General Sociology*
1912–1984	Schelsky, Helmut *Applied Sociology*
1913–2003	Coser, Lewis Alfred *Social Conflict*
1913–	Keyfitz, Nathan *Demography*
1913–	Moore, Barrington, Jr. *Political Sociology*
1914–2000	Whyte, William Foote *Industrial Sociology*
1914–2006	Williams, Robin Murphy, Jr. *Race Relations*
1918–2002	Blau, Peter Michael *Formal Organizations*
1916–1991	Bendix, Reinhard *Historical Sociology*
1916–1962	Mills, Charles Wright *Structure of Power*
1917–	Form, William Humbert *Industrial Sociology*
1917–	Garfinkel, Harold *Ethnomethodology*
1917–2003	Goode, William Josiah *Sociology of Marriage*
1918–1968	Rose, Arnold Marshall *Sociology and Law*
1919–	Bell, Daniel *Class Conflict*
1919–1988	Janowitz, Morris *Military Sociology*
1919–2003	Merton, Robert King *Sociology of Science*
1921–2004	Duncan, Otis Dudley *Social Stratification*
1921–1979	Porter, John Arthur *Social Stratification*
1922–1982	Goffman, Erving *Stigma*
1922–2006	Lipset, Seymour Martin *Political Sociology*
1923–1994	Antonovsky, Aaron *Stress and Health*
1923–	Halsey, Albert Henry *Educational Equality*
1924–2000	Bernstein, Basil *Sociolinguistics*
1925–	Bauman, Zygmunt *Consumerism*
1925–1961	Fanon, Frantz Omar *Discrimination*
1925–1995	Gellner, Ernest André *Ethnography*
1925–	Huber, Joan *Sociology of the Family*
1925–	Touraine, Alain *Sociological Intervention*
1926–1995	Coleman, James S. *Sociology of Education*
1926–	Straus, Murray A. *Family Sociology*
1927–	Bellah, Robert *Sociology of Religion*
1927–	Gans, Herbert J. *Urban Sociology*
1927–1998	Luhmann, Niklas *Systems Theory*
1928–	Becker, Howard Saul *Sociology of Art*
1928–2004	Wilson, Bryan Ronald *Sociology of Religion*
1929–	Alberoni, Francesco *Sociology of Movements*
1929–	Berger, Peter Ludwig *Sociology of Consciousness*
1929–	Baudrillard, Jean *Structural Semiotics*
1929–	Dahrendorf, Baron Ralf Gustav *Class Conflict*
1929–	Etzioni, Amitai *Socioeconomics*
1929–	Habermas, Jürgen *Communicative Reason*
1930–	Becker, Gary Stanley *Economic Sociology*
1930–2002	Bourdieu, Pierre *Education and Culture*
1930–1988	Humphreys, Laud *Sociology of Homosexuality*
1930–	Wallerstein, Immanuel Maurice *World System Theory*

1931–	Erikson, Kai T. *Human Disasters*
1932–	Piven, Frances Fox *Sociology of Reform*
1932–	Scott, W. Richard *Sociology of Organizations*
1933–	Lieberson, Stanley *Ethnic Relations*
1935–	Wilson, William Julius *Urban Poverty*
1936–	Marchak, Patricia *Political Sociology*
1936–	Duster, Troy *Sociology of Race*
1938-	Giddens, Anthony *Structuration*
1939–	Kimmerling, Baruch *Political Sociology*
1940–	Hallinan, Maureen T. *Sociology of Education*
1940–	Patterson, Orlando *Sociology of Slavery*
1940–	Ritzer, George *Sociology of Consumption*
1942–	Castells, Manuel *Urban Sociology*
1942–	Thorne, Barrie *Sociology of Gender*
1942–	Whyte, Martin King *Sociology of China*
1943–	Granovetter, Mark *Social Networks*
1943–	Kanter, Rosabeth Moss *Sociology of Management*
1944–	Chodorow, Nancy Julia *Psychoanalysis of Feminism*
1944–	Haraway, Donna J. *Cyborg Theory*
1944–	Oakley, Ann Rosamund *Medical Sociology*
1944–	Portes, Alejandro *Immigration and Urbanization*
1945–2003	Barchas, Patricia R. *Sociophysiology*
1945–	Turner, Bryan Stanley *Medical Sociology*
1946–	Urry, John Richard *Sociology of Mobility*
1947–	Skocpol, Theda *Political Sociology*
1947–	Wright, Erik Olin *Social Class*
1948–	Collins, Patricia Hill *Sociology of Black Women*
1948–	Rumbaut, Rubén G. *Sociology of Immigration*
1949–	Sassen, Saskia *Human Migration*
1950–	Winship, Christopher *Statistical Sociology*
1951-	Brym, Robert J. *Political Sociology*
1952–	Gartner, Rosemary *Sociology of Crime*
1952–	Massey, Douglas S. *International Migration*
1957–	Lamont, Michèle *Race and Culture*
1957–	Waters, Mary C. *Sociology of Immigration*
1962–	Christakis, Nicholas Alexander *Medical Sociology*
1975–	Cadge, Wendy *Sociology of Religion*

People for whom no year of births available

Bielby, William T.   *Psychology of Rock and Roll*
Bloemraad, Irene   *Sociology of Immigration*
Gershuny, Jonathan   *Social Class*
Haveman, Heather A.   *Industrial Sociology*
Kaufman, Jason Andrew   *Political Sociology*
Kay, Tamara   *Political Sociology*
Reskin, Barbara F.   *Social Justice*
Sampson, Robert J.   *Sociology of Crime*

Index